Reading the New Testament

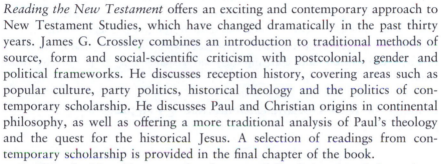

D0165255

Reading the New Testament offers an exciting and contemporary approach to New Testament Studies, which have changed dramatically in the past thirty years. James G. Crossley combines an introduction to traditional methods of source, form and social-scientific criticism with postcolonial, gender and political frameworks. He discusses reception history, covering areas such as popular culture, party politics, historical theology and the politics of contemporary scholarship. He discusses Paul and Christian origins in continental philosophy, as well as offering a more traditional analysis of Paul's theology and the quest for the historical Jesus. A selection of readings from contemporary scholarship is provided in the final chapter of the book.

Reading the New Testament has been carefully designed to help students think critically and in wide-ranging ways about the texts of the New Testament and will prove a valuable resource for everyone engaged in serious study of the Bible.

James G. Crossley is Senior Lecturer in New Testament Studies at the University of Sheffield. His research interests include the New Testament and biblical scholarship in historical, cultural and political contexts. His publications include *Jesus in an Age of Terror* (Equinox, 2008).

Reading Religious Texts series

This exciting series introduces students to the key texts from each of the major world religious traditions. It provides students with tools to engage with the texts, while helping them to understand their religious, social, cultural, historical and literary contexts. Each book addresses the issues arising from the text's interpretation and contemporary approaches and responses to these issues.

Reading the New Testament: Contemporary Approaches
James G. Crossley

FORTHCOMING:
Reading the Hebrew Bible
Reading the Qur'an
Reading Hindu Texts

Reading the New Testament

Contemporary Approaches

James G. Crossley

Routledge
Taylor & Francis Group

LONDON AND NEW YORK

First edition published 2010 by Routledge
2 Park Square, Milton Park, Abingdon, Oxon OX14 4RN

Simultaneously published in the USA and Canada by Routledge
270 Madison Ave, New York, NY 10016

Routledge is an imprint of the Taylor & Francis Group, an informa business

© 2010 James G. Crossley

Typeset in Sabon by Taylor and Francis Books
Printed and bound in Great Britain by TJ International Ltd, Padstow, Cornwall

British Library Cataloguing in Publication Data
A catalogue record for this book is available from the British Library

Library of Congress Cataloging in Publication Data
Crossley, James G.
   How to read the New Testament : contemporary approaches / James G.
Crossley. – 1st ed.
      p. cm.
   Includes index.
   1. Bible. N.T.–Criticism, interpretation, etc. 2. Bible. N.T.–Theology. I. Title.
   BS2361.3.C76 2010
   225.6–dc22
                         2009042300

ISBN 10: 0-415-48530-4 (hbk)
ISBN 10: 0-415-48531-2 (pbk)
ISBN 10: 0-203-85315-6 (ebk)

ISBN 13: 978-0-415-48530-2 (hbk)
ISBN 13: 978-0-415-48531-9 (pbk)
ISBN 13: 978-0-203-85315-3 (ebk)

For Serena and Dominique

Contents

Acknowledgements

I would like to thank a number of people who have helped me in a number of ways relating to this book: Loveday Alexander, William Arnal, Jacques Berlinerblau, Ward Blanton, Maurice Casey, Diana Edelman, Steph Fisher, David Horrell, Will Lamb, John Lyons, Halvor Moxnes, Jorunn Økland, Todd Penner, Philip Davies, Barry Matlock, Hugh Pyper, Justin Meggitt, Francesca Stavrakopoulou, Wendy Sproston North, Jim West, Keith Whitelam, Catrin Williams, and N.T. Wrong.

Additionally I would like to thank Lesley Riddle and Amy Grant from Routledge for their encouragement, support and patience.

More personally, I would also like to thank Francis Crossley, Pamela Crossley, Richard Crossley, Gill Turner, Caroline Watt, Glennis Watt, and Mike Watt.

But this book was only ever going to be dedicated to the incomparable duo, Serena and Dominique Crossley.

Chapter 1

Introduction
How to Read the New Testament

Readers should emphatically not read this book as a series of definitive ways in which to read this collection of texts which have been the subject of disputes, often bloody, for effectively two millenia. This book is not called, *How to Read the new Testament*. Perhaps the plural of the subtitle – *Contemporary Approaches* – might already imply that this is a guide to different ways in which readers can approach the texts. In fear of sounding quaint and sentimental, one of the aims in this book is to open the way for readers to search for more and more ways of reading the texts which inevitably could not all be covered in this introductory book.

One of the key purposes of this book is to introduce students, and relative newcomers to advanced biblical studies, to a greater range of approaches to the New Testament than the standard introductions. Standard introductions to the New Testament, at least in the experience of this writer, place a heavy emphasis on issues such as place of writing, authorship, theological agendas, literary structure, original historical context, broader historical contexts, key themes, and other traditional historical and literary approaches. There is, obviously, nothing wrong with such approaches, and they absolutely will not be ignored in this book, though there would be little point in producing yet another traditional introduction. However, New Testament studies, and biblical studies more widely, has so many more different approaches than is usually found in introductory textbooks and the omission of a range of creative and innovative approaches in textbooks fails to provide approaches for students who are not necessarily interested in the more traditional and seemingly 'mainstream' approaches to biblical texts. The mere 'fact' that the study of the New Testament, like any academic discipline, has so many different approaches *not* typically covered in introductory textbooks seems, to this writer at least, a failure and simply reinforces the idea that certain 'mainstream' approaches are the 'best' approaches.

This book is divided into four distinct sections. The first section, 'History', will introduce classical historical critical approaches to the New Testament – from source criticism to the quest for the historical Jesus – and more recent developments which might loosely be labelled 'historical' – from postcolonial criticism to issues in gender and identity. The second section, 'Revolutionary origins of Christian beliefs?', will cover classical questions of Christian origins (e.g. the origins of Christology, Paul's theology, emergence of a gentile religion) as well as some of the related but seemingly unusual discussion of Paul among contemporary continental philosophers. The links with the 'History' section ought to be obvious enough but this section also links neatly to the third section, 'Reception'. This section will discuss the various methods surrounding the reception of the New Testament texts, most notably in the twentieth and twenty-first centuries, using examples from politicians to pop music, from theology to contemporary scholarship. The final section will be extracts from contemporary New Testament scholarship relating to the different chapters and sections of this book.

But before we get carried away, it ought to be stressed that this book is not as radical as might have been implied. While there are a range of approaches discussed which are not typically discussed in most introductory textbooks, many of these approaches are now becoming less cutting-edge and even, ever-so-slowly, part of the establishment. This might be one good reason to justify the inclusion of such non-traditional approaches in an introductory textbook, namely, to keep up with current trends before it is too late. Furthermore, what this book will also do is to show how various non-traditional approaches either are a direct development of more traditional approaches or can be wed with traditional approaches with relative ease. This has partly been done throughout this book by using ideas of 'history' to bring approaches old and new (-ish) together and to show that, no matter how hard we may try, history cannot be avoided. Even those of a more literary bent may have to concede that the historical is always there, even if those of us fascinated by history will have to concede that history can be reconfigured in different ways and in light of challenges made by the literary. But throughout all this, the main idea is to give students some insight into a wide range of different approaches to the New Testament, some of which they may otherwise have missed in most introductory textbooks. Arguably the most prominent ways of approaching the New Testament which have not been given much, if any, space in intro-ductory textbooks are those involving identity, postcolonial criticism, Paul in continental philosophy, and the major growth area in New Testament studies, 'reception history', which gets a section to itself.

We are now getting ahead of ourselves. Before we properly begin, let us go back to the most basic question: 'What is "the New Testament"?'.

What is 'The New Testament'?

The New Testament consists of twenty-seven books which are regularly subdivided. Firstly, we have four Gospels (Matthew, Mark, Luke and John) which are effectively lives of Jesus. Mark's Gospel is usually said to have been written first, some time between 65–75 CE, although there is a minority opinion (this writer included) which would date it as early as some time close to 40 CE. It is usually thought to have been written in Rome or somewhere in the eastern Mediterranean (e.g. Syria or Galilee). Matthew is typically thought to have been written some time after the destruction of the Jerusalem Temple by the Romans in 70 CE, though again a minority scholarly tradition dates it earlier. Antioch is one of the favoured places of writing for Matthew. Luke is likewise thought to have been written after 70 CE, and possibly after Matthew, though the obligatory early daters can always be found. Quite where Luke was written is much more of a mystery. John's Gospel, perhaps the latest of them all, is again thought to be post-70 CE (with occasional detractors) and often thought to have been written in Ephesus. Whether the Gospels were written by the names attributed to them continues to be debated, with opinions including: accepting the attributed names (and even then working out who they might be!), originally anonymous authors and texts; and pseudonymous authorship, a known cultural practice.

Then we have the book of Acts which is a history of the development of the early Church from Jerusalem to Rome, with a particular focus on the acts of Paul and his epic journeys, though Peter features in significant places too. Acts is typically thought to have been written by Luke or whoever wrote Luke's Gospel. While there are those who date Acts just about pre-70 CE (inevitable, perhaps, if there are those who date Luke early), it is usually thought to be a post-70 CE text, with some recent scholars following an older scholarly tradition in suggesting a second century date. Again its place of origin is difficult to discern, though Rome is being touted by certain major scholars of Acts.

Then we have letters written by arguably one of the most influential thinkers in Christian history, (Saint) Paul. It is common for scholars to talk of the 'seven authentic Pauline letters', or the 'undisputed letters', named so because they are the letters which virtually all scholars would agree are genuine letters from Paul. These letters were written in the middle of the first century and are: Romans, 1 Corinthians, 2 Corinthians, Galatians, Philippians, 1 Thessalonians, and Philemon. The Deutero-Pauline letters, or the disputed Pauline letters, are those which are less confidently attributed to Paul with a long scholarly history of being thought to have been pseudonymously written in Paul's name. These letters are Ephesians, Colossians, 2 Thessalonians, 1 Timothy, 2 Timothy, and Titus. 2 Thessalonians and Colossians are more likely to be believed to be genuine Pauline than the rest. These 'disputed' Pauline texts are usually believed to have been written in the latter half of the first century. Mention might also be made of the anonymous letter to the Hebrews which did get attributed to Paul by some in the early church (and thus helping Hebrews make its way into the New Testament canon) but is now typically accepted as 'authorship unknown'.

Further subdivisions include the 'Pastoral Epistles', thus called because they are addressed to individual church figures and discuss issues of responsibilities, faith and practice, and these letters are 1 Timothy, 2 Timothy and Titus. The 'Catholic Epistles' are thus called because they are seemingly addressed to a general Christian audience and the letters are: James, 1 Peter, 2 Peter, 1 John, 2 John, 3 John, and Jude. Again, these letters are typically believed to be written pseudonymously, and so deliberately recalling a major 'name' in Christian origins, towards the end of the first century, or some time into the second century, though cases have been made, for instance, that James and 1 Peter could be 'authentic' texts.

Finally, there is the book of Revelation (note the singular 'Revelation' and *not* the plural 'Revelations'). Revelation, with all its seemingly weird and wonderful language, is typically thought to have been written in the latter part of the first century or early second century, and in reaction to persecution of Christians, though this, along with the idea that the book reflects a specific persecution of Christians, has been challenged and it may be a reaction against a less dramatic cultural imperialism surrounding the general worship of the Roman Emperor in the Eastern Mediterranean. Revelation seems to have been written by a figure called John exiled on the island of Patmos.

But the New Testament as a collective whole emerged over a longer period of time as certain Christians sought to include and exclude texts in the formation of their definitive writings, or, as it is more typically called, their 'canon'. Christians would eventually distinguish two testaments we know as Old and New, though there is some grounding for this in New Testament texts (e.g. Heb. 9.18–20), and Jesus' words themselves were taking on an authoritative status from the earliest decades (e.g. 1 Cor. 7.10–11). By the turn of the second century, it seems that Paul's letters were taking on a degree of authority in certain circles (2 Pet. 3.15–16). By the end of the second century the fourfold Gospel starts to become a distinctive collection in its own right, partly to help define a form of Christianity which would eventually develop into Christian orthodoxy over against different other Christian sects and movements, often described as 'heresies', which had their own favoured Gospels or versions of the canonical Gospels. Yet it was hardly all plain sailing for the text we have. People had their doubts about the validity of major texts such as John's Gospel, Hebrews and Revelation which were at times considered suspect. But by the time we get to the mid-fourth century CE, and thanks to figures such as Athanasius, we start to get the collection of the twenty-seven books we now know as the New Testament.

In this general context, we should not underestimate the importance of apostolic authority for defining an authoritative canon because this meant that tracing back texts to the first century and to the major Christian figures was important. Christians may not have got everything accurate but we can say that they did collect texts from the first and early part of the second century. While there remain plenty of disagreements over the specifics of dates, authorship, and places of writing, in general terms we can see that we have a group of texts written in the eastern Mediterranean, and perhaps as far west as Rome, in the first and second centuries CE.

Now we have a general idea of what the New Testament might be and its general setting, let us now dive straight in and proceed to look at ways of reading it.

Part One

History

Chapter 2

Reading Historical Documents Historically

From Historical Criticisms to Literary Criticisms and Back Again

What is History?

Writing history means different things to different people. In contemporary contexts, some people may be interested in cataloguing lists of monarchs, rulers, presidents and so on. Others may be interested in explaining why things happened, such as the various factors underlying the Second World War. Others still may want to write an explicitly ideological history defending their own perspective, an extreme example of which might include retellings of the past in Soviet Russia. While Soviet histories literally airbrushed the inconvenient out of history (think of Stalin's removal of Trotsky from photographs of Lenin), partisan histories and interested parties can potentially provide insights others might miss. Perhaps a committed evangelical might pick up nuances of Paul's theology of justification that a non-believer might miss through lack of interest. A non-believer might think about reading New Testament texts like any other text and provide insights from different disciplines beyond the interests of others. A Jewish scholar might bring insights from a range of Jewish texts and interests in Jesus or Paul as a Jewish figure. A middle-of-the-road Anglican or Episcopalian might happily absorb the lot. All these examples have happened and such perspectives or biases can bring insights as well as distortions.

All of these approaches to history ultimately stand or fall by evidence and yet none of these approaches to history, not even the most accurate, can be regarded as innocent. History writing will often tell us about the presentation of a given group's or individual's agenda and so we can also read the historians as history, so to speak (see Chapter 11). History writing can also tell us something about the historian and the historian's time by, for instance, what they do *not* tell us. Why catalogue monarchs and not local folk heroes? Or why catalogue local folk heroes and not kings? Why catalogue both? Decisions have to be made when writing history and it is worth asking what informs those decisions.

So much for contemporary history writing; what of ancient history? There are plenty of differences between ancient and modern history writing. Modern historians have significantly better access to a greater range of evidence, resources and methodology so modern history is inevitably and obviously going to be different. But there are general similarities too. Ancient historians and writers with an interest in history still had to select evidence and reports. Compare, for instance, the opening of Luke's Gospel (Luke 1.1–4) with the words of one famous ancient historian, Thucydides:

> With reference to the speeches in this history, some were delivered before the war began, others while it was going on; some I heard myself, others I got from various quarters; it was in all cases difficult to carry them word for word in one's memory, so my habit has been to make the speakers say what was in my opinion demanded of them by the various occasions, of course adhering as closely as possible to the general sense of what they really said. And with reference to the narrative of events, far from permitting myself to derive it from the first source that came to hand, I did not even trust my own impressions, but it rests partly on what I saw myself, partly on what others saw for me, the accuracy of the report being always tried by the most severe and detailed tests possible. My conclusions have cost me some labour from the want of coincidence between accounts of the same occurrences by different eye-witnesses, arising sometimes from imperfect memory, sometimes from undue partiality for one side or the other.
>
> (Thucydides, *Peloponnesian War* 1.22.1–4)

There does seem to be some concern for something like the sifting through of evidence and something potentially useful for modern concerns with accuracy, even if elaboration through imagining what a person said or did in the absence of sources was practised and even if some historians thought it fair to bring in the occasional supernatural agent in the story. That said, the differences between then and now should not be overstated: contemporary historians such as Simon Schama and Natalie Zemon Davis have both used the role of fictive characters and a liberal historical imagination in their historical work. Similarly, the agendas of an ancient historian, like the modern, can be seen in the most basic terms, whether the focus is on epic wars, military leaders, emperors, religious figures, some great intellectual, or something the historian's patron might want to hear, and already tells us something in terms of the interests of the writer. In addition to Thucydides' concern for sifting through the sources, it is not difficult to detect his perspective and bias anymore than it is to detect the perspectives and biases of the New Testament writers (cf. John 20.30–31):

> The cause of all these evils was the lust for power arising from greed and ambition; and from these passions proceeded the violence of parties once engaged in contention. The leaders in the cities, each provided with the

fairest professions, on the one side with the cry of political equality of the people, on the other of a moderate aristocracy, sought prizes for themselves in those public interests which they pretended to cherish, and, recoiling from no means in their struggles for ascendancy, engaged in the direct excesses; in their acts of vengeance they went to even greater lengths, not stopping at what justice or the good of the state demanded, but making the party caprice of the moment their only standard, and invoking with equal readiness the condemnation of an unjust verdict or the authority of the strong arm to glut the animosities of the hour. Thus religion was in honour with neither party; but the use of fair phrases to arrive at guilty ends was in high reputation.

(Thucydides, *Peloponnesian War* 3.82.8)

Biblical writers, like many ancient writers, sought to explain why things happened, often through moral explanations. In the Hebrew Bible/Old Testament a case can be made for much of its epic history providing an explanation for what is usually called 'the exile' based on people acting against the commandments of God. In terms of the Gospels, presumably the writers were not simply relating the story of Jesus because he was an interesting historical figure. No doubt there were profound theological reasons for keeping the story alive. Likewise, why was the history of the early church told in Acts of the Apostles and why such an emphasis on Paul? Why not stress the acts of James or John or Philip in more detail? Why stress the origins of the church in Jerusalem? Why ignore Galilee? Again, no doubt, the writer we know as Luke had his reasons.

We will see that parallels in the Gospels can give us insights into the theological and ideological agendas of the different writers. This type of reading is not quite as easy with non-Gospel literature in the New Testament because we do not have such bountiful parallels. But when we do, the results can be particularly helpful. Acts 15.1–30 and Galatians 2.1–10 are widely believed to be a description of a significant meeting in Jerusalem, some time around 50 CE, designed to discuss the issue of Jewish and non-Jewish integration in earliest Christianity. The reasons why scholars believe both Acts and Galatians discuss the same event is because in Galatians we read of a meeting in Jerusalem including Paul, Barnabas, Titus, James, Peter, and John, with circumcision of Gentile converts a key issue, while in Acts we also read of a meeting in Jerusalem including Paul, Barnabas, James, Peter and apostles and elders, with circumcision of Gentile converts as a key issue. These are significant overlaps. However, there are also significant differences, most notably the resolution in Acts that some prohibitions be placed on Gentiles, which goes unmentioned in Galatians, and the subsequent Antioch controversy in Galatians, the equivalent of which precedes the Jerusalem council in Acts.

There is some debate over whether Acts 15.1–30 and Galatians 2.1–10 are descriptions of the same event but the following analysis is still applicable because both texts discuss the same issues just outlined. Through a comparison of these two very similar issues, therefore, we can see how each writer uses the past to forward their own particular agenda. In Acts, for instance, Luke is typically thought as wanting to promote a more harmonious history of the church, perhaps to bring different groups together, whereas Paul uses the Jerusalem conference to show, in the context of bitter arguments with Galatian Christians, how his views on circumcision and Law were accepted by the major figures of the Church and to back up his charges levelled at Cephas (Peter) in Antioch (Gal. 2.11–15):

> ... and when James and Cephas and John, who were acknowledged pillars, recognized the grace that had been given to me, they gave to Barnabas and me the right hand of fellowship, agreeing that we should go to the Gentiles and they to the circumcised.[10] They asked only one thing, that we remember the poor, which was actually what I was eager to do.
>
> (Gal. 2.9–10)

Luke, on the other hand, has a controversy in Antioch first and then immediately followed by resolution. Whether or not this is referring to the same controversy at Antioch is in some ways beside the point because it seems clear that Luke is gearing his history towards resolving conflict rather than confronting potential conflict head on as Paul does in Galatians.

Storytelling and Haggadah

One important difference between the ancient world and the contemporary academic world at least involves the question of historicity. We will spend some time (see Chapter 5) working out details of Jesus' life and whether certain themes could plausibly be attributed to the figure active in late 20s Galilee. As we have seen, while there were people concerned with historical accuracy in the ancient world, such detailed analysis is more typically modern. Furthermore, there were ancient writers less concerned with historical accuracy and more concerned with an ideological or religious 'truth'. It is to such ideas we can now turn.

Jewish contexts of Christian origins have increasingly been emphasised since the 1970s. Roger Aus has provided a massive amount of material from Jewish storytelling or 'haggadah'. 'Haggadah' (or 'aggadah') is typically defined as material which is not concerned with laws, though we should be careful not to push this definition too hard because legal material does turn up in haggadic material. But we can say that 'haggadah' typically refers to material such as parables, miracles, creative rewriting of history, stories of various rabbis or great figures from the past and so on. Aus has a profound knowledge of haggadic traditions from the time of Jesus through to the huge amount collected in the works of the rabbis in the centuries following and has provided New

Testament scholarship with numerous analyses. While Aus accepts that many of these traditions are late and need to be analysed with care, he is able to show through arguments of collective weight that there is clear awareness of various haggadic stories in the Gospel traditions.

One of the most prominent examples of the use of haggadic-style literature in the New Testament is the birth and infancy story in Matthew 1.18–2.23. It seems clear enough that the writer of Matthew 1–2 has written Jesus' birth and infancy in light of the story and retellings of the life of Moses and the book of Exodus as Aus and Dale Allison in particular have shown.[1] There are clear general parallels, most notably the murder of infants, particularly brutal rulers, and the Egyptian backdrop. Notice also the precise linguistic connections. For instance:

... for all those who were seeking your life are dead ...

(Exod. 4.19)

... for those who are seeking the child's life are dead ...

(Matt. 2.20)

The parallels become even clearer when we look at some of the retellings of the Moses story roughly contemporaneous with Matthew's Gospel. For example, according to the first century CE Jewish historian Josephus (*Ant.* 2:210–16), the noble father of Moses (Amram) was anxious about his wife's pregnancy because Pharaoh had ordered the death of male infants and so God appeared in a dream to calm him and foretold the greatness of Moses. We might compare the story of Joseph, the righteous father of Jesus, when he wonders what to do concerning his wife's pregnancy with an angel of the Lord calming his nerves and foretelling the future greatness of Jesus (Matt. 1.18–21).

Why use Moses? For a start, the potential for a new Moses figure was present in the Pentateuch and attributed to Moses himself in Deuteronomy 18.15, 'The Lord your God will raise up for you a prophet like me from among your own people ... ', and to God himself 18:18, 'I will raise up for them a prophet like you from among their own people ... ' The figure of Moses could be used in a number of ways by subsequent writers (e.g. Lawgiver, prophet), but most relevantly for present purposes, writers could use stories of Moses as deliverer or saviour figure and reapply them to figures such as Gideon or the Messiah. The Messiah in later rabbinic literature was frequently associated with Moses in some way. As Moses led the great redemption from slavery in the past so the Messiah will deliver Israel in the time to come. The idea of a new Exodus was certainly known in Judaism at the time of Matthew and was bound up with 'messianic' ideas and removal of Roman rule. Moses was also regarded as Israel's 'saviour' (e.g. Josephus, *Ant.* 2.216; Acts 7.25, 'He supposed that his kinsfolk would understand that God through him was rescuing them, but they did not understand.') and, most interestingly, Josephus associates the name 'Moses' with the Egyptian word 'save': ' … the princess gave him the name recalling his immersion in the river, for the Egyptians call water *mou* and those who are saved *eses*; so they gave him the name compounded of both worlds' (*Ant.* 2.228). Here we might compare Matthew's noting of the name of 'Jesus', derived from the Hebrew 'Joshua', meaning 'Yahweh saves': 'She will bear a son, and you are to name him Jesus, for he will save his people from their sins' (Matt. 1.21).

Many scholars would view such storytelling as having no serious grounding in the earliest life of the historical Jesus but would see it as fiction in the same way that other major figures, from rabbis to the Patriarchs, would have fictional tales told about them. Whether 'many scholars' are right or wrong can be judged by readers but one point ought to be confronted: the issue of 'verification'. A regular comment made is that there would have been witnesses around able to verify claims made by the first Christians. It could be argued that this misses the point of the function of haggadah and storytelling in the ancient world where such standards of truth did not necessarily apply. At the very least, dramatic events were a known feature in the recalling of events surrounding people deemed significant. More broadly in the ancient world, the following two examples are from a first century CE natural historian (Pliny the Elder) and a fourth century CE Christian historian (Eusebius) and of obvious relevance for questions of historical accuracy of elements of the infancy narrative:

> Stars are occasionally seen along with the sun, for whole days together, and generally round its orb, like wreaths made of the ears of corn, or circles of various colours; such as occurred when Augustus, while a very young man, was entering the city, after the death of his father, in order to take upon himself the great name which he assumed. The same radiances occur about the moon and also about the principal stars, which are stationary in the heavens.
>
> (Pliny the Elder, *Natural History* 2.28–29)

> In the case of other remarkable and famous men we know that strange stars have appeared, what some call comets, or meteors, or tails of fire, or similar phenomena that are seen in connection with great unusual events. But what event could be greater or more important for the whole Universe than the spiritual light coming to all men through the Saviour's Advent, bringing to human souls the gift of holiness and true knowledge of God? Wherefore the herald star gave the great sign, telling in symbol that the Christ of God would shine as a great new light on all the world.
>
> (Eusebius, *Proof of the Gospel* 9.1)

Both writers are clearly aware of the symbolic function of dramatic events surrounding those figures deemed great so where does this leave the question of whether such things really happened or not? When talking about finding people who might verify a story in the ancient world, is there not a danger of imposing certain modern concepts of truth on certain ancient ones?

Historical Approaches and the New Testament I: Source Criticism

New Testament scholarship has become associated with its own very specific types of historical approaches. Traditionally these have been source and form criticism. Source criticism involves solving the 'Synoptic Problem'. The Synoptic Gospels (Matthew, Mark, and Luke) are called so because there are extremely close similarities between the three in wording and order (with the majority of material in Mark's Gospel found in Matthew and Luke) to the extent that there is almost certainly some literary relationship between the three. Naturally enough, scholars have sought a 'solution' to this 'problem' and the accompanying mini-problems: which Gospel came first? Who used what? Are there different sources we no longer have?

John's Gospel, however, is clearly different from the Synoptic Gospels. John has some highly elaborate theology (read John 1.1–18) and some major claims and disputes over Jesus making himself equal with God (e.g. John 5.16–18; 10.30–39). The disputes over Jesus' equality with God in John's Gospel stand in contrast to the Synoptic Gospels where conflicts are typically over Jesus' authority in matters of Law, healing and exorcism. Other problems include John removing virtually all of the common Synoptic sayings about the 'kingdom of God/heaven', with some notably different exceptions (John 3.3, 5), and John removing the common stories of Jesus as an exorcist and his association with 'sinners'. John also has the so-called cleansing of the Temple at the beginning of Jesus' ministry (John 2.13–22) whereas the Synoptic Gospels have it in Jerusalem at the end (Mark 11.15–17 and parallels). In the Synoptic Gospels, the Temple incident is an event leading to Jesus' death; in John, Jesus' death is sparked by the raising of Lazarus from the dead (John 11). Clearly, then, there are some serious issues at stake when comparing John and the Synoptic Gospels. This problem did not go unnoticed in the early Christian centuries. The following is a not entirely satisfactory ancient explanation:

> ... the apostle John was asked to relate in his own gospel the period passed over in silence by the former evangelists and the things done during it by the Saviour, that is to say, the events before the imprisonment of the Baptist ... Thus John in the course of his gospel relates what Christ did before the Baptist had been thrown into prison, but the other three evangelists narrate the events after the imprisonment of the Baptist. If this be understood the gospels no longer appear to disagree ...
>
> (Eusebius, *Ecclesiastical History* 3:24.11–13)

We might ask; did John then know the Synoptic Gospels? Certainly the general outline contains the basic elements (from Galilee, controversies, went to Jerusalem, crucified, resurrected, etc.) and the Synoptic Gospels, or at least Mark, would have been known to Christians in the ancient world so some familiarity seems plausible even if John decided to go his own way. We may even be able to be more precise still and say that John probably knew at least one Synoptic Gospel (Mark?). John 12:1–8 has notable similarities with Mark 14. We might also compare the following:

> And he said to them, 'Truly I tell you, there are some standing here who will not taste death until they see that the kingdom of God has come with power.'
>
> (Mark 9.1)

> ' ... Very truly, I tell you, whoever keeps my word will never see death.' The Jews said to him, 'Now we know that you have a demon.' Abraham died, and so did the prophets; yet you say, 'Whoever keeps my word will never taste death.'
>
> (John 8.51–52)

This would be a vigorous rewriting in line with John intentions but that is a technique available in the world of the New Testament as we have already seen in passing.

If we leave John to one side for now and return to the Synoptic Gospels, the idea that Mark was the earliest Gospel and the source of Matthew and Luke has gained widespread approval in biblical scholarship. Reasons for this are due to parallel texts such as the following from the miracle of the stilling of the storm:

> 'Teacher, do you not care that we are perishing?'
>
> (Mark 4.38)

> 'Lord, save us! We are perishing!'
>
> (Matt. 8.26)

> 'Master, Master, we are perishing!'
>
> (Luke 8.24)

The general scholarly logic is that Mark has harsh words with the appearance that Jesus might not care about the disciples whereas Matthew and Luke change this to make it clear that the disciples cry out to Jesus for help. It is unlikely that Mark would have changed Matthew and Luke to produce a harsher Jesus and so this is one type of reason for Markan priority. Similarly we see the Jesus of Mark elevated further by the other Gospel writers. The following example is a clear case:

And he said to them, 'Truly I tell you, there are some standing here who will not taste death until they see that the kingdom of God has come with power.'

(Mark 9.1)

'Truly I tell you, there are some standing here who will not taste death before they see the Son of Man coming in his kingdom.'

(Matt. 16.28)

Here the kingdom of God coming in power is now changed to the kingdom of the Son of Man. Again, it is unlikely Mark would have de-emphasised the role of Jesus while it is highly likely that Matthew would heighten the role of Jesus.

There are other reasons regularly given to account for Markan priority. Mark is the shortest and more abbreviated account. The logic applied to the above texts is similar. For instance, it is easier to see why Matthew and Luke would expand Mark to include material such as the Lord's Prayer, the birth and infancy narratives, and the Sermon on the Mount, plain as it is to see why Mark would have omitted them and abbreviated Matthew and Luke. Luke and Matthew 'improve' Mark's Greek. Mark's Greek is often said to be 'rough' and contains a notable influence from Aramaic which Matthew and Luke 'improve'. When combined with the other arguments, it is difficult to see how this can be anything other than Mark coming first and Luke and Matthew using Mark rather than vice versa. This reasoning makes it very difficult to accept one classic solution to the Synoptic Problem, namely, the Griesbach Hypothesis (or Two Gospel Hypothesis) and its developments, whereby variations of this argument claim that Matthew was the first gospel, Luke used Matthew and Mark used and edited both.

Though not without notable differences, there is also precise word-for-word correspondence in Matthew and Luke which is not found in Mark such as the following:

But when he saw many Pharisees and Sadducees coming for baptism, he said to them, "You brood of vipers! Who warned you to flee from the wrath to come? [8] Bear fruit worthy of repentance. [9] Do not presume to say to yourselves, 'We have Abraham as our ancestor'; for I tell you, God is able from these stones to raise up children to Abraham. [10] Even now the ax is lying at the root of the trees; every tree therefore that does not bear good fruit is cut down and thrown into the fire.
(Matt. 3.7–10)

John said to the crowds that came out to be baptized by him, "You brood of vipers! Who warned you to flee from the wrath to come? [8] Bear fruits worthy of repentance. Do not begin to say to yourselves, 'We have Abraham as our ancestor'; for I tell you, God is able from these stones to raise up children to Abraham. [9] Even now the ax is lying at the root of the trees; every tree therefore that does not bear good fruit is cut down and thrown into the fire."
(Luke 3.7–9)

Given texts such as these, scholars have concluded that there must be some kind of literary dependence between Matthew and Luke. However, we also have texts which are clearly discussing the same thing but the literary closeness is not so clear. Compare the following:

"Woe to you, scribes and Pharisees, hypocrites! For you tithe mint, dill, and cummin, and have neglected the weightier matters of the law: justice and mercy and faith. It is these you ought to have practiced without neglecting the others.
(Matt. 23.23)

"But woe to you Pharisees! For you tithe mint and rue and herbs of all kinds, and neglect justice and the love of God; it is these you ought to have practiced, without neglecting the others.
(Luke 11.42)

With the above in mind, clearly there is *something* connecting Matthew and Luke. Additionally, there is some agreement in narrative order in Matthew and Luke which *might* suggest a common source or literary dependency, though of course we might add that it would be no great surprise if Luke and Matthew independently put stories of John the Baptist at the beginning of their story if they did not have access to a single written document which scholars have hypothesised and labelled 'Q'.

The hypothetical source 'Q' (from the German 'Quelle' meaning 'source') is part of a popular view which has gained momentum since the nineteenth century which has forcefully argued that there is another common source (in addition to Mark) for Matthew and Luke. When combined with Mark as part of the solution to the Synoptic Problem, we are dealing with what has become known as the Two Source Hypothesis (not to be confused with the Two Gospel Hypothesis). This may seem simple enough but then there are different models of Q. It has been argued that Q was a single, fixed, literary document, a scholarly tradition recently culminating in a critical edition of Q.[2] It has also been argued that Q is effectively shorthand for oral tradition. Another view which should have been important and which recurs in scholarship while being regularly ignored, is that Q ought to be seen as a chaotic model without the idea of a single written document. This chaotic model involves small sources, some in Greek, some in Aramaic, often literary and some, potentially, oral. Additionally, scholars have noted material particular to Matthew (e.g. some of the material in Matt. 23) and particular to Luke (e.g. the parable of the Good Samaritan) and labelled this M and L, respectively, and so now we are dealing with the Four Source Hypothesis.

There have been alternatives to the Mark/Q-based solutions to the Synoptic Problem. We have already seen the Griesbach hypothesis in passing but this has, for reasons mentioned above and more, fallen out of favour. The most serious challenger to the Mark/Q solution has involved removing the concept of Q and replacing it with the idea of Luke using Matthew, though Luke may still additionally have had independent source material. Markan priority remains in place. This is often named the Farrer Hypothesis or the Farrer-Goulder-Goodacre Hypothesis after its major proponents (Austin Farrer, Michael Goulder and Mark Goodacre). This approach has been criticised because it is not deemed to have sufficiently explained why Luke followed the order of Mark but did not follow the order of Matthew's insertions into Mark and scattered well-ordered material from Matthew such as the Sermon on the Mount. Naturally, proponents of this thesis provide various intricate counter arguments but maybe one general counter argument is worth noting. If we assume that Luke was written after Matthew (see Chapter 1) then is it not likely that Luke would have at least known of Matthew given its prominence in early Christianity? More to the point, this may well be implied in the opening of Luke:

> Since many have undertaken to set down an orderly account of the events that have been fulfilled among us,[2] just as they were handed on to us by those who from the beginning were eyewitnesses and servants of the word,[3] I too decided, after investigating everything carefully from the very first, to write an orderly account for you, most excellent Theophilus,[4] so that you may know the truth concerning the things about which you have been instructed.
>
> (Luke 1.1–4)

Perhaps we ought to be thinking about less fixed models for the Synoptic Problem. Perhaps Luke did use Matthew from a combination of memory, community recollections and repeating, and direct copying, alongside a range of other sources. Interestingly, this approach to the Synoptic Problem could be tied in with the chaotic model of Q, as Maurice Casey has recently shown under the influence of his student Stephanie Fisher.[3]

It is, obviously, of no great ease to solve the Synoptic Problem. There will be times in this book where I will deliberately remain ambiguous even though I may have a strong opinion on a given topic. In this case, my fence sitting is due to my not knowing precisely what to make of the Synoptic Problem, other than finding important arguments in both the Q arguments and the arguments inspired by the Farrer-Goulder-Goodacre Hypothesis. The Synoptic Problem underlies much other work done on the Gospels and students are referred to the footnote for some further reading.[4] I have mainly included a very basic outline of the Synoptic Problem as issues relating to the solutions to the Synoptic Problem will be referenced elsewhere in this book. Students should perhaps be warned that books on the Synoptic Problem often reflect entrenched positions but from experience it seems to me, and others, that there are enough 'floating voters' not directly associated with the Synoptic Problem who do not have fixed positions and are ready to be persuaded. The Synoptic

Problem is indeed one of the oldest issues in academic New Testament studies but I suspect there is more to come and that the old dog still has life in it yet.

Historical Approaches and the New Testament II: Form Criticism, Redaction Criticism and Literary Criticism

Probably the dominant scholarly reading of the Gospels from around the 1920s to the 1970s was 'form criticism', developed most vigorously by major German scholars such as K.L. Schmidt, Martin Dibelius and Rudolf Bultmann. Form criticism attempted to isolate individual passages or pericopes and sayings and locate their setting in life (*Sitz im Leben*) prior to their inclusion in the Gospels. The role of the individual passages in the faith of the earliest church was a prominent issue for the form critics. The form critical approach would often look for the earliest form of the passage or saying and see how given passages accumulated extra details over time. Form critics established different structures or even genres for different forms including parables, 'pronouncement stories' which culminated in the authoritative words of Jesus (e.g. Mark 2.15–17), and miracle stories which homed in on Jesus' power and with features such as awe and amazement. While much of form criticism remained sceptical about finding the Jesus of history (e.g. the work of Bultmann), there were occasions, notably outside Germany, where there was more optimism (e.g. Vincent Taylor). Another feature of form criticism was that there was a tendency to view the final authors of the Gospels as passive recipients of tradition who merely tinkered with the sources to form a vaguely coherent whole and with little interest in creatively producing a work of literature.

One of the curious features of the heyday of form criticism in the early mid-twentieth century is that it never really looked at the social setting of the forms in any widespread way as might be expected when emphasising the setting in life. Instead, the emphasis was more on the setting in faith, the ways in which the early church constructed its faith through its use of pre-gospel tradition. A major reason for this was that political context in which form criticism emerged, namely the rise of fascism and the Nazi party in Germany. By the 1930s and 1940s there were several prominent New Testament scholars, such as the infamous Walter Grundmann, Gerhard Kittel, and K.G. Kuhn, working on the gospel tradition and related areas, even providing the world with the most perverse result of mainstream New Testament scholarship: an Aryan Jesus. Of course, there were plenty of German scholars who were not committed Nazis and indeed were opponents of the Nazi party but the general context of anti-Jewish thought was rife and anti-Jewish sentiments were found in the historical and theological work of figures such as the leading form critic Rudolf Bultmann. In a more general sense, and a point to which we will return, while there were certainly vigorous critics of anti-Jewish sentiments in New Testament scholarship, it took until the 1970s for this to be challenged in a widespread sense. Placing scholarship in its historical and political contexts is important because we can now see why German-led form criticism did not place any great emphasis on social context of the forms: the social context of the forms would inevitably lead to *Jewish* social contexts in which these forms emerged and this was not conducive to scholarship in a period and place where anti-Jewish sentiment was rife.

This major failing of form criticism has now been qualified by the greater positivity towards Judaism in New Testament scholarship since the 1970s and by the work on the haggadic background to the New Testament. Recall that the term 'haggadah' can refer to a range of material such as parables, miracles, and stories and sayings of great figures. This, obviously, has a lot in common with the material designated and studied by form critics and ought to form one of the important contexts for understanding the Gospel traditions. When we apply form critical approaches to Mark 6.17–29 in Chapter 4 the haggadic background will feature prominently.

The next logical step from the role of the forms and units in pre-Gospel history is the role of the forms and units in the 'final form' of the texts. This brings us on to redaction criticism which began to take off from the 1960s onwards. Redaction criticism explicitly looked at the theological motivations of the final editors or redactors and how they arranged and modified the material accordingly. Given the widespread assumption of Markan priority, this was easier with Matthew and Luke because we could not only see what they had done with the Markan texts but also what they had done in comparison with one another. And if redaction criticism is the next logical step from form criticism then literary criticism – reading the Gospels as the products of creative authors in their own right – was the next logical step from redaction criticism.

Literary approaches to the New Testament, and the Gospels in particular, came off the back of a broader movement in literary studies in the humanities which emerged in the 1950s in the UK and North America and would become one of the dominant modes of interpretation: the so-called New Criticism. New Criticism tended to downplay the role of the external factors in interpretation (social and historical contexts, individual influences, etc.) and focus on how the text 'speaks' for itself. The meaning of texts could be found through a range of literary devices such as repetition, metaphor, characterisation, and so on. In biblical studies, the influence of New Criticism would be felt from the 1970s onward when a now significant scholarly tradition of ahistorical readings would emerge, most notably in Hebrew Bible studies in the works of, for instance, Robert Alter. To caricature slightly, where a source or form critic might see a contradiction or repetition as a way of reconstructing a possible underlying source, literary critics might see this as evidence of a text trying to tell us something significant. Or again, where a more conservative critic might see an incidental detail, such as the famous 'green

grass' (Mark 6.39) in the Feeding of the Five Thousand, as evidence of incidental historical reminiscence, a literary critic might see this as an example of
literary 'realism' with little or no bearing on the issue of historical accuracy.

In New Testament studies, and biblical studies in general, language of plot,
narrator, character, point of view and various other 'literary devices' have
become deeply embedded in the scholarly language. In a prominent study of
character in John's Gospel, R. Alan Culpepper looks at the ways in which
characters are defined in relation to their responses to, and, in certain cases,
misunderstandings of, Jesus.[5] Certainly, there is explicit evidence of the text
'artificially' drawing in the audience. In John 3.1–10, where Jesus debates with
Nicodemus, Jesus switches from 'you' in the singular (referring to Nicodemus)
to 'you' in the plural which presumably is there for the audience to decide: 'Do
not be astonished that I said to you [sg.], "You [pl.] must be born from
above"' (John 3.7). Various scholars have pointed to a range of responses to
Jesus, from extreme rejection of a 'collective character', 'the Jews' (e.g. John
5.16–18; 10.30–33), through followers deserting (John 6), the uncertainty of
Nicodemus (John 3.1–10), and the trust of the Samaritan woman (John 4), to
the ultimate acceptance of the Beloved Disciple. Compare the following where
the example of faith shown by the Beloved Disciple is presumably exemplary:
'the other disciple, who reached the tomb first, also went in, and he saw and
believed' (John 20.8). We might compare John 20.29 and a reaction to
'doubting' Thomas: 'Jesus said to him, "Have you believed because you have
seen me? Blessed are those who have not seen and yet have come to believe."'
Presumably, then, the reader may indeed doubt but is encouraged to believe
nonetheless, with the character of Thomas providing the impetus for this kind
of faith. For Culpepper, one of the important aspects of the misunderstandings
in John's Gospel is to prevent and teach readers the ways in which they can
understand correctly (and typically understand the 'correct' view of Jesus) and
bring them in to the realm of the 'insider'.

There have been many trends in literary criticism since the middle of the
twentieth century but one which has had a significant influence on biblical
studies, in addition to, and as a part of, the impact of deconstructive and/or
poststructuralist approaches on biblical studies,[6] has been the shift to the role
of the reader or audience in generating meaning, even to the extent of emphasising Roland Barthes' famous over-the-top idea of 'the death of the author'.
In some variants of 'reader-response criticism', it is a given community of
readers who create meaning. There are more radical versions of reader-
response criticism than others, ranging from texts having no fixed meaning
with readers more or less being the sole generators of meaning (cf. Mark 12.17)
through to genres imposing, in lesser and greater degrees, limits on
interpretation (is there not some restriction on the reading of Philem. 22?),
often couched, among literary theorists, in terms of an unwritten contract
between text and reader. In Section III, we will see how this emphasis on the
creative role of the reader – and not always with concern for the 'original

meaning' – has been developed in reception historical analysis of the New Testament texts.

Gaps in the text have been deemed to be important by some New Testament scholars. In the most basic sense, the New Testament writers give little in the way of physical description and when (say) an artist approaches a given text then interpretative decisions have to be made about what is unsaid. There are other types of gaps in the text pointed out by scholars. In a famous footnote, Robert M. Fowler counted seventy-seven unanswered questions from a total of 114 questions in Mark's Gospel.[7] These unanswered questions were developed by Daniel Marguerat and Yvan Bourquin in a manner not dissimilar to Culpepper in that such questions left unanswered in the text effectively invites or challenges readers to answer them. One of the comparisons they make is between Mark 8.14–21 and Matthew 16.5–12. There is a run of five unanswered questions in Mark:

Why are you discussing the fact that you have no bread?
Do you not yet perceive or understand?
Are your hearts hardened?
You have eyes do you not see?
You have ears, do you not hear?

Then we get two questions which are impossible to get wrong not least because they are at the basic level of a literal answer: the answers to how many loaves and fishes.

Then we get the final unanswered abrupt question: 'Do you not yet understand?' (Mark 8.21). By way of contrast, with Matthew we get two questions:

You of little faith, why do you reflect on the fact that you have no bread?
Do you not yet understand?

This is followed by another two questions which refer back to the disciples' memory ('do you not remember … ?') followed by an explanation about the Pharisees and Sadducees and the disciples remembering what they ought to have remembered. Matthew is much kinder on the disciples, and perhaps on the reader, by spelling out the meaning. Mark, however, is not so kind. The disciples to not come to knowledge and cannot understand what is happening. But on the level of story, the readers are presumably meant to know what is going on and are provoked to answer the unanswered questions. Similarly Mark elsewhere throws down the gauntlet for the reader by questioning the understanding of the disciples and readers (Mark 4.11, 14) and leaves gaps for the reader to fill.

Despite ahistorical emphases in many literary approaches to the Bible (and other texts), history is not always easy to avoid in certain texts. A non-biblical and very basic general example might be George Orwell's *Animal Farm*, which is a famous allegory of the Russian Revolution and an attack on Stalinist Russia. Of course it can be read without any knowledge of this but it would hardly have emerged without the events of Soviet Russia and, given it is an allegory, there is some correspondence between characters and historical figures. In New Testament studies, the rising literary critical approaches were utilised readily by historians of Christian origins. If we take the examples of the harsh questioning of the disciples in Mark it was (and occasionally still is) common to seek a more concrete historical audience for this criticism, typically Peter and his legacy in the Jerusalem church. I strongly emphasise that the debates over the historical and cultural locations of literature are far more complex than could possibly be outlined here but as a basic point we can say that literary critical approaches and historical critical approaches are not so easily distinguished. The literature of the earliest Christians was, obviously, produced in historical contexts while the history of the earliest Christians is, obviously, accessible to us through written documents such as those recorded in the New Testament.

Indeed most contemporary commentaries on the biblical texts will typically employ historical and literary methods as a matter of routine. As a major recent example of the ways in which literary theory and historical criticism were bound together as one is the work of Richard Burridge on Gospel genre. Following different literary critics, Burridge argues that the Gospels have a cluster of features which overall would have generally been recognised as belonging to the genre of (ancient) biography, similar in style to texts such as Philostratus' *Life of Apollonius of Tyana* and Philo's *Life of Moses*. These general features include the following: mention the subject's name in the opening few words or lines, title or prologue (e.g. 'the life of ... ', prologues in Luke and John, Mark's opening and Matthew's opening sentence); the focus on one person; largely continuous prose narrative; ancestry (e.g. genealogies in Luke and Matthew; cf. Mark 6.3); chronological structure with material such as teaching and great deeds inserted along the way; serious tone with encouragement to emulate the subject (cf. Mark 8.34–36; 10.35–45); an exemplary figure worthy of praise (cf. Luke 7.16–17); didactic material; apologetic in the sense of putting forward the 'correct' view of the subject or correct any 'misunderstanding' (cf. Mark 3.20–23; Matt. 27.62–66; 28.11–15; 1 Cor. 1.23); and a general interest in character details by a portrayal of actions and words. According to this approach, genre is important for understanding because if we do not understand the conventions and expectations of a genre from a different time and a different culture then we will inevitably miss some of the important points being made by the author or text. According to this approach we should be looking for the issues of teaching, polemic, apologetics, the real identity of the subject (Jesus), including the details of the 'earthly' Jesus' life (though this still remains a particular portrait and does not necessarily equal the 'historical Jesus') rather than simply the faith of the church as many form and redaction critics might believe.

Historical Approaches and the New Testament III: Social Scientific Criticism

In tandem with the emphasis on Jewish contexts of Christian origins since the 1970s, the social world of Christian origins has also been emphasised and applied to traditional form criticism, most significantly, perhaps, in the pioneering work of Gerd Theissen, who was at the forefront of the re-emergence of the use of social sciences in New Testament studies. Social-scientific criticism of the New Testament analyses the texts in their social and cultural contexts and, typically, tries to understand ways in which the ancient texts might have been understood by ancient audiences. Social-scientific criticism might involve the use of various theories and models borrowed from disciplines such as sociology or social/cultural anthropology or it might involve outlining a general history of a particular social group, such as a history of women in Christian origins, or it might involve analysing a given text in its geographical location, such as looking at the social structures in Corinth and how this might shed light on Paul's letters to the Corinthians, or it might involve looking at various other aspects of 'everyday life' such as diet, agriculture, leisure and so on. A now classic study of the levels of poverty as the backdrop for Paul is that of Justin Meggitt and an extract is available in Chapter 12. As all this already implies, social-scientific criticism can be defined broadly.

Some scholars prefer to use clear models. In the 1970s, attempts were made to apply sociological approaches to millenarian groups to Christian origins and earliest Christian views of imminent end times in New Testament texts. John Gager argued that early Christianity was a millenarian movement and the failure of the imminent kingdom to materialise was compensated by a fervent desire to evangelise.[8] This disjunction between reality and belief gave rise in New Testament studies to a phrase used in social sciences, 'cognitive dissonance'. Gager's approach has come under criticism for importing the study of modern religious issues onto ancient texts but the potential to (partially) explain Christian origins and New Testament texts in social terms had been ushered in by such works and other prominent scholars producing social scientifically inspired work (e.g. Gerd Theissen).

There are different ways of using social scientific approaches to the New Testament. At the beginning of the 1980s, Bruce Malina, and like-minded scholars called the Context Group, began to develop models from cultural/social anthropology for application in New Testament studies.[9] Malina has been influential in making some scholars believe that we should view the world of the New Testament in terms of the pivotal values of the Mediterranean which would highlight the alien nature of the New Testament documents for modern and largely North American readers. Pivotal values of the Mediterranean (including much of the *contemporary* Mediterranean), so Malina argued, included honour and shame where contests for honour are played out publically in games of challenge and riposte and such issues underlie a great deal of the New Testament texts.

Methodological criticisms have been levelled at the model-based approaches in particular. One obvious criticism is that by using models of *contemporary* societies, the scholar is imposing a model on a society from a very different time with some very different assumptions (and that might also be assuming that the model based on contemporary society 'got it right' in the first place!). But in response it could be argued that this is actually a problem for any historical approach to New Testament texts: the interpreter, as scholars repeatedly remind us, brings all sorts of presuppositions and influences to bear on the ancient evidence. This does not, of course, solve the problem for heavily model-based social sciences but it is something anyone has to bear in mind when approaching the text. A related problem is imposing results not just from a different *time* but also a different *place*. For example, new religious movements in the contemporary USA will have some radically different cultural, social, psychological, etc. assumptions from new religious movements in the ancient world and only exacerbated by the massive amount of historical changes which have taken place over two thousand years.

Underlying this discussion is, then, the idea that a social-scientific model can 'force' the ancient evidence to give the answers to fit the model. An example of this is Philip Esler's reconstruction of Jewish eating habits and association with Gentiles in the ancient world as a means of understanding related controversies in earliest Christianity. Esler applies the anthropological work of Mary Douglas and Edmund Leach and uses the example of the Indian caste system. According to Esler, 'Among the Indian castes ... inter-marriage is normally only possible between people who can eat together without risk of defilement' and so 'Given the antipathy of the Jews for marrying Gentiles, the Indian comparison suggests that it would be most surprising if they did not also feel a pronounced hostility towards eating with them.'[10] It would seem that this background interferes too much with Esler's handling of key texts. Of the Jewish texts, *Letter of Aristeas* (182–83), where a Gentile king holds a banquet for his Jewish audience, Esler claims that the text does not specify whether food and wine were passed between the king and the Jewish contingent, adding 'it would seem more likely that he ate his and they ate theirs'. However, the preceding verse says the exact opposite to what Esler claims and serves as a warning against pushing a model too hard: 'Everything of which you partake ... will be served in compliance with your eating habits; it will be served to me as well as to you' (*Letter of Aristeas* 181).

Unfortunately, resort to the apparently most obvious context of the New Testament, 'the Mediterranean', and the supposed pivotal values of honour and shame, does not solve the problems. For a start, are the supposedly pivotal values of honour and shame really that different from values in North American or Northern European cultures? Anyone who has experienced school, sport, the workplace, academia, and so on will be all too aware of how issues of honour and shame are hardly alien to European and North American cultures. As this might suggest, the use of the 'the Mediterranean' as a culture area is not always successful in establishing anything distinctive about the social world of Christian origins. In fact, it has a tendency to brush over cultural particularities and differences, and in this case Judaism, an obviously significant backdrop to the New Testament, suffers. Markus Bockmuehl, who knows as much about early Judaism as any contemporary New Testament scholar, made the following criticisms of Malina's book, *The New Testament World*:

> And it is Jews, after all, whose role in the 'New Testament world' arguably matters more than most. Both in their own eyes and in those of their pagan critics, they were culturally unique. Little of that distinctness, however, comes into the fore in this book. Malina refers to ancient Jews and their literature in curiously arm-waving and unspecific terms ('Semites', 'Semitic subculture', 'Ben Zakaiists', 'late Israelites'), citing the Mishnah only twice and the Dead Sea Scrolls not at all, and virtually ignoring the first-century role of the Pharisees, who (rather than the priests) were in Josephus's view the *real* 'bearers of the Great Tradition'.[11]

Moreover, the application of a grand Mediterranean culture can actually lead to similar mistakes to the application of other broad model-based approaches by making all the evidence fit. Bockmuehl adds the following criticisms:

> A good many of Malina's cultural generalizations are plainly untrue for the followers of Jesus and for some or indeed most other religious Jews. For example, individual decision rather than family ties *did* matter for Jesus and at Qumran; Jews did *not* believe that 'stars were living beings, intelligent and powerful'; they did *not* wear tassels on their garments primarily to ward off the evil eye; at least the Dead Sea sect *did* prohibit marriage with nieces and cousins; 'Ben Zakaiists' (i.e. rabbis) did *not* develop 'a viable Israelite domestic religion ... largely through interaction with post-Jesus groups' (i.e. Christians). And so forth. Exaggerated claims for a homogeneous and apparently timeless Mediterranean culture seriously compromise the anthropological and historical applicability of Malina's model to the highly specific and unusual context of religious first-century Palestinian Judaism.

The use of the Mediterranean has not been entirely successful in removing modern assumptions from interpretation. On the contrary, at times some very clear modern cultural assumptions have been brought to bear on the evidence. As we will see in Chapter 11, the Mediterranean frequently blurs into the contemporary Arab world, an area of renewed interest in American and European politics and media in the past forty years.

So is the inevitability of our contemporary assumptions rending interpretation little more than a narcissistic exercise? Is the situation hopeless? Maybe, maybe not. One possible answer might be to embrace or acknowledge our assumptions or use our contemporary results to ask questions of the texts and then evaluate the texts in light of the evidence. In many ways, this is (partly) boiling down to pushing for a careful concern for the details of texts, and rightly so. What this would also mean is a 'conversation' between modern evidence and modern assumptions, on the one hand, and ancient ones, on the other. In some ways this is what we have been doing with the criticism of the use of 'the Mediterranean'. A generalising question about the Mediterranean was asked as we saw that the ancient world is, unsurprisingly perhaps, much more diverse than a crude imposing of a model might suggest. With the question of Jewish eating habits, the question was asked and attention was focused on a passage and gave us an answer that, for one text at least, there were circumstances where Jews and Gentiles might eat together.

A different approach to social scientific criticism of the New Testament is, put simply, less model based and more a way of thinking about and approaching the ancient evidence while looking less at generalisations and more at the nuances and peculiarities of the first Christians. Scholars such as Wayne Meeks, Gerd Theissen and Justin Meggitt have looked at issues relating to social 'level' or 'class' of the earliest Christians in discussions by pagan and New Testament authors, analysing whether the first Christians were from the poorer sections of society, elite sections, or a cross-section of society. This raises further questions: how do we determine class and status? Does status differ in different contexts?

A related methodological way of benefiting from such a 'conversation' with social sciences is a further example from social-scientific criticism of Christian origins. Here we turn to the ground-breaking study of Rodney Stark. Rodney Stark is an internationally renowned sociologist of religion whose work includes, among many things, studies of the rise of New Religious Movements, including the rise of Mormonism through social networks (friendship, workplace and so on). Stark decided to move outside his field and apply his work to Christian origins where he made similar arguments on the rise of Christianity through social networks as a broad explanation as to why it would become the religion of the Roman Empire.[12] Stark made mistakes (he was working away from his home field so this is hardly unexpected) but the general approach is now regarded as an important one. Some of the sympathetic criticism of Stark's work made the suggestion that the historical peculiarity of ancient networks needed to be factored in more, such as the role of elite householders and the ways in which once the householder was converted the household inevitably followed suit and a new range of networks were opened up. Consequently people such as Jack T. Sanders and this author were able to modify Stark's work and take it in new directions.[13] We will see how Stark's work can be usefully applied to the origins of Christianity in Chapter 7.

One way we could develop Stark's work might be to ask questions such as: what might have been the social status of key figures in the conversion process? As it happens, the ancient evidence throws up significant examples of women and households. The study of gender has become increasingly part of the study of Christian origins since the 1960s and 1970s, no doubt partly due to the contemporary social upheavals where feminism became increasingly popular in the universities. What we have here, then, is another potential conversation with the ancient evidence grounded in contemporary concerns about gender, households and social networks.

A woman could gain some power in running a household. Compare the following from the New Testament:

So I would have younger widows marry, bear children, and manage their households, so as to give the adversary no occasion to revile us.

(1 Tim. 5.14)

Likewise, tell the older women to be reverent in behavior, not to be slanderers or slaves to drink; they are to teach what is good,[4] so that they may encourage the young women to love their husbands, to love their children,[5] to be self-controlled, chaste, good managers of the household, kind, being submissive to their husbands, so that the word of God may not be discredited.

(Titus 2.3–5)

Notice the mention of widows and older women. This might be significant because husbands tended to be older than wives in the ancient world and so if a husband died this would be one way the wife would gain further power in the running of the household (cf. Philostratus, *De gymnastica* 2.23; 272.30–31). Whatever way we imagine elite women with some power in the household, it seems as if they would have been able to become potentially pivotal figures in the spread of new ideas, which is particularly important for the earliest spread of Christianity because Christianity was, of course, to emerge out of Judaism. We have evidence of wives devoted to Judaism where husbands were not. The following example is from first-century Antioch at the beginning of the Jewish revolt against Rome in 66–70 CE:

yet did they distrust their own wives, who were almost all of them addicted to the Jewish religion; on which account it was that their greatest concern was how they might conceal these things from them; so they came upon the Jews, and cut their throats ... in number ten thousand, and all of them unarmed, and this in one hour's time, without anyone to disturb them.

(Josephus, *War* 2.560–61)

One reason why there may not have been so many men keen on converting to Judaism is due to the issue of circumcision: in addition to being extremely painful, it was life threatening for an adult male. It is notable that the issue of circumcision is a problematic barrier in other accounts of conversion and converts to Judaism (e.g. Josephus, *Ant.* 20.34–48; *Genesis Rabbah* 46.10), a point to which we will return in Chapter 7.

In terms of the emerging Christian faith, we have examples where we might suggest women had played a pivotal role in the social networks. Mary, the mother of John Mark, ran a household where people gathered and prayed (Acts 12.12–17) while in Colossians 4.15 greetings are sent out to Nympha and 'the church in her house' and a figure called Chloe in 1 Corinthians 1.11 has a network of people who are able to inform Paul. These women may well have been pivotal in the spread of the earliest Church by at least providing a centre for Christians and thereby links between different networks related to the early Church. We have an even more precise example of this recorded in Acts:

> A certain woman named Lydia, a worshiper of God, was listening to us; she was from the city of Thyatira and a dealer in purple cloth. The Lord opened her heart to listen eagerly to what was said by Paul.[15] When she and her household were baptized, she urged us, saying, 'If you have judged me to be faithful to the Lord, come and stay at my home.' And she prevailed upon us.
>
> (Acts 16.14–15)

A second century critic of Christianity, Celsus, not only criticised Christianity for its inclusion of women but also suggests that women were playing a pivotal role in conversion in what we might describe as a social network:

> He [Celsus] asserts, 'We see, indeed, in private houses workers in wool and leather, and fullers, and persons of the most uninstructed and rustic character, not venturing to utter a word in the presence of their elders and wiser masters; but when they get hold of the children privately, and certain women as ignorant as themselves, they pour forth wonderful statements, to the effect that they ought not to give heed to their father and to their teachers, but should obey them; that the former are foolish and stupid, and neither know nor can perform anything that is really good, being preoccupied with empty trifles; that they alone know how men ought to live, and that, if the children obey them, they will both be happy themselves, and will make their home happy also. And while thus speaking, if they see one of the instructors of youth approaching, or one of the more intelligent class, or even the father himself, the more timid among them become afraid, while the more forward incite the children to throw off the yoke, whispering that in the presence of father and teachers they

neither will nor can explain to them any good thing, seeing they turn away with aversion from the silliness and stupidity of such persons as being altogether corrupt, and far advanced in wickedness, and such as would inflict punishment upon them; but that if they wish (to avail themselves of their aid,) they must leave their father and their instructors, and go with the women and their playfellows to the women's apartments, or to the leather shop, or to the fuller's shop, that they may attain to perfection; – and by words like these they gain them over.'

(Origen, *Contra Celsus* 3.55)

It could be that Celsus is trying to slur Christianity by deliberately associating the movement with women, with women playing no role in reality. While there is obviously an element of slur in Celsus' report, we should probably conclude that he was firing at Christianity *because* women played a role in conversion, a view supported by the above evidence from the New Testament.[14]

Summary

History can mean different things to different people. Why emphasise kings and leaders rather than peasants and labourers, or vice versa? It is clear history, ancient and modern, is written with some sort of agenda, and the New Testament texts purporting to explain the past are no exception. Different ways of understanding the past were explored, such as storytelling and fictitious rewriting of the past, as a means of explaining a problem or issue in the present. The classic approaches to history in New Testament studies were covered, such as those which are more concerned with the history behind the texts, especially form criticism and, to lesser extent, source criticism, and those which look at the 'final form' of the texts, most notably redaction criticism and literary criticism. We also saw one approach which can be applied to pre-Gospel forms and the final form of the texts, namely, social-scientific criticism.

Key words

Form criticism: The analysis of Gospel passages, sayings, stories, and verses in their possible pre-Gospel contexts.

Haggadah (or: Aggadah): Often distinguished by what it is not, that is, it is not legal material ('halakah'). More positively, it involves storytelling, rewriting history, parables, stories of various teachers, miracles and so on.

Historical criticism: A general description for approaches to biblical texts with concern for origins and original historical contexts.

Literary criticism: The application of various techniques analysed in literary studies and applied to the biblical texts. Stress is often placed on the creative role of the author.

Q: Label given to the hypothetical source or sources used by some scholars to explain why Matthew and Luke have material in common not found in Mark. 'Q' is from the German 'Quelle', 'source'.

Redaction criticism: The analysis of the role of the editor or 'redactor' of the 'final form' of the text as a whole and the different ideological and theological interests of the editor.

Social-scientific criticism: A broad label covering uses of approaches from various disciplines (e.g. sociology, anthropology, psychology, and econom-ics) and used to establish the contexts of the texts and earliest Christianity, as well as an aid to interpretation.

Source criticism: In New Testament studies, the search for the sources of the canonical Gospels, especially the sources for Matthew and Luke.

Further Reading

Aus, R.D., *The Death, Burial, and Resurrection of Jesus, and the Death, Burial, and Translation of Moses in Judaic Tradition*, Lanham: University Press of America, 2008.

Goodacre, M., *The Synoptic Problem: A Way through a Maze*, London and New York: T&T Clark, 2001.

Horrell, D.G., ed., *Social-Scientific Approaches to New Testament Interpretation*, Edinburgh: T&T Clark, 1999.

Osiek, C., and M. Y. MacDonald with J. H. Tulloch, *A Woman's Place: House Churches in Earliest Christianity*, Minneapolis: Fortress, 2006.

Stark, R., *The Rise of Christianity: A Sociologist Reconsiders History*, Princeton: Princeton UP, 1996.

Streeter, B.H., *The Four Gospels: A Study in Origins*, New York: Macmillan, 1930.

Theissen, G., *The Gospels in Context: Social and Political History in the Synoptic Tradition*, Edinburgh: T&T Clark, 1992.

Thiselton, A.C., *New Horizons in Hermeneutics: The Theory and Practice of Transforming Biblical Reading*, Carlisle: Paternoster, 1992.

Chapter 3

Contemporary Historical Approaches to the New Testament

Identity and Difference

Identity and Difference

The discussion of gender and Christian origins also brings us neatly to an area where modern assumptions and ideology are brought to the forefront of interpretation. A great deal of discussion of the more overtly ideological scholarship involves identity and difference. By 'identity and difference' I mean, generally speaking, the ways in which people view themselves, relate to others, and negotiate perceived similarities and differences with others in the world. Think, for example, of the ways in which the terms 'American', 'British', 'European', 'African', 'Gentile', or 'Jewish' are used. Identity is often established by the negative – who we are *not* – and so we might find identity formulated in familiar polarisations such as black and white, straight and gay, man and woman, and so on. But if we return to the examples of 'American', 'British' or 'European' then it is not too difficult to think of identities not being made explicit and being ignored. When talking of national identities, does this obscure class or racial divisions? What might the term 'European' mean for former colonies of European powers or immigrants from former colonies? Why did I choose the examples I chose? Does it say something about the location of this author and his audience? Why not choose 'Chinese', 'Asian', 'Latin American', 'Brazilian' and so on? Why choose nations or geographical terms? These sorts of questions have led to further questioning of biblical texts (among many others) and the search for what is not being mentioned in the text. Does the text assume an ethnic, gender or religious bias? Are other groups or other identities being excluded?

We could go on endlessly with questioning but for present purposes the ways in which identity is *constructed* by groups is important. Important terminology related to such questions involves 'essentialist' and 'non-essentialist' models of identity. An 'essentialist' model of identity would emphasise a fixed and unchanging set of features which defines a group. When we hear discussions of 'Englishness' or 'Jewishness', or what it means to be a 'true American' or a 'true Christian', or what 'true Islam' is, this would presumably mean such terms can be used by people with the assumption that there are certain characteristics that define the given group. Or in gender terms, some people might argue that 'real men' are so because they eat meat, drink beer and watch football and/or that women are 'real women' because they are caring, like babies, worry about their presentation and so on. In this context, we might also think of the role of ethnic, gender, religious, etc. stereotypes, and indeed the ways in which these different roles intersect with one another.

A related example from New Testament studies where the issue of essentialist identity arises is over 'Jewishness'. William Arnal criticises a significant trend in contemporary New Testament scholarship whereby Judaism is constructed as having a fixed identity and anything which comes outside of the scholarly definition of 'Jewishness' is deemed not Jewish, even though no known contemporary scholar denies Jesus was Jewish.[1] It is indeed very common in New Testament scholarship, as we will see in important discussions of Paul in Chapter 7, that symbols such as circumcision, Sabbath, food laws, profound interest in Israel's history and so on are deemed some of the ways that 'Jewishness' ought to be defined. Yet is Arnal's criticism of such fixed identity markers not significant? What if someone identified as Jewish but did not really care about Sabbath or Israel's history? Are they no longer to be deemed 'Jewish' by modern interpreters? Compare the following comments from N.T. Wright:

> Have ... the advocates of the Cynic Jesus, come to terms with the problematic analogy between themselves and those German scholars who, in the 1920s and 1930s, reduced almost to nil the specific Jewishness of Jesus and his message?[2]

Strong words indeed! Whether or not advocates of the Cynic Jesus (a kind of non-theologically minded social critic Jesus) are historically correct, why is it that their very liberal Jesus is compared with the Nazis of all people? Nazi Jesus scholarship genuinely did take things as far as arguing that Jesus was racially Aryan (see Chapter 11) and not Jewish but no advocate of the Cynic Jesus does this or comes remotely close. Irrespective of whether the 'Cynic Jesus' is the correct way to describe Jesus, every contemporary advocate of the Cynic-like Jesus claims their Jesus was Jewish. However, it is Wright's use of Jewish identity that allows him to make this claim because it is made on the assumption of a very fixed or essentialist view of Jewish identity (interest in scriptures, interest in Israel's history, interest in 'symbols' such as Sabbath, etc.). By this logic anyone who does not uphold Wright's view of Jewish identity is no Jew. But we could again ask ourselves: what if someone identifies as Jewish but has a radical view of Judaism or thinks something like Cynic philosophy is wonderful, why can they not be Jewish?

Clearly, identity is a slippery concept and is difficult to pin down with fixed definitions. On the one hand, there are obvious biological and reproductive differences between male and female. But even here we must be careful.

As already alluded to, it is hardly uncommon to find suggestions that issues deemed 'natural' to men or women (e.g. it is apparently 'natural' that women are more 'suited' to bringing up children). We might also bring in related issues of sexuality too. In a similar way there are debates over whether homosexuality is genetic (the so-called 'gay gene'), 'natural', 'unnatural', or a part of complex social-psychological contexts. In other words, there are areas where the essentialist model becomes controversial and not so clear cut. Such debates over what constitutes 'natural' are hardly modern. Some ancient writers held a 'one sex' model where gender is effectively an axis where the male pole is deemed the perfect human form and the female pole lacked perfection, with more or less 'male' or 'female' biological developments along the axis.[3] But in the ancient model too we start to see how construction begins to impinge on what may have seemed biological 'fact'.

On the other hand, as some of the above already implies, it is relatively easy to note behaviour deemed 'masculine' and 'feminine' as social constructions of gender. An obvious example of gender as socially constructed might be the example of baby clothing. The physical differences between clothed babies are not as obvious as with many adults yet there has been an increasing tendency, in the UK at least, to dress baby boys in blue and baby girls in pink. Why not the more seemingly gender 'neutral' white? Apart from the important question of marketing, what might this early gender specifying say about such a society? In theory, a given society could stress the similarities with minimal attention given to differences. So what does the stress on differences tell us about a given society, texts, groups and so on and their views of gender?

But if we further question the essentialist model and start providing exceptions and argue that these fixed definitions do not work for everybody so labelled and are more social constructions, we might be moving towards a 'non-essentialist' model. A 'non-essentialist' model would emphasise that identity is not fixed and is constantly changing with the role of perception being crucial in understanding identity. Clothing and gender are, as ever, a basic but good example. If a man walked into a job interview for a bank dressed in a skirt or sporting attire then many would no doubt think this was unusual and clearly this is due to assumptions about what men should and should not wear and when a man should or should not wear such clothing.

With this discussion in mind, and for the purposes of clarity, we might use the following definitions but with the firm qualification that the boundaries between the concepts are not fixed and are fluid and overlapping:

> ... we define 'gender' as referring to the performative aspect of being a 'man' or a 'woman,' the cultural role models one adopts to act as one or the other. The second term, 'sex,' is understood here to refer to the physical aspects of being identified as 'male' or 'female,' while 'sexuality' refers to one's sexual orientation.[4]

Now think of these comments in light of the following comments by Paul: 'Does not nature itself teach you that if a man wears long hair, it is degrading to him' (1 Cor. 11.14). We might further think of related issues. Through appeal to nature, does not Paul think hair length for being a man is obvious and fixed? But then nature has not been so obvious throughout history with ideas of long hair changing all the time. So what defines long hair? What defines unnatural hair? Where does short hair end and long hair begin?

Identity, Networks and Christian Origins

In a more subtle way, we might think of the ways in which masculine behaviour could often be constructed as centring on households. A man might conventionally be thought, among other things, to be the one to head a household and actively procreate. Halvor Moxnes uses 'queer theory' to explain the seemingly unusual views of Jesus on household in the Gospel tradition.[5] Here 'queer theory' theory is used not simply in terms of Jesus' sexuality but as a questioning of fixed categories of identity and challenging social boundaries deemed to be the norm.

One way we might think about these gender-related categories being changing and flexible is through the Jesus tradition. On the one hand, it might be argued that Jesus' migratory ministry (cf. Matt. 8.20//Luke 9.58[6]) was framed in traditionally masculine ways such as self-control. However, this migratory ministry also raised seemingly contradictory issues concerning the ways in which masculinity was understood. Jesus was not, as was perhaps expected, heading his household and procreating. Moxnes argues that such issues may underlie the following saying in Matthew 19.12: 'For there are eunuchs who have been so from birth, and there are eunuchs who have been made eunuchs by others, and there are eunuchs who have made themselves eunuchs for the sake of the kingdom of heaven. Let anyone accept this who can'. For Moxnes, Jesus could be playing on an allegation levelled at his movement for being un-manly because eunuchs were an ambiguous category in the ancient world and one that was certainly mocked by different writers (cf. Apuleius, *Met.* 7.24–31; Lucian, *Eunuch* 8–9). Eunuchs could be referred to as woman-like, half-men, effeminate and so on and this may well have been known to Jesus, his followers and his opponents through travelling religious groups in Syria-Palestine (compare Lucian, *Syr. Dea* 20ff.; Apuleius, *Met.* 7.24–31; Justin, *Apol.* 1.29). It could be argued that Jesus symbolically re-interpreted the category of eunuch, perhaps in response to opponents' allegations, to describe his movement, a movement now removed from traditional gender categories.

It is difficult to be sure if this is a fair reading on the basis of one verse but it is clear that Jesus is remembered in terms of using a highly ambiguous category such as 'eunuch'. This use of ambiguous gender categories is found elsewhere in the gospel tradition (e.g. Mark 12.18–27; Luke 20.34–36). It is also notable that Jesus is remembered not as head of a conventional household but as head of a socially displaced group including widows and mothers but, intriguingly, no fathers (cf. Mark 3.34; Matt. 23.9). However, these seemingly 'un-masculine' categories in earliest Christianity were hardly universally applied. There are well-known hostile views in earliest Christianity towards homosexuality (Rom. 1.26–28) and behaviour deemed non-masculine (e.g. 1 Cor. 6.9–11; 11.14–15), views echoed elsewhere in the ancient world (Lev. 18.22; 20.13; Apion 2.119; Arist. 152; Sib. Or. 3.185, 584–606, 762–66; Philo, Spec. Leg. 3.37–42; Hypoth. 7.1; Cont. 59–62). Perhaps it was no surprise that a continual playing around with traditional gender roles was not widespread in earliest Christianity.

We might develop our general discussion of identity by adding that people take on different roles in different social contexts. People behave differently at sporting events, religious ceremonies, libraries, pubs and bars, and so on. People may well emphasise one aspect of their identity at a sporting event that they would not do at another, say a job interview. Then we could bring in all sorts of factors such as class and ethnicity. For instance, there may be different social expectations of the ways in which elite men and women ought to behave than lower class women and men.

As already implied, we should not think of the various categories (class, gender, ethnicity, etc.) as mutually exclusive. Based on a range of literary, inscriptional and archaeological evidence, scholars of Christian origins have long pointed out that there were a range of differing social networks used by the first Christians (among others) in the spread of ideas and influence. These social networks would have included family connections, households, workplace, trade and 'religious' meeting places. Urban centres were densely populated and privacy would have been a luxury. Tapping into a particular network and finding contacts would have been relatively easy and we might even expect identities and perceptions to be shifting in such densely populated contexts. Compare, for instance, finding of a contact and the different identities at play in the following passage from Acts:

> After this Paul left Athens and went to Corinth.[2] There he found a Jew named Aquila, a native of Pontus, who had recently come from Italy with his wife Priscilla, because Claudius had ordered all Jews to leave Rome. Paul went to see them,[3] and, because he was of the same trade, he stayed with them, and they worked together – by trade they were tentmakers.
>
> (Acts 18.1–3)

As Philip Harland in particular has argued, there were, inevitably perhaps, dual or multiple affiliations to different groups (trade, associations, synagogues, etc.) in the Eastern Mediterranean.[7] It is no surprise, therefore, that different identities could be brought to the fore in different contexts.

Even within the family, issues of different affiliations were present for the early Christians. In 1 Cor. 7.12–16, for instance, Paul has to deal with marriage partners who believe and marriage partners who do not. For all Paul's optimism that the unbeliever might come to the fold, it is clear that he accepts the possibility that they may well separate. In Chapter 7 we will look at such passages in relation to conversion to the new movement and the countervailing influences at work.

It is perhaps no surprise, then, that with different social influences we find examples of individuals behaving differently in different contexts. A particularly good example of identity changing in different contexts might be Herod the Great, the infamous Herod of the birth and infancy story. There is a long history of criticising Herod the Great's relationship with Judaism. From the earliest point, it appears people doubted whether he really was a 'Jew' or not or whether he really ought to be thought of as an Idumean or, indeed, whether he ought to be thought as something in between: Josephus claims that Herod the Great was even thought of (polemically) as a 'half-Jew'. Some Jews could refer to Herod as their king in disputes against non-Jewish opponents while other Jews could think of him as anything but (compare e.g. *Ant.* 14.8–10; *Ant.* 15.326–300; *Ant.* 19.328–30; *Ant.* 20.173). From the ancient sources we find presentations of different positions probably inspired by Herod the Great's behaviour in different contexts: he might support massive projects aimed at emphasising his 'Jewish' credentials such as carrying out the massive project of rebuilding the Jewish temple in Jerusalem while supporting a range of building projects which may well have been deemed 'idolatrous' in non-Jewish urban centres. According to Josephus,

> There was also another disturbance at Caesarea – those Jews who were mixed with the Syrians that lived there, rising a tumult against them. The Jews pretended that the city was theirs, and said that he who built it was a Jew, meaning King Herod. The Syrians confessed also that its builder was a Jew; but they still said, however, that the city was a Greek city; for that he who set up statues and temples in it could not design it for Jews.
>
> (*War* 2.266)

On one level, is this so very different from Paul's assertion that 'To the Jews I became as a Jew … To those under the law I became as one under the law … to those outside the law I became as one outside the law …' (1 Cor. 9.20–21)?

Postcolonial Criticism

Issues of race, ethnicity, and blurred identity boundaries bring us to the heart of an increasingly popular approach to New Testament texts in the past decade: postcolonial criticism. I will use a broad definition when referring to 'postcolonial criticism' of the New Testament. The term can cover a number of approaches and typically involves the readings in the context of empire and imperialism and all the complexities such systems of power entail, from the overtly brutal and explicitly acquisitive to the more rhetorically subtle brutal international economic systems. As for the terms 'empire', 'colonialism' and 'imperialism' I follow another broad definition by one of the pioneering figures for postcolonial criticism in the humanities, Edward Said (by way of Michael Doyle):

> As I shall be using the term, 'imperialism' means the practice, the theory, and the attitudes of a dominating metropolitan centre ruling a distant territory; 'colonialism', which is almost always a consequence of imperialism, is the implanting of settlements on distant territory. As Michael Doyle puts it: 'Empire is a relationship, formal or informal, in which one state controls the effective political sovereignty of another political society. It can be achieved by force, by political collaboration, by economic, social, or cultural dependence. Imperialism is simply the process or policy of establishing or maintaining an empire.'[8]

In biblical studies, postcolonial readings range from biblical texts as works of resistance to empire and imperialism to biblical texts supportive of empire and imperial power, or at least replicating the power structures of imperialism. Throughout such readings, it is worth emphasising, are the ways in which empire and imperialism intersect with other areas of analysis such as race, class, gender and so on.

Such postcolonial readings can be in the classical historical critical mode of the sorts we have seen in this chapter, namely reading the texts in original historical contexts. Alternatively, such readings might focus on the ways in which the Bible has been used in the context of more recent European or American imperialisms. We will return to readings of the New Testament in light of more modern empires and imperialism later in this book; in this chapter we will look at readings of the New Testament in terms of ancient empires and imperialism or, to be more precise, the Roman Empire and its influence.[9]

In terms of the New Testament, Mark's Gospel has received a lot of attention from the perspective of postcolonial criticism.[10] As Stephen Moore puts it, there are two polarised positions in postcolonial biblical criticism and Mark's Gospel in particular: a hard-line anti-imperial literature or literature which replicates the imperial and colonial ideologies even if attempting to resist them. On the one hand we might place Ched Myers, Herman Waetjen and Richard Horsley who read Mark's Gospel as a profoundly anti-imperialistic resistance literature. According to Myers:

> His primary audience were those whose daily lives bore the exploitative weight of colonialism ... Mark's Gospel originally was written to help imperial subjects learn the hard truth about their world and themselves ... to those willing to raise the wrath of empire, Mark offers a way of

discipleship (8.34ff.) ... There was ample social, economic, political, and cultural justification for a strategy that delegitimized both the Roman *and* the authority of the Jewish aristocracy ... [11]

On the other hand we might follow Moore and locate Tat-siong Benny Liew who argues that Mark replicates imperial ideology by replacing the power of Rome with the power of Jesus the Messiah who cuts a 'kingly' and highly authoritative figure, who is God's only heir and who will also return to crush all opposition. According to Liew:

> Looking at the way Mark (1) attributes absolute authority to Jesus, (2) preserves the insider-outsider binarism, and (3) understands the nature of 'legitimate' authority ... Mark has indeed internalized the imperialistic ideology of his colonizers ... Presenting an all-authoritative Jesus who will eventually annihilate all opponents and all other authorities, Mark's utopian, or dystopian, vision, in effect duplicates the colonial (non) choice of 'serve-or-be-destroyed'.[12]

Here we might make mention of the early twentieth-century work of Antonio Gramsci (1891–1937) which developed ideas relating to hegemony and how elite ideology becomes absorbed across society as one way of maintaining elite power. This is echoed in the postcolonial concept of 'mimicry' and has become one of the most influential concepts to have emerged from postcolonial studies, and especially through the work of the theorist Homi Bhabha, and picked up in the work of Liew, Moore and others.[13] According to this sort of reading, the colonised digest, replicate and mimic the culture of the coloniser and so the ideas of the coloniser are potentially destabilised. This might mean an earnest acceptance of colonial ideas and ideology, it might mean a caricature of colonial ideology, and/or it might mean potentially replacing one system of domination with another system of domination and thereby maintaining the power structures in a different guise. Whatever way we look at it, the mimicry of colonial identities is never quite the same in the hands of the colonised.

I Peter and Revelation in Postcolonial Contexts

The postcolonial concept of 'mimicry', among other things, can help us in analysing two New Testament texts which have been seen as having very different reactions to life in the Roman Empire: 1 Peter and Revelation. Philip Harland analysed and compared both these texts in order to establish different ways in which Christians were (or were not) able to participate in the ancient world and to challenge a common reading of 1 Peter where the text was read as a work of a radical Christian sect.[14] For Harland (and others) there has been an over-emphasis on exclusivity and separation and such views do not pay sufficient attention to the endorsement of activities relating to empire. Clearly, then, such concerns have much in common with postcolonial readings.

It seems clear that 1 Peter in fact endorses conventional models of house-holds and positive views towards authority. Compare the following passage: 'Slaves, accept the authority of your masters with all deference, not only those who are kind and gentle but also those who are harsh' (1 Pet. 2.18). Preceding this verse, 1 Peter even endorses the values of the surrounding civic life, including institutions honouring the Emperor:

> Beloved, I urge you as aliens and exiles to abstain from the desires of the flesh that wage war against the soul.[12] Conduct yourselves honorably among the Gentiles, so that, though they malign you as evildoers, they may see your honorable deeds and glorify God when he comes to judge.[13] For the Lord's sake accept the authority of every human institution, whe-ther of the emperor as supreme,[14] or of governors, as sent by him to punish those who do wrong and to praise those who do right.[15] For it is God's will that by doing right you should silence the ignorance of the foolish.[16] As servants of God, live as free people, yet do not use your freedom as a pretext for evil.[17] Honour everyone. Love the family of believers. Fear God. Honour the emperor.
>
> (1 Pet. 2.11–17)

Given the differing degrees of assimilation and accommodation it is quite possible that some Christians thought along the lines that 'as to the eating of food offered to idols, we know that "no idol in the world really exists," and that "there is no God but one"' (1 Cor. 8.4). What we have here is not a wholesale removal from the Empire but an adaptation (though a potentially provocative adoption) to the ways of the Empire, working out ways in which those associated with 1 Peter can uphold their distinctive Christian identity in a potentially hostile world, as indeed other non-Christian groups did. A scho-lar such as Harland might view this as a social strategy of the author to lessen group-society tensions whereas a potentially complementary postcolonial reading might view such an approach as a classic case of mimicry in that the text absorbs social norms and repeats them but in a new modified, hybridised and Christianised way.

However, it is also clear, as has already been implied, that 1 Peter does not wholeheartedly embrace the world of the Roman Empire, as might be expected from a time when the Empire certainly was not Christian. We therefore also get 'pro-Empire' sentiments as well as a harsh caricaturing of the behaviour of the rest of the world:

> You have already spent enough time in doing what the Gentiles like to do, living in licentiousness, passions, drunkenness, revels, carousing, and lawless idolatry.[4] They are surprised that you no longer join them in the

same excesses of dissipation, and so they blaspheme.[5] But they will have to give an accounting to him who stands ready to judge the living and the dead.

(1 Pet. 4.3)

While listing the vices of Gentiles has a history in early Judaism, even here we could make a case for postcolonial mimicry because earlier in 1 Peter the author says, 'Conduct yourselves honourably among the Gentiles, so that, though they malign you as evildoers, they may see your honourable deeds and glorify God when he comes to judge' (2.12). There are clear connections between 1 Peter 4.3 and 2.12. In both cases the other group is maligned and in both cases judgement will come. We could argue then that 1 Peter is mimicking (consciously or otherwise) the behaviour of the society that apparently judges the Christians.

Mimicking societal judgement and turning it on the judger is taken to a greater extreme in the book of Revelation. Furthermore, the sort of accommodation to the Roman Empire we find in 1 Peter is everything that the book of Revelation abhors. While the details of precise historical location are debated, it is certainly the case that the unnerving and symbolic language of Revelation is firing at the Roman Empire in the strongest possible sense and looking to its end and replacement. It is probably more accurate to call Revelation a sectarian work in that distinct boundaries are drawn around the Christian movement and participation in areas of civic life, such as honouring the Emperor, are out of the question. Developing the prophetic tradition of the Hebrew Bible/Old Testament, the metaphor of 'fornication' is used for honouring the Emperor rather than God and the Lamb alongside general passages advocating who is deemed *truly* worthy of worship (Rev. 4.11; 5.12–13; 7.11–12; 13.4–8; 14.7; 14.9–11; 20.4–6; 22.8–9). Unlike 1 Peter and Paul in 1 Corinthians, there is not even lip service paid to the Empire and Emperor. Indeed, John fires at the 'Nicolaitans' and those who follow 'Jezebel' and 'Balaam' (both negative symbolic names) and eat food dedicated to idols (e.g. Rev. 2.14, 20; 9.20–21). Revelation also slams the general commercial practices of the Roman Empire (e.g. Rev. 18) and, for example, hits hard at the church in Laodicea for their complicity (Rev. 3.14–18). The horrifying future depicted in Revelation has those with the mark of the beast buying and selling:

... and it was allowed to give breath to the image of the beast so that the image of the beast could even speak and cause those who would not worship the image of the beast to be killed.[16] Also it causes all, both small and great, both rich and poor, both free and slave, to be marked on the right hand or the forehead,[17] so that no one can buy or sell who does not have the mark, that is, the name of the beast or the number of its name.[18] This calls for wisdom: let anyone with understanding calculate the number of the beast, for it is the number of a person. Its number is six hundred sixty-six.

(13.15–18)

However, as Stephen Moore has shown (see also the extract in Chapter 12), while Revelation is the most explicitly anti-Empire text in the New Testament, it is still dependent on the model of empire in general, and the Roman Empire in particular. In other words, we are dealing with a text ripe for analysis in the light of the postcolonial concept of mimicry. For a start, the replacement of empire with empire is clear in Revelation 11.15: 'The kingdom of the world has become the kingdom of our Lord and of his Messiah, and he will reign forever and ever.' It is no surprise, then, that the empire to come is modelled on the empire past. In addition to the language of violence and conquest in Revelation, we might add that the New Jerusalem will replace the mocked 'Babylon' ('Babylon' in Revelation is usually taken to be a coded reference to Rome) and Christians gain the chance to share in the power of the empire to come (Rev. 3.21; 5.10; 20.4–6; 22.5). At the top of the pyramid of power, as has long been noted, the language about God in Revelation (e.g. Rev. 4–5) is similar to the language used of Roman Emperors. Revelation certainly uses the model of the Empire to subvert the Empire but things are not so black and white. In Revelation, the Roman Empire is vigorously challenged, mocked, parodied, replaced, replicated and, ultimately, anything but avoided in a classic example of postcolonial mimicry. As Moore colourfully puts it,

> The seer storms out of the main gates of the imperial palace, wrecking tools in hand, only to be surreptitiously swept back in through the rear entrance, having been deftly relieved of his tools at the threshold … Revelation's overt resistance to and expressed revulsion toward Roman imperial ideology is surreptitiously compromised and undercut by covert compliance and attraction.[15]

Summary

Like history, identity can mean different things to different people, and in practice it is difficult to establish fixed identities. For instance, being a Jew in the ancient world could mean different things in different contexts. Some Jews might emphasise the importance of Sabbath and food laws in contexts of conflict or association with Gentiles, for instance. Some Jews might place minimal emphasis on such practices either generally or when with Gentile friends. Roles attributed to individuals and groups are invariably socially constructed and not easily reduced to biological inevitability. We saw the ways in which gender could be constructed with reference to Jesus and Paul. The approaches to identity as fluid concept feed neatly into the rise of postcolonial criticism in New Testament studies where simple binary oppositions of oppressed and oppressor have been challenged and a range of responses to Empire have been seen in New Testament texts, from ferocious opposition to accommodation. Even in the cases of opposition to the Roman Empire, we also saw how such texts still used the language of power and imperialism in their responses.

Key Words

Essentialist: An approach to identity whereby identity is deemed fixed and unchanging.

Gender: The cultural and social presentation of being a man or a woman.

Mimicry: A postcolonial concept whereby the colonised absorb ideologies of colonial powers and 'mimic' the power and power structures of the colonisers. This mimicry can range from open acceptance to outright mockery.

Non-essentialist: An approach to identity whereby identity is not fixed and adapts to different contexts. Perception is an important part of non-essentialist approaches to the understanding of identity.

Postcolonial criticism: Reading in the context of empire and imperialism and the complex relations of power in such contexts.

Further Reading

Arnal, W., *The Symbolic Jesus: Historical Scholarship, Judaism and the Construction of Contemporary Identity*, London & Oakville: Equinox, 2005.

Harland, P.A., *Associations, Synagogues, and Congregations: Claiming a Place in Ancient Mediterranean Society*, Minneapolis: Fortress, 2003.

Moore, S.D., *Empire and Apocalypse: Postcolonialism and the New Testament*, Sheffield: Sheffield Phoenix Press, 2006.

Moxnes, H., *Putting Jesus in His Place: A Radical Vision of Household and Kingdom*, Louisville: WJK, 2003.

Smith, J.Z., *Drudgery Divine: On the Comparison of Early Christianities and the Religions of Late Antiquity*, Chicago: University of Chicago Press, 1990.

Sugirtharajah, R.S., *Postcolonial Criticism and Biblical Interpretation*, Oxford: OUP, 2002.

Vander Stichele, C. and T. Penner, *Contextualizing Gender in Early Christian Discourse: Thinking beyond Thecla*, London: T&T Clark/Continuum, 2009.

Chapter 4

Applying Methods Old and New

With the work on the cultural world of Christian origins and the New Testament in mind, we are now in a position to wed some of these insights to a traditional historical approach to the Gospel tradition. I would strongly stress that the intersecting approaches I will use here are but the tip of the iceberg and they could all be developed in much more detail and with much more nuance. But in the following example I hope to show how those different approaches we have seen in Chapters 2 and 3 can be used in practice and with more detail.

Mark 6.17–29: Form and Context

With these qualifications in mind, the text I have selected is Mark 6.17–29, the story of the death of John the Baptist:

> 6.17 For Herod himself had sent men who arrested John, bound him, and put him in prison on account of Herodias, his brother Philip's wife, because Herod [Antipas] had married her.[18] For John had been telling Herod [Antipas], "It is not lawful for you to have your brother's wife."[19] And Herodias had a grudge against him, and wanted to kill him. But she could not,[20] for Herod [Antipas] feared John, knowing that he was a righteous and holy man, and he protected him. When he heard him, he was greatly perplexed; and yet he liked to listen to him.[21] But an opportunity came when Herod [Antipas] on his birthday gave a banquet for his courtiers and officers and for the leaders of Galilee.[22] When his daughter Herodias came in and danced, she pleased Herod [Antipas] and his guests; and the king said to the girl, "Ask me for whatever you wish, and I will give it."[23] And he solemnly swore to her, "Whatever you ask me, I will give you, even half of my kingdom."[24] She went out and said to her mother, "What should I ask for?" She replied, "The head of John the baptizer."[25] Immediately she rushed back to the king and requested, "I want you to give me at once the head of John the Baptist on a platter."[26] The king was deeply grieved; yet out of regard for his oaths

and for the guests, he did not want to refuse her.[27] Immediately the king sent a soldier of the guard with orders to bring John's head. He went and beheaded him in the prison,[28] brought his head on a platter, and gave it to the girl. Then the girl gave it to her mother.[29] When his disciples heard about it, they came and took his body, and laid it in a tomb.

(Mark 6.17–29)

In form critical terms this story is sometimes labelled a 'martyrdom tale', comparable to the martyrdom tales in early Judaism (e.g. 2 Macc. 6.18–31; see also Acts 6–7). However, there are features central to martyrdom tales missing from Mark's account of the death of John the Baptist, such as a description of the sufferings of the martyr and the martyr's defence of their actions. Something like 'court tale' or 'court legend' might be more appropriate.[1] In the ancient world, stories of the misuse of power in royal courts were certainly known, including the suffering of an innocent. As we will see, it seems as if Mark 6.17–29 has been heavily influenced by court tales based on the book of Esther. We should not, however, impose categories too forcefully. As we will also see, there are plenty of other and related popular motifs present in Mark 6.17–29.

One way we might establish Mark 6.17–29 as a tradition of court intrigue prior to its appearance in the Gospel of Mark is that elsewhere in Mark, the Gospel tradition generally, and an important non-New Testament source in Josephus, John the Baptist and the Galilean ruler Herod Antipas are always portrayed as enemies with no indication that Herod Antipas ever showed remorse. Mark portrays those associated with Herod Antipas in a negative light when dealing with Jesus (e.g. Mark 3.6; 8.15; 12.13) while in Luke's Gospel there is some ambiguity in Jesus' trial before Herod Antipas but still Antipas and his soldiers are said to have treated Jesus contemptuously (Luke 23.6–12). In the account given by the first-century Jewish historian Josephus we are only told of a typical response of a tyrant to any potential threat (real or otherwise) to their power:

> Now, when [many] others came in crowds about him, for they were very greatly moved [or pleased] by hearing his words, Herod [Antipas], who feared lest the great influence John had over the people might put it into his power and inclination to raise a rebellion, (for they seemed ready to do anything he should advise,) thought it best, by putting him to death, to prevent any mischief he might cause, and not bring himself into difficulties, by sparing a man who might make him repent of it when it would be too late.

(Ant. 18.116–19)

We might compare this response with Matthew's account of the death of John the Baptist: 'Though he [Herod Antipas] wanted to put him to death, he feared the crowd, because they regarded him as a prophet' (Matt. 14.5). None of our other first-century sources explaining John the Baptist's death ever portray Herod Antipas having remorse for what he had done or care for learning about John the Baptist's teaching. Now of course it could be the case that Mark has a source portraying Herod Antipas in a positive light that no one else had or that no one else cared about. But we are still left with the issue that Mark actually has such a passage expressing sentiments others did not and a passage going against Mark's clear tendency to portray Herod Antipas in a negative light, a tendency, as we mentioned, found elsewhere in the Gospel tradition. It could be argued that such arguments are a good indication of Mark 6.17–29 pre-dating the Gospel of Mark.

At this point it is worth discussing issues of historicity and 'did it really happen or not' sort of questions, though these will be the focus of a later section. It is certainly true that a lot of traditional German form criticism had little concern for establishing historical accuracy of these traditions and thought they told us the concerns of faith. In our precise example it could theoretically have been the case that the story of the dancing girl and Herod Antipas being duped really did happen, just as, obviously, the opposite could theoretically have been the case. However, it is also possible for people who hold both views to engage in the kind of reading of a Gospel tradition as being done here. It remains that we *do* have an unusual spin on the death of John the Baptist and so we could now ask a different kind of historical question of this passage: why did this seemingly unique spin on Herod Antipas' relation-ship with John the Baptist emerge or why was it deemed worthy of retaining in the pre-Gospel tradition? Put another way, what was the social function of this particular use of the form of a court tale?

One possible solution is that an early group related to the Christian movement were facing charges of subversion. It is worth pointing out that the emphasis on the coming kingdom of God would no doubt have some serious implications for the then present rulers of the world: Rome. We might add that Jesus was executed as a criminal and so it is understandable his followers would have been worried that their beliefs could have led to a similar fate. And of course followers of John the Baptist (cf. Acts 19.1–7) could also have been worried of facing a similar fate. The unusual story of the death of John the Baptist in Mark 6.17–29 is, on one level, clear that John the Baptist was no political threat and was executed due to little more than the whim of a resentful wife. Does not this story let Herod Antipas off the hook?

We could also develop the related question of social historical context. Outside New Testament studies, the historian of French cultural history, Robert Darnton, developed ideas from cultural and social anthropology to understand stories told by, among others, French lower classes in the eight-eenth century.[2] Developing the work of the famous anthropologist Clifford Geertz, one of Darnton's interests was to look at the ways in which cultural and historical distance can assist in understanding historical sources. According to Darnton, that which strikes the modern reader as unfunny, repulsive or opaque is one way to begin the interpretative task. By then trying to understand the joke, the riddle, the ceremony, the proverb and so on is one way to understand broader social and cultural trends, such as constructions of gender roles and class differences, as well as establishing historical contexts. While many Bible stories have become deeply embedded in different contemporary cultures, for this modern reader, and no doubt for many more, the story of a mother using her daughter to dance in front of the king to secure a promise of beheading does seem highly unusual and it might be significant that the dancing and beheading has been an obsession in the history of interpretation of this passage in much art and literature. We might add to Darnton that looking at texts such as Mark 6.17–29 where an unusual argument is made in distinction from other ancient sources – in this case the blame for the death of John the Baptist – could be an equally and complementary entry point for interpretation. Likewise, once we establish that a text makes a seemingly unique case we can then start asking why this is so and what kind of historical context gave rise to such seemingly unique readings.[3]

Storytelling

Here we can now bring in some more precise work on the cultural context, namely the role of storytelling and haggadah noted above because similar stories in the ancient world give details on those parts of the story which might seem to us to be unusual. One widely noted parallel story used to understand the death of John the Baptist in Jewish traditions is the interpretation of the book of Esther, a book which is clearly referenced in Mark 6.17–19 in the promise of half a kingdom (Esther 5.3; 7.2).[4] There are other linguistic echoes which are precise in Greek as well as English. Like 'the girl' of Mark 6.17–29, 'the girl' Esther likewise 'pleased' the king in Esther 2.9 (see also Esther 2.4, 9, 15, 17) and both would, of course, obtain the promise of half a kingdom. Such are the similarities that retellings and rewritings of this Esther story involve a banquet for King Ahasuerus' birthday where it is even said that the innocent Queen Vashti was beheaded accompanied by the serving of her head on a platter (e.g. Esther Rabbah 4.9–11)!

Here we can also bring in to play the ways in which significant differences as based on the general similarities can provide helpful interpretative insights as mentioned above. While Mark 6.17–19 has clear links with the retelling of the Esther story there is one noticeable difference which enhances the reading suggested here. The retellings of the Esther story have a clear stress on the king being fearful of Jewish rebellion. The king in one Aramaic version of the Esther story promises half the kingdom but adds an exception clause: there will be no rebuilding of the Temple in Jerusalem. The king will not do this because he fears a Jewish rebellion. We might add to this that according to Josephus John the Baptist was killed because Herod Antipas feared John to be a revolutionary threat so he executed him (*Ant*. 18.118). In Mark 6.17–29 we have a different fear: Herod Antipas fears John the Baptist because he is 'a wise and righteous man'. The version in Mark 6.17–29 is significantly different and the rebellious aspect is conspicuously not present. From this perspective, John the Baptist certainly is *not* a rebellious threat.

John the Baptist's unfortunate fate is that of beheading, the kind of fate those perceived revolutionary figures of the first century faced. Sometimes perception was all that mattered to those in power and if someone was a potential threat then why take the risk in letting such a person live (a kind of 'ask questions later' policy)? No surprise that Mark 6.17–29 wants to make it clear that John's decapitation really was unfair. Again, it is possible that Mark 6.17–29 turned to the retelling of the Esther story to help make his case because there were various versions where the king was regretful of the beheading/killing/banishment of the queen because she was innocent (compare Esther 2.1; *Ant*. 11.190–95; Esther Rabbah 5.2; 2 Targum Esther 2.1). As we saw, according to some traditions, Queen Vashti was, like John the Baptist, beheaded with her head presented on a platter and according to some traditions, Queen Vashti was, like John, innocent, causing the king remorse. The implications of this for Mark 6.17–29 would be to stress yet again that John the Baptist had done nothing wrong and was wrongly killed.

Telling Stories about Men and Women

With this material in mind, we can now turn to the first seemingly unusual part of the story: the mother and her dancing daughter. For a start, rightly or wrongly, this passage ultimately puts the blame for John the Baptist's death at Herodias' door, in stark contrast to other first-century sources where Herod Antipas is unambiguously implicated. Herodias bears the grudge and Herodias wants John killed. Two questions we might ask are: how was Herodias understood in the first century and how would blaming Herodias have been accepted? Probably the best resource we have for such aristocratic women in early Judaism is, as ever, Josephus. As it happens, Josephus did not like Herodias and blames her for having a significant part in Herod Antipas' eventual downfall. Josephus portrays Herodias stereotypically as a nagging wife, envious of the success of others and trying to get her husband to better their already highly privileged lives at all costs while Herod Antipas was happy with the way things were. Josephus is extremely clear on who he thought was the driving force: 'she never flagged till she carried the day and made him her unwilling partisan, for there was no way of escape once she had cast her vote on this matter' (*Ant*. 18.246). This would all lead to disaster and exile, and Josephus is equally clear who was to blame: 'And so God visited this punishment on Herodias for her envy of her brother and on Herod [Antipas] for listening to a woman's frivolous chatter' (*Ant.* 18.255). The person or people responsible for Mark 6.17–29 would no doubt have found at least one sympathiser in putting the blame on Herodias and portraying her as a deceiving woman capable of leading her husband astray.

We do not have so much data on Heriodias' dancing daughter, Salome. But the dancing daughter does have a pivotal role so one place to turn might be to the storytelling and haggadic parallels to Mark 6.17–29, particularly the retellings of the book of Esther. One later retelling of the Esther story in rabbinic literature has naked dancing women at the banquet of King Ahasuerus and the drunken king wanting his queen, Vashti, to perform likewise. Queen Vashti refused and so she was killed (*Pirqe Rabbi Eliezer* 49 on Esther 1:8, 10–12, 19). Emphasising Vashti's innocence, another later Jewish interpretation of Esther 1.2 is stark in its assessment: Satan came and danced at the banquet and had Vashti killed (b. *Megillah* 11b)!

While it is certainly possible to trace later traditions to around the time of the first century, lateness remains a problem. However, here we can think more in terms of the cultural construction of gender, and more precisely the ways in which dancing women and their relationship to male watchers were understood. Josephus (*Ant.* 12.187–89) discusses a story of Joseph of Jerusalem who became besotted with a dancing girl but faced a problem marrying a non-Jew (Joseph was ultimately saved by his brother who disguised his own daughter – Joseph's niece – as a replacement). According to this perspective, dancing women can cause all sorts of problems for unsuspecting men. Again, there would have been at least some who would have empathised with Herod Antipas' situation in Mark 6.17–19.

Furthermore, even more upright men could be misled from these kinds of perspectives. A text from the Dead Sea Scrolls, the Damascus Document, is worried about guilty thoughts and lascivious eyes. But the writer is doubly worried because even 'brave heroes' have stumbled (CD 2.16–17). By the first century, there was also a long established tradition of associating evil with seductive females to the extent of personifying evil as a wicked woman. The book of Proverbs is one example of this (e.g. Prov. 7.25–26). The Dead Sea Scrolls include similar sentiments in a text labelled by modern scholars as 4Q184, or 'The Wiles of the Wicked Woman', and here the personification of evil is similarly enticing men, even the most upright, always from godly ways. The evil alluring woman was therefore an established cliché in the cultural context of Mark 6.17–29.

However, ancient writers could also personify wisdom as a woman and also wisdom as an alluring and sexually desirable woman (e.g. Sir. 51.13–19; 11Q5 11 21.11–18). In other words, the female personification of Wisdom was very much like the female personification of evil. No surprise then that they can be described as behaving similarly in the same text. Compare the following from the book of Proverbs:

She [the sexually immoral woman] is loud and wayward; her feet do not stay at home; now in the street, now in the squares, and at every corner she lies in wait …

(Prov. 7.11–12)

Does not wisdom call, and does not understanding raise her voice? On the heights, beside the way, at the crossroads she takes her stand; beside the gates in front of the town, at the entrance of the portals she cries out …

(Prov. 8.1–3)

These personifications are therefore ambiguous. According to the book of Esther, Esther uses her sexuality positively. In Mark 6.17–29, the dancing daughter does not. With all these perspectives in mind, how does the man know which is which with such dangerous ambiguities? How was Herod Antipas supposed to know, if even the most upright man can be deceived? Is this not the kind of perspective from which Herod Antipas might be excused from promising so much and falling into the trap of having to agree to John the Baptist's death?

We can go further into the illumination of ancient cultural contexts and Darnton's approach to cultural difference. Herod Antipas is trapped by swearing to do whatever the dancing girl asked of him and that was, of course, acquiring the head of John the Baptist. Ideally, oaths and vows were to be taken extremely seriously, at least according to relevant ancient texts (e.g. Deut. 23.21), perhaps the most alarming of which is the Old Testament/ Hebrew Bible story of Jephthah's daughter (Judg. 11.30–40) where Jephthah vows to offer up as a sacrifice the first person who comes through his door if God provides a military victory. God does so and unfortunately Jephthah's daughter is the one who has to be sacrificed. Furthermore, even someone as powerful as the infamous Roman Emperor Gaius Caligula (12–41 CE) was forced to keep his vow which he might not have made had he been a little more sober at a banquet, not least because of illustrious witnesses (*Ant.* 18.298). With such illustrious perspectives in mind, did Herod Antipas have any choice but to consent once he realised he had been trapped in front of his own illustrious guests? After all, our passage is emphatic that Herod Antipas was both innocent and in a deeply awkward position: 'The king was deeply grieved; yet out of regard for his oaths and for the guests, he did not want to refuse her' (Mark 6.26).

Historical and Literary Locations: from Precise Datings to Postcolonial Mimicry

If we are interested in fulfilling the aims of form criticism and locating the form in its life setting, what can we then do with Mark 6.17–29? What might have been the immediate circumstances in which a court tale or legend might have flourished? We have seen some broader cultural contexts involving the construction of gender and the dangers of living in threat of death from political powers. More precise historical locations involve an inevitably speculative approach to history. We might speculate that as this is the only place in the gospel where Jesus is *not* the focus of attention, the pre-Gospel history of this passage may have been associated more with followers of John the Baptist. Some scholars have suggested that there is some influence of the Aramaic language on Mark 6.17–29 and so this passage would probably have emerged in or around the area of Syria-Palestine.

As for more precise historical setting, we might suggest that general context of living under political powers and living under some local Roman ruler or Roman puppets such as Herod Antipas' successor, Agrippa I, would certainly make sense. We could perhaps rule out the context of living under Herod Antipas because Herodias would probably want a few more dead if she ever came across such storytelling, as might Herod Antipas. When Agrippa I began to rise to power towards the end of the 30s CE when Herod Antipas was exiled, thanks in part to the plotting of Agrippa I, would be a particularly smart time to write or even openly tell such a story and if Agrippa's people heard of such sentiments they may well have been impressed. Josephus says that Herodias 'begrudged her brother [Agrippa] his rise to power far above the state that her husband enjoyed' and that Agrippa's penchant for ostentation 'made her especially helpless to keep this unfortunate envy to herself' (*Ant.* 18.240). Significantly, Agrippa I appears to have persecuted those associated with the Christian movement in Jerusalem (Acts 12) so pleading innocence could well have been important. In all this we should not forget that there appear to have been important links between the earliest Christian movement and followers of Jesus and the Herodian court (cf. Luke 8.3; Acts 13.1).

But as with many attempts to read Gospel passages in light of precise historical situations, we are building on shaky foundations. If we date the Gospel of Mark early (c. 40 CE) then a reading in the context of Agrippa I would be more plausible for the simple reason that later alternatives are ruled out; if we date the Gospel later (c. 65–75 CE) the later alternatives are ruled back in. We know of a prophetic figure called Theudas, active under the procurator Cuspius Fadus (44–48 CE), and mentioned in Acts 5.36 as having a following of 400 people. Theudas persuaded his following to go out to the River Jordan and watch the river part, a prophetic move no doubt deliberately recalling stories of Moses and Joshua. There is no indication that this was a violent revolutionary movement but Cuspius Fadus killed them anyway and beheaded Theudas (*Ant.* 20.97–99). It is not difficult to imagine someone seeing the benefits of a story about the death of John the Baptist having resonance in this context. Alternatively, we might turn to the time when the Roman procurator of Judea, Felix, was in charge and there was social upheaval with various prophetic-type figures alongside the more violent bandits and assassins, some of whom went to the desert to look for signs of deliverance

(*War* 2.254–68; *Ant*. 20.161–74). Would not the story of the death of John the Baptist also make sense in this context?

We could go on with speculating and one obvious benefit of outlining these different contexts is not that they provide the precise context for the story (though they might) but that they show that the story would have made very good sense at almost any time in the first century and so we can at least suggest that the general threat of persecution of a movement associated with someone like John the Baptist was always present and it is at least not overly speculative to suggest this. However, while speculation is certainly inevitable when understanding pre-Gospel traditions, speculating about precise historical locations has its obvious limits.

Given that our passage is located at the court of Herod Antipas, a puppet of Roman power, not to mention that one of the key non-biblical sources used in this chapter is Josephus, a Jewish historian writing the heart of the Roman Empire under elite Roman patronage, one way we can locate this passage more broadly at least is by using critiques associated with postcolonial criticism. To use a modern colonial analogy to this context, we might follow the suggestion that the role of places such as Galilee at the time of Jesus are analogous to the various Eastern European satellite states once directly associated with the Soviet Union.[5]

In terms of Mark 6.17–29 at least, I do not think we are dealing with a text that is overtly anti-empire and anti-colonial rule in the strong sense. The postcolonial concept of mimicry, intersected with what has been discussed on the issues of gender and class, may prove to be useful here in showing how the people responsible for the passage were modifying the language of the powerful to ensure their own survival. In doing so, the people responsible for this passage may not quite have replicated the structures of power to the extend Tat-siong Benny Liew claimed of Mark's Gospel as a whole (is this further evidence of a pre-Markan tradition, out of step with the emphasis of the rest of the Gospel?), but certainly there is a replication of elite discourses about gender roles in that we see similar patterns of gender in Josephus' retelling of related figures. The passage also reinforces the hegemonic view that potentially revolutionary types ought to be killed by going to great lengths to say John very definitely is *not* a dangerous revolutionary type. This passage is embedded in its time and perhaps through expediency and desire for the people behind it to be left alone it 'buys into' the discourse of power.

To state the obvious, we at least know that Mark 6.17–29 is a text firmly located within the Gospel of Mark, whatever we may make of its pre-history, and so we can also look at the ways in which Mark used this text. We could still develop certain perspectives from classical form critical approaches and say this passage was of minimal interest for Mark. After all, there is no reason why texts must be coherent and there is no reason why collectors or authors must have felt a given passage was significant and this is, after all, the only time John is seriously developed in Mark's gospel and not in direct relation to Jesus.

Perhaps, but we still have the fact that Mark *did* include such a lengthy diversion on John. Here we might want to develop the insights of redaction and literary criticism, though do note that this, like our guesses at precise historical placement, involves speculation. It could have been included for the purposes of foreshadowing Jesus' death or foreshadowing martyrdom (cf. Mark 10.40–45; 13.9–13). The head served on the platter could be a gruesome contrast to the food provided in the following feeding miracle (Mark 6.31–44). We might want to combine a literary approach with the socio-political historical context of Mark. Did Mark include the distinctive literary technique of a 'flashback' to emphasise that the Christian movement whose figurehead was executed as a bandit were not to be mistaken with a violent revolutionary movement and were able to live in peace with the political order?

We are now speculating – and nothing more than that – about how the first audiences might have understood Mark 6.17–29. When read or heard in contexts where little is known of the Jewish details and more is known about a range of other classical literature, how might this story have been understood? Well, audiences would have had different perceptions based on social and cultural expectations with varying attitudes to food and ostentatious banquets, gender and seduction, philosopher–ruler relationships, power and so on. With these variable attitudes across the Roman Empire and across different socio-economic groups we presumably must assume that different expectations would presumably have been among the earliest audience of Mark's Gospel and already the subtle shifts in meaning and response would have been taking place.

Summary

In this chapter we have seen how the various approaches from the previous chapters can be applied to a specific text (Mark 6.17–29). In form critical terms, the passage looks like a 'court tale' with concern for the mistreatment of an innocent. One function of such a 'form' appears to be to show how John the Baptist, his followers, and perhaps the group responsible for the passage, were not a violent and subversive threat to political power. Through the use of haggadic retelling of the story of Esther, an anthropological approach to history and constructions of gender, in addition to a close reading of the text, we have seen how the blame is placed on Herodias and her daughter. Furthermore, the postcolonial concept of 'mimicry' can be employed to show how dominant gender roles were replicated in Mark 6.17–29. In addition to the broader context of imperialism, more precise historical contexts which might have given rise to such a passage were explored.

Key Words

See previous chapters.

Further Reading

Aus, R.D., *Water into Wine and the Beheading of John the Baptist: Early Jewish-Christian Interpretation of Esther 1 in John 2:1–11 and Mark 6:17–29*, Atlanta: Scholars Press, 1988.

Anderson, J.C., 'Feminist Criticism: The Dancing Daughter' in J.C. Anderson and S.D. Moore, eds, *Mark and Method: New Approaches in Biblical Studies*, Minneapolis: Fortress Press, 1992, pp. 103–34.

Crossley, J.G., 'History from the Margins: The Death of John the Baptist' in J.G. Crossley and C. Karner, eds., *Writing History, Constructing Religion*, Aldershot: Ashgate, 2005, pp. 147–61.

Glancy, J.A., 'Unveiling Masculinity. The Construction of Gender in Mark 6:17–29', *Biblical Interpretation* 2 (1994), pp. 34–50.

Spencer, F.S., *Dancing Girls, 'Loose Ladies', and Women of the Cloth: Women in Jesus' Life*, London and New York: Continuum, 2004.

Taylor, J.E., *The Immerser: John the Baptist within Second Temple Judaism*, Grand Rapids: Eerdmans, 1997.

Chapter 5

The Quest for the Historical Jesus

Arguably the classical historical enterprise in New Testament studies over the past 200 years has been the quest for the historical figure of Jesus. Typically the quest has sought to find the man who really walked around Galilee in the late 20s and was later framed in more elevated terms. In more theological terms, the quest has looked for the *Jesus of history* in distinction from the *Christ of faith*, though some conservative scholars have tried to break this distinction down and argue it is impossible to have one without the other because the Jesus of history is only known through the Christ of faith. We will return to the ways in which Jesus was seen after his death in the next section and so readers can judge for themselves about the usefulness of the distinction between the Jesus of history and the Christ of faith. For now let us turn to the ways in which the life and teaching of the historical Jesus might be reconstructed. There are several criteria used in scholarship to try and reconstruct the life and teaching of the historical Jesus. We can begin with the criteria of 'dissimilarity' and 'embarrassment'.

The Criteria of 'Dissimilarity' and 'Embarrassment'

One of the more prominent criteria, especially in previous generations of scholarship, though still used today, is the *criterion of dissimilarity*. Using the criterion of dissimilarity means that a saying (or action) is deemed more likely to be historically authentic if Jesus is different from his Jewish context and the early church. Arguably the classic passage used in conjunction with 'dissimilarity' is the parallel text found in Matthew 8.21–22 and Luke 9.59–60:

8:21 Another of his disciples said to him, "Lord, first let me go and bury my father."²² But Jesus said to him, "Follow me, and let the dead bury their own dead." (Matt. 8.21–22)

9:59 To another he said, "Follow me." But he said, "Lord, first let me go and bury my father." ⁶⁰ But Jesus said to him, "Let the dead bury their own dead; but as for you, go and proclaim the kingdom of God." (Luke 8.59–60)

According to the dominant approach to the Synoptic Problem this would be classed as a 'Q' passage, though the following discussion works with or without that particular hypothesis. Many scholars, including prominent scholars who believe the historical Jesus typically functioned within what we know about early Judaism, hold that 'let the dead bury their own dead' was a shocking sentiment in early Judaism, and indeed throughout the ancient world. The typical reasoning for Matthew 8.21–22 and Luke 9.59–60 being so radically dissimilar to early Jewish sentiments is that burial of parents was regarded highly in early Judaism (e.g. Gen. 23.3–4; Tobit 6.13–15; *m. Ber.* 3.1; *m. Nazir* 7.1).

However, there are good reasons to suspect that the criterion of dissimilarity promises too much. If we begin with the texts and contexts of Matthew 8.21–22 and Luke 9.59–60 we should add that there is no indication in the passage or in the immediate narrative contexts that this saying was as shocking as scholars who use dissimilarity here have argued. We could also point out that Jesus is recorded in the Gospels as having many disputes with opponents and friends alike who are portrayed as being puzzled at least by some of his behaviour so why is there no shock here if the sentiment is so dissimilar and outrageous? And is the saying so shocking anyway? After all the implication is that the dead father will be buried by 'the dead' (the 'spiritually' dead?) and not left unburied.

We might also compare the criterion of dissimilarity with its slightly more useful relation, the *criterion of embarrassment*. This reasoning behind this criterion is that anything that might be deemed to embarrass Jesus and yet makes it into the Gospels, which obviously have a highly elevated view of Jesus, is more likely to be historically authentic. For instance, compare the following passage about Jesus' rejection: 'And he could do no deed of power there. Except that he laid his hands on a few sick people and cured them. And he was amazed at their unbelief' (Mark 6.5–6). As is widely argued, the version from Mark is probably not the sort of thing a Christian writer would invent about Jesus and so there is a good chance something like Mark 6.4 reflects something from the life of the historical Jesus. It is of some significance that Matthew has to alter the emphasis of this saying by claiming that the lack of healing was Jesus' choice: 'And he did not do many deeds of power there, because of their unbelief' (Matt. 13.58). The criterion of embarrassment is more use than dissimilarity and it is at its strongest when we find ourselves confronted with passages where the earliest of which are not likely to have been invented by a Christian writer. Good examples might be the different accounts of Joseph of Arimathea (Mark 15.47–43; Matt. 27.57; Luke 23.50–51; John 19.38) or the different accounts of Jesus' baptism (Mark 1.9; Matt. 3.13–15). We might ask ourselves, what are the differences between Mark and the later Gospel writers and why? What ramifications do these passages have for understanding the historical Jesus?

As ever, we should not get too carried away and caution ought to be exercised. It could be that we have found something Mark did not find embarrassing but others did and this does seem to be a tendency in Mark and the editing of Mark by the other Gospel writers, notably in the negative presentation of disciples in Mark. This leads to the general problem with the criterion of embarrassment: that which is embarrassing to one need not necessarily be embarrassing to another. How do we judge what is embarrassing? John's Gospel removes Jesus' association with 'sinners' and removes the stories of Jesus as exorcist and the reason may well be that he found these themes embarrassing. But it is equally clear that the other Gospel writers did not find these themes embarrassing so what we might be establishing is what John found embarrassing and not necessarily an argument in favour of material about the historical Jesus. Embarrassment is very often a question of taste.

The reason for bringing the criteria of embarrassment and dissimilarity under the same heading is that both require, to some extent, dissimilarity from the movement that followed Jesus as a key point. But is this helpful? If we take the criterion of dissimilarity, it is certainly possible that Jesus was different from what followed but it is also possible that he had a connection with what followed. It is also theoretically possible that some other people in the early church could have created material that was dissimilar and embarrassing. If we can assume that Jesus could create dissimilar and embarrassing material, why not some figure from the early church? This is not, of course, to say that a passage such as Matthew 8.21–22 and Luke 9.59–60 does not reflect the sentiments of the historical Jesus (or, indeed, that it does) but rather it is to say that these criteria have very limited use.

We could also play around with the criteria of embarrassment and dissimilarity by pointing out that both Matthew and Luke were prepared to include the saying 'let the dead bury their own dead'. In the same way that there are no indications this saying was dissimilar to the point of shocking, there are no indications that this saying was embarrassing. Would both have included this saying in their gospels if it were so shocking and embarrassing?

We can also apply similar general criticisms of the criterion of dissimilarity but this time the claim of dissimilarity from early Judaism. The criterion of dissimilarity only works if it can be clearly established that a deed or saying of Jesus was genuinely unparalleled in early Judaism. However, we do not know with any degree of certainty whether this can actually be shown. Our knowledge of early Judaism is hardly complete (what happens if another find on the scale of the Dead Sea Scrolls occurs?) and it might be the case that we simply do not have a precisely similar saying in early Judaism. Here we should not forget what was pointed out above in the case of the saying 'let the dead bury their own dead': no one appears shocked at Jesus' words so could it be that the general sentiment was simply accepted in certain circles?

While the criterion of dissimilarity continues to be used, it is increasingly criticised, not least because it seems to be of little value. More generally, the very criterion itself already assumes that Jesus must have been different from early Judaism and utterly unique, even before its application. This might theoretically have been the case but it can only be established with evidence from early Judaism. It seems though that this case cannot be upheld and this can be seen by the next, more useful criteria.

The Criterion of Historical Plausibility

In recent years, and in line with the positive attitude towards Judaism in historical Jesus scholarship over the past forty years, *the criterion of historical plausibility* has been developed in particular by Gerd Theissen and Dagmar Winter.[1] According to this criterion, Jesus' life and teaching ought to be compatible with Judaism of Jesus' time and place and Jesus must emerge as a recognisable figure within that context while still being a figure who influenced what came after him in earliest Christian history. In general terms, this sounds very useful (and it is) but some qualifications need to be made. Jesus could, *theoretically*, have been a truly revolutionary figure of his time and done things beyond what is known about early Judaism. However, this qualification could be used to our advantage. If Jesus' teachings start to look as if they are very part of what is known of his time and place then this would suggest they were indeed from his time and place. Another qualification should be made. What if parts of Jesus' teaching had no influence in earliest Christianity? Theoretically, that must be an option at least. As Dale Allison put it, 'We cannot ascribe everything in early Christianity to its founder. We can no more praise him for all that went right than we can blame him for all that went wrong. His followers sometimes reaped where he did not sow.'[2]

A famous parable often assumed to be 'authentic' is worth using in our discussion of historical plausibility, namely, the parable of the Good Samaritan (Luke 10:31–37). This parable is a good example of the importance of cultural plausibility because it concerns some very particular issues of purity law of little interest to what we know about the Christian movement in the first century but very much a part of what we know about Palestinian Judaism in the first century.

This becomes increasingly evident when we look at the parable in more detail. Here is the parable in full:

> 10.29 But wanting to justify himself, he [a legal expert/lawyer] asked Jesus, "And who is my neighbor?"[30] Jesus replied, "A man was going down from Jerusalem to Jericho, and fell into the hands of robbers, who stripped him, beat him, and went away, leaving him half dead.[31] Now by chance a priest was going down that road; and when he saw him, he passed by on the other side.[32] So likewise a Levite, when he came to the place and saw him, passed by on the other side.[33] But a Samaritan while traveling came near him; and when he saw him, he was moved with pity.[34] He went to him and bandaged his wounds, having poured oil and

wine on them. Then he put him on his own animal, brought him to an inn, and took care of him.[35] The next day he took out two denarii, gave them to the innkeeper, and said, 'Take care of him; and when I come back, I will repay you whatever more you spend.'[36] Which of these three, do you think, was a neighbor to the man who fell into the hands of the robbers?"[37] He said, "The one who showed him mercy." Jesus said to him, "Go and do likewise."

(Luke 10.31–37)

It is widely observed that the issue of avoiding a corpse and thus corpse impurity – hence the avoidance of the 'half-dead' man by the Priest and the Levite – is an important part of this passage. Defining 'purity' and 'impurity' (or 'clean' and 'unclean') is notoriously difficult but for now it is worth thinking of impurity as something like an invisible contaminate which is best avoided if possible and especially so the closer a Jew was to the Temple in Jerusalem. Impurity could be contracted from sources such as a menstruating woman, sexual intercourse, 'leprosy' and corpses. Of course, biblical writers and early Jewish law were perfectly aware that avoidance of impurity was extremely difficult and provisions were put in place to become pure again. These include sacrifices at the Temple, washing clothing and bedding and waiting until sunset, and immersing the body in an immersion pool.

Corpse impurity was deemed the most defiling of all impurities in early Jewish law and for the priestly class this was something to be particularly avoided because of their particular closeness to what was deemed in such circles as the holiest of places on earth, the Temple in Jerusalem (Lev. 21). The case of the Levite is interesting because a Levite becoming clean after contracting corpse impurity was, theoretically, non-controversial (Num. 19.11–13). Read from this perspective, the Levite should have had no excuse in touching a possible corpse. We will return to what might have been the Levite's reason in due course.

One way of reading this passage in the light of early Jewish discussions of Jewish purity law is to argue, as many have, that Jesus is advocating something relatively revolutionary: he wants the priest to become impure by *not* avoiding corpse impurity beyond close relatives. Some scholars even go as far as arguing that this questions the whole system of pure and impure in early Judaism. There are indications in the passage to suggest otherwise, perhaps the most obvious being the legal expert not appearing remotely shocked by Jesus' teaching and criticism of the priest. If it were so revolutionary in relation to the whole system of pure and impure, would not this have been made evident?

So what might the priest have done? Despite plenty of serious punishments outlined for priests who violate their duties, there is no punishment for priests and who become impure (Lev. 21; Ezek. 44:25–27). Leviticus 21.1–2 is also specific on the issue of the priests and corpses: 'The Lord said to Moses: "Speak to the priests, the sons of Aaron, and say to them: No one shall defile himself for a dead person *among his people*, except for his nearest kin: his mother, his father, his son, his daughter, his brother." [3] If a priest is not meant to come into contact with a corpse when 'among his people' this makes the priest's role more complicated when faced with a situation such as that outlined in Numbers 19.16: 'Whoever in the open field touches one who has been killed by a sword or who has died, or a human bone, or a grave, will be unclean seven days.' What happens if a priest is walking between Jerusalem and Jericho? Is the priest now exempt from touching a corpse if he did not believe he was 'among his people'? Why would we get laws such as Leviticus 5.3 – on the contracting of impurity wittingly or unwittingly – if there were not concerns about people becoming impure?

Jewish law knew of the different problems when giving related laws on purity. Numbers 6 discusses what is called the 'Nazirite vow'. This vow includes, among other things, avoidance of corpse impurity but at an even greater level than the priest: a Nazirite was not even supposed to contract corpse impurity from close relatives. However, Numbers 6 is aware of the possibility of someone dropping dead suddenly and so if this happens the Nazirite is to shave his head and make offerings (Num. 6.9–12).

This background led to some discussion by legal experts close to the time of Jesus. One text, m. *Nazir* 7.1 records a disagreement focused on the teaching of a controversial late first-century rabbi called Eliezer and what should be done in the cases of an abandoned corpse and the High Priest and/or Nazirite. For Eliezer, the High Priest is allowed to become unclean whereas the Nazirite may not. Eliezer's opponents thought the exact opposite. What is important for such a discussion is that these details were being discussed by Jewish legal experts close to the time of Jesus and the parable of the Good Samaritan would seem to be advocating a position close to that of Eliezer: the priest should have been prepared to have become impure and checked the state of abandoned man, at least to see if he was dead or 'half-dead'. Even if he were to turn out to be dead, there was a tradition in the ancient world where it was an extremely good thing to bury an abandoned corpse (Tob. 1.17–18; 2.3–9; 12.13; 2 Macc. 12.39).

There is further support for this kind of reading because Jesus does not allow the excuse that the Priest and Levite were about to serve in the Temple in Jerusalem where they would be required to be in a state of purity. Why not? Well the parable provides a crucial piece of information in Luke 10.31–32: 'a priest was *going down* that road ... So likewise a Levite ... ' There is a sharp descent from Jerusalem to Jericho and this is a clear visual image, so to speak, of movement *away from* the Temple in Jerusalem. The work in the Temple had been done. Put another way, there was no excuse for the Priest and Levite from the perspective of the parable of the Good Samaritan.

So why use the Priest and Levite in a story where purity issues are close to the surface? Here further points of purity law can help. We know that in the first century there were Jewish groups and individuals dedicated to expanding the law of purity found in the Bible to encompass all parts of everyday life outside the Temple. Not everyone accepted this and the parable of the Good Samaritan is a good example of an exception to keeping in a state of purity outside the Temple, namely loving the neighbour. Here the Priest and Levite are perfect figures for the story: they have served in the Temple and are moving away from the Temple yet still they are keen to avoid impurity surrounding a corpse.

This is where the figure of the Samaritan becomes important. Samaritans were known for upholding something like the Pentateuch or Torah (Genesis to Deuteronomy) and so in this context the Samaritan in the parable of the Good Samaritan becomes the symbol of the Law summarised in the loving of the neighbour over against, or as an exception to, the emphasis on maintaining purity beyond what the biblical Law commands.

The details of purity debates underlying the parable of the Good Samaritan make this a classic case of a text that is illuminated by the criterion of historical plausibility. Furthermore, the knowledge of purity underlying this parable strengthens the case for plausibility in that the ins and outs of purity law were of little if any use for non-Jews, who we know became a major issue for first-century Christians. Purity, in Jewish law, concerned Jews and Jews were the ones who should worry about contract impurity, not non-Jews. *From what we know* of first-century Christianity, such knowledge of purity was not important.

But we should not think that this takes us directly to the historical Jesus. While we do not know the details of any Christian group with such a keen interest in the specifics of Jewish purity who might have been responsible for developing such a story after Jesus' death, this does not mean that that no such group existed. There is, we must always acknowledge, a lot we do *not* know about first-century Christianity. Given the existence of the parable of the Good Samaritan someone at least must have known the details of purity. Of course that might have been the historical figure of Jesus but we must accept there are limits on just how certain we can be, at least when using criteria such as plausibility alone.

In fact, what this discussion should show us so far is that the criteria cannot be applied mechanically to the gospel sources when evaluating historical accuracy. The historian will need to be creative and accept that results are provisional. Arguments can be made stronger and more convincing. One way to do this would be to combine different criteria to provide an argument of collective weight. If we take the parable of the Good Samaritan we could add that debates over issue of purity were discussed in traditions presumably pre-Lukan (e.g. Mark 7.1–23; Matt. 23.25–26//Luke 11.39–41) and so such disputes are potentially early. We could then add that disputes and conflicts over issues of the Law are common in the Synoptic Gospels but were also culturally plausible as there are plenty of disputes between different groups and individuals over points of Law and purity attested (for the general point see *Ant.* 13.297–98). Again, such disputes over the details of interpretation were not, as far as we know, typical of earliest Christianity where disputes tended to be over whether the Law should be observed at all. It may be the case that conflict traditions were invented but collectively this would make a stronger argument for the historical plausibility of the historical Jesus involved in conflicts with opponents over the details of interpretation. It is to some of these other criteria we now turn.

The Criterion of Multiple Attestation

This leads us directly to one of the most popular criteria used in historical Jesus scholarship: 'multiple attestation'. Multiple attestation involves an idea or saying of Jesus found *independently* (so not simply a saying in Matthew and/or Luke and copied from Mark) in different sources. According to the standard model of the Synoptic Problem this would involve Mark, Q, M and L. If we took the Farrer-Goulder-Goodacre hypothesis this might involve using Mark and material particular to Matthew and Luke. Multiple attestation is sometimes expanded to include forms such as parables and pronouncement stories and so if a saying, idea or theme is found across sources and forms, so the logic goes, the more likely it is to be 'authentic'. But multiple attestation is not without its own difficulties. What the criterion of multiple attestation really tells us is whether a tradition is early and pre-gospel (such as the not unproblematic multiply attested miracle stories). This can be helpful, as we will see, but by itself it only takes us so far. What this tells us is that a criterion on its own is limited. What we need to do is to combine as many as possible to provide much stronger arguments.

The Criterion of Multiple Criteria

There are a range of passages which we can analyse in light of a range of criteria. Let us take one of notable cultural significance – as good a reason as any to study the historical Jesus – namely, the Lord's Prayer. There are two versions of the Lord's Prayer but only in Matthew and Luke (Matt. 6.9–13; Luke 11.2–4) and so by the conventional solution to the Synoptic Problem this would make it a 'Q' passage, though it is worth stressing again that the following analysis would again work with those alternative approaches to the Synoptic Problem which dispense with Q. The two versions are as follows[4]:

6.9 "Pray then in this way: Our Father in heaven, hallowed be your name.[10] Your kingdom come. Your will be done, on earth as it is in heaven.[11] Give us this day our daily bread.[12] And forgive us our debts, as we also have forgiven our debtors.[13] And do not bring us to the time of trial, but rescue us from the evil one. (Matt. 6.9–13)

11.2 He said to them, "When you pray, say: Father, hallowed be your name. Your kingdom come.[3] Give us each day our daily bread.[4] And forgive us our sins, for we ourselves forgive everyone indebted to us. And do not bring us to the time of trial." (Luke 11.2–4)

There are, obviously, differences between the two and reconstructing an 'original' or indeed the words of Jesus, is a difficult task to put it mildly. But taking some key themes in the Lord's Prayer and by using different criteria we can make some provisional conclusions about the teaching of the historical Jesus.

In both versions, Jesus tells his disciples to call God 'our father' or 'father'. The use of the language of 'father' for God is very well (and multiply) attested in the sayings of Jesus (e.g. Mark 14.25, 36; Matt. 5.16; Matt. 5.44–47//Luke 6.27–28, 33, 35–36; Matt. 6.26//Luke 12.24; Matt. 6.2–8, 16–18; Matt. 6.31–32// Luke 12.29–30; Matt.7.9–11; Luke 11.13; Luke 23.34) and clearly implied in parables (e.g. Mark 12.1–12; Matt. 21.28–32; Luke 15.11–32), all of which are found across the Gospel tradition. By the conventional use of the criterion of multiple attestation of sources and forms, the use of such language would pass with great ease. We also know of similar language used in the Hebrew Bible/ Old Testament and early Judaism before, during and after the time of Jesus (e.g. Deut. 32.6; 2 Sam. 7.4; Isa. 64.7; Ps. 89.26–28; Sirach 51.10; 4Q372; 1QH 9.34–35; *Ant.* 5.93; *m. Abot* 5.20; Targ. Ps. Jonathan Lev. 22.28) including prayers (e.g. *m. Ber.* 5.1; *b. Taan.* 23b) such as the famous Jewish prayer, the Qaddish, a close Aramaic parallel to the Lord's Prayer ('their father who is in heaven'). The use of 'father', then, is obviously culturally plausible.

In both versions Jesus refers to 'your kingdom come'. The coming of the kingdom is a common feature of teaching attributed to Jesus and has multiple attestation of sources and forms (e.g. Mark 1.15; 4.30–32; 9.1; Matt. 5.3//Luke 6.20; Matt. 13.33//Luke 13.20–21; Matt. 25). Hopes for the coming kingdom, or at least a great divine intervention, of God were also known in early Judaism. Again there is a famous parallel in the Qaddish: 'May he establish his kingdom in your life and in your days and in the life of all the house of Israel, speedily and in a short while!' We also know that there was enthusiastic expectation of something dramatic in the decades immediately after Jesus' death (e.g. 1 Thess. 4.13–15.13), an enthusiasm which dampened down towards the end of the first century (John 21; 2 Pet. 3). The probable explanation for this was that someone very early on, such as Jesus, predicted something dramatic, such as the imminent kingdom of God.

In both versions, we have the hope for daily bread. Such hope would have been common enough across the ancient world given that the overwhelming majority of rural dwellers would have been close to the breadline. We might add famines and crop failures were unfortunately too common and could have devastating effects (cf. Acts 11.27–30). This outline of the economic context of the ancient world does not of course tell us much about Jesus. However, it is possible – and no more than that – that here Jesus' precise social context could provide insight. Though much debated, it is possible that land displacement and social and economic changes accompanying the building of Tiberias and the rebuilding of Sepphoris as Jesus was growing up could have contributed to a sharpening of the issues of rich and poor and it is clear that such concerns about the effects of poverty are common in the Synoptic Gospels (Mark 10.17–31; Matt. 6.24//Luke 16.13; Luke 14.16–24// Matt. 22.1–14; Luke 12.13–21; Luke 16.19–31). But it may well be likely that that one of the effects of this social change was Jesus' itinerant mission and if Jesus was travelling around Galilee with nowhere to lay his head (Matt. 8.20//Luke 9.58), then prayers for daily bread might make good sense in that context.

In both versions of the Lord's Prayer, we have talked of forgiveness but the language is subtly different. Matthew talks about debts whereas Luke talks about sins. As it happens, both could plausibly be a fair translation of an Aramaic idiom. In Aramaic, 'debts' and 'debtors' were ways of talking about 'sins' and 'sinners' so while we may well have a case of Matthew and Luke making what would both be reasonable judgements about translation, Matthew gives us a very precise example of historical plausibility. The use of Aramaic as a subset of the criterion of historical plausibility is a highly technical and difficult enterprise but here we have a relatively straightforward example. Moreover, a concern for forgiveness is also found possibly independently and clearly different from the context of the early church: 'So when you are offering your gift at the altar, if you remember that your brother or sister has something against you, leave your gift there before the altar and go; first be reconciled to your brother or sister, and then come and offer your gift' (Matt. 5.23–24).

Both versions mention worries about 'the time of trial'. This is trickier to establish as such related issues were certainly a concern for the early church (cf. Acts 6.8–8.3; 12.1–3; 13.45–14.7; 18.9, 12–16, 26; 19.9–8; 23.23; 25.6, 23; 2 Cor. 11.23–33) but given that John the Baptist had been killed by the time Jesus' mission was up and running it is hardly implausible that Jesus could have predicted troubles ahead for himself and his followers; issues of suffering were certainly known in Jewish literature (including apocalyptic literature) and martyrdoms were recalled annually at the festival of Hanukkah. So overall we might conclude that it is difficult to say either way on the historicity of this one.

What we have now seen is that if we are prepared to combine a number of criteria we can use a passage as small as the Lord's Prayer to reconstruct some key teachings of the historical Jesus, not to mention the social, economic, religious, and political contexts of his time. Of course, it is not the easiest task to say whether we have the actual words of the historical Jesus but we could plausibly suggest that the sentiments expressed in the Lord's Prayer echo the general sentiments of the historical Jesus. It is common among scholars this past decade to start talking about ways in which Jesus was 'remembered' or how memory retains the 'gist' of a given saying or action.[5] This sort of approach is usually associated with more conservative scholars but it is worth noting that those less conservative are more than capable of using such language. For instance, the North American Jesus Seminar, a group of scholars who became known for downplaying what we can actually know about the historical Jesus according to the canonical Gospels, still had voting options which included this: 'Jesus probably said something like this' and 'Jesus did not say this, but the ideas contained in it are close to his own'.[6] It is this sort of language which can be helpful when used in conjunction with the criteria because it avoids an over-confident attitude that when the criteria are used we have supposedly found the precise words and deeds of the historical Jesus.

More generally, it is possible to build up a general picture of the historical Jesus. Some of it may seem banal enough, such as he was born in Galilee, attracted followers, clashed with people over interpretation of the Law, gained a reputation as a successful healer and exorcist, preached the coming of the kingdom, often spoke in parables, and went to Jerusalem where his actions in the Temple led to his crucifixion by the Romans. That is more or less the Gospel outline but no surprise really given that they are the best sources! However, we should not get too carried away with what we know. Ultimately the criteria, even a combination of them, remain general possibilities. Furthermore, the criteria can be used negatively: they can suggest material attributed to Jesus does *not* reflect the historical Jesus. We will return to such tricky questions in Chapter 6 when we discuss Christology.

Another issue worth mentioning, and one to which we will return, is that of the individual in history. Modern lives of Jesus (and there are many) are very much about describing the individual Jesus and, in the case of the more theologically inspired lives of Jesus, how this Jesus effectively influenced the rise of a religion in his name. Jesus, it seems, appears as a bolt from the blue, out of nowhere. The problem, it seems to me, is that this is a strange one-dimensional kind of history where broader factors in the emergence of the Jesus movement are relatively neglected. Certainly, scholars have often mentioned the social and economic contexts of Jesus' mission but not really as an explanation for why the Jesus movement emerged when and where it did. Alternatively, we could ask questions such as the following: 'Why did Jesus happen when and where he happened? Why then? Why there? ... Why not another time? Why not another place?'[7] As it turns out we do have some important reasons why the Jesus movement might have emerged when and where it did. The building of Tiberias and the rebuilding of Sepphoris, major urban centres in Galilee as Jesus was growing up, would have made serious changes to the social and economic structure with new demands on the surrounding towns for goods and resources. Scholars debate whether these building projects might have been a good or bad thing but we can at least say that there was change and not everyone would be happy with the change in the status quo. Here we have one powerful social and economic reason for the emergence of the Jesus movement.

Such reasoning will be developed further in this book and will also be done not just in relation to the emergence of the Jesus movement but also in relation to the emergence of Christian origins and the role of Jesus the individual in the grand scheme of things. Before we turn to such issues in later chapters we will first turn to the ultimate scholarly example of Jesus the individual and his influence on history: the resurrection.

The Resurrection and the Supernatural

One of the most controversial areas of historical Jesus scholarship concerns the resurrection stories (Matt. 28; Mark 16.1–8; Luke 24; John 20–21; 1 Cor. 15:3–8) and the age old question of the supernatural in history. Prior to this past decade, the major and mainstream New Testament works of scholars such as Bultmann were not overly interested in showing that the bodily resurrection of Jesus really did happen, though of course there were conservative views on the subject even if they were not necessarily at the forefront of scholarship. The subject, however, well and truly became part of the mainstream of historical Jesus studies with the work of the Bishop of Durham, N.T. Wright, and the publication of his book, *The Resurrection of the Son of God* (2003). One of the most notable things about Wright's book is that he is explicit about the role of the supernatural in history. Even Matthew 27.52–53 is treated with a degree of historical optimism. The passage reads: 'The tombs also were opened, and many bodies of the saints who had fallen asleep were raised. After his resurrection they came out of the tombs and entered the holy city and appeared to many.' According to Wright, and some might say alarmingly so, 'Some stories are so odd that they may just have happened. This may be one of them, but in historical terms there is no way of finding out'.[8]

Wright is even more optimistic about the historical plausibility of the bodily raised Jesus happening and happening as a supernatural event in history. For Wright, the idea that Jesus really was bodily raised from the dead is the only plausible explanation for why we have a story of someone being bodily raised before end times in a Jewish context. Otherwise the story of Jesus' resurrection is so unusual in the context of early Jewish thought on resurrection that it cannot be explained in any better way. Wright's book was discussed at length in leading scholarly journals such as *Journal for the Study of the New Testament* and *Journal for the Study of the Historical Jesus* and has gained praise from some of the most famous New Testament scholars of this generation.

There are, as you might expect, alternative views. On the opposite end of the spectrum, we have scholars who suggest that the sightings of a resurrected Jesus might have been little more than 'hallucinations' or visions which may be little more than a psychological projection or, a more modified version, that historical reconstruction cannot move beyond the idea of a vision to the idea that this really was the bodily raised Jesus. If we were to take the strong form of this argument (e.g. hallucinations or psychological projection of the earliest Christians), it could be argued (though it does not have to be) that this would mean that the Gospel narratives are largely fictional and that the only serious evidence would be Paul's recollection in 1 Corinthians 15.3–8:

> For I handed on to you as of first importance what I in turn had received: that Christ died for our sins in accordance with the scriptures, and that he was buried, and that he was raised on the third day in accordance with the scriptures, and that he appeared to Cephas [Peter], then to the twelve. Then he appeared to more than five hundred brothers at one time, most of whom are still alive, though some have died. Then he appeared to James, then to all the apostles. Last of all, as to someone untimely born, he appeared also to me.

There has been much debate on these verses. Does the absence of the details of the Gospel narratives – most notably the empty tomb – mean that they are discredited by Paul's non-inclusion? Alternatively, scholars such as Wright would counter that the empty tomb is obviously implied when Paul speaks of Jesus being raised (the Greek implies a bodily raising). Then might Wright be qualified or countered by the suggestion that the assumption of Jesus being raised in a way that would leave an empty tomb only means that this is what the earliest Christians *believed*, not what actually happened?

What is the evidence that the Gospel stories of the empty tomb and resurrection are fiction or non-fiction? Alongside 1 Corinthians 15.3–8, Mark 16.1–8 is our other earliest source. One of the main problems using Mark 16.1–8 is that it does not have a resurrection appearance. We are told of a young man dressed in white (an angel?), explaining to Mary Magdalene and Mary mother of James and Salome that Jesus had been raised. Mark's Gospel ends (16.8) abruptly: 'So they went out and fled from the tomb, for terror and amazement had seized them; and they said nothing to anyone, for they were afraid.' It would seem then that we have no resurrection appearance in the earliest source and some scholars have argued that the mention of the women telling no one is Mark's way of saying that no one really knew where Jesus' tomb was and possibly covering up that Jesus was thrown into a pit for common criminals. Others would counter that the text implies that the women went to tell the disciples while Wright has suggested that there is a lost ending to Mark which would have included the resurrection appearances.

There is also the problem that in Mark's account the young man dressed in white tells the women 'go, tell his disciples and Peter that he is going ahead of you to Galilee; there you will see him, just as he told you' (16.7). Luke, however, has two men in dazzling clothes rather than Mark's one young man, who tell the women not to go to Galilee as Mark's account had it, but rather 'Remember how he told you, while he was still with you in Galilee: The Son of Man must be delivered into the hands of sinful men, be crucified and on the third day be raised again' (Luke 24.6–7). Luke has resurrection appearances around Jerusalem and not in Galilee. There are also problems with different authorities being present at the resurrection. According to John and Luke, Peter is present at the empty tomb (Luke 24.11–12; John 20.6–8). It is clear, then, that there are problems (and these are just some of them) with the resurrection accounts. Some conservative scholars might try to harmonise the different accounts whereas more mainstream scholars might say that the Gospels creatively develop the resurrection accounts to fit their theological agendas. For instance, in Acts Luke begins his historical narrative of the early church in Jerusalem and clearly sees this as a place of great theological significance, Matthew wants to justify the Gentile mission (Matt. 28.16–20) and John wants to advocate an extremely elevated view of Jesus (John 20.28–29). Certain conservative scholars would argue that no one would invent women as the first witnesses whereas other scholars might add that the young man or men was or were the first witness or witnesses and that Mark, for instance may not have had a problem with women as earliest witnesses.

Some scholars also see the Markan resurrection story in terms of spiritualising of deeply held religious convictions or in terms of haggadah (see Chapter 2). Roger Aus has recently published work on how retellings of the death and burial of Moses underlie stories of the resurrection.[9] He points out that there were well-known Jewish traditions arguing that Moses was in fact taken to heaven without dying while at the same time there were other accounts which accept that Moses died and that it was his soul taken up to heaven. Aus argues that early Jewish Christian believers combined both traditions about Moses because we know that Jesus obviously died and yet at the same time was also believed to be bodily transferred to heaven. It will be interesting to see how scholarship reacts to Aus' suggestions.

A related general question posed to the problems surrounding the resurrection might be this: is the resurrection beyond historical reconstruction in the sense that we simply could never prove such a thing? On one level we might provide a solid answer: of course we cannot prove such a thing with the certainty of Wright. After all, all we have is historical guess work and if we are trying to prove the supernatural then best of luck given how we have seen the level of uncertainty with the basic details of Jesus' pre-death life! It is certainly true, as scholars sometimes point out, that discussions over whether the resurrection really happened or not polarise different scholarly biases like nothing else. However, in the interests of scholarly peace and harmony, we could perhaps do the seemingly impossible and bring a variety of views together. Whether we believe something supernatural or not generated the different accounts, most of us could at least agree that *something* happened historically and *something* generated the different accounts. If we can more or less all agree that *something* happened and that the first followers *believed* they saw the risen Christ, then can we not move on and develop a broader explanation of Christian origins without worrying about whether or not this constitutes proof for atheists or conservative Christians, respectively, thereby channelling more intellectual energy into historical explanations of Christian origins?

Summary

The quest for the historical Jesus has been one of the major issues in the history of New Testament scholarship. A variety of criteria have been used to establish the words and deeds of the figure active in Galilee around the year 30 CE. The 'criterion of dissimilarity' holds that if words or deeds attributed to Jesus are unparalleled in early Judaism and in the early church then it is possible we are dealing with the historical Jesus. There are various problems with this approach, such as our incomplete knowledge of Judaism and a gnawing concern that relevant Jewish evidence is not always brought forward by scholars. A related criterion is that of 'embarrassment' which holds that if something is potentially embarrassing for the earliest Christians then it is unlikely that it would have been invented. This criterion is of some use but it needs to be used with caution, not least because embarrassment is sometimes in the eye of the beholder. The 'criterion of historical plausibility' holds that Jesus must be a recognisable figure in his cultural context. This criterion can be developed more negatively to suggest that if Jesus is more reflective of a different or later context then we could be dealing with invention and embellishment. The 'criterion of multiple attestation' holds that if a saying or theme is attested independently in more than one source or more than one 'form' then it is likely to be an early, pre-Gospel saying or theme. This does not necessarily mean a saying or theme goes back to the historical Jesus but, like the other criteria, it becomes particularly useful when combined with other criteria to provide an argument of collective weight. Perhaps, then, we should be thinking of the 'criterion of multiple criteria'. Other issues in historical Jesus studies were also considered, such as the role of the individual in historical change and the ever controversial issue of the bodily resurrection of Jesus.

Key Words

Dissimilarity: If a word, words or a deed attributed to Jesus are deemed dissimilar to what is known about early Judaism and dissimilar to the interests of the early church, some scholars have believed this to be an indication of something close to the life and teaching of the historical Jesus.

Embarrassment: If a word, words or a deed attributed to Jesus are deemed to have been embarrassing for the early church, some scholars believe this to mean an indication of something close to the life and teaching of the historical Jesus.

Historical Jesus: The historical figure active around the year 30 CE whose life and teaching were later developed in the Gospels and the New Testament.

Historical plausibility: In terms of the criteria for studying the historical Jesus, if a word, words or a deed attributed to Jesus are recognisable in the context of the Judaism of Jesus' time and place, and a figure emerges who could still have influenced the movement in his name, then some scholars believe this to be an indication of something close to the life and teaching of the historical Jesus.

Multiple attestation: If a word, words or a deed are attributed to Jesus in different sources (e.g. Mark, material particular to Matthew and/or Luke, and, if accepted, Q) independent of one another and different independent forms (e.g. parables, sayings, controversy stories), then many scholars have deemed it more likely that we are dealing with an early, pre-Gospel tradition, possibly as early as the lifetime of the historical Jesus.

Further Reading

Allison, D.C., *Resurrecting Jesus: The Earliest Christian Tradition and Its Interpreters*, London: T&T Clark, 2005.

Casey, M., *Jesus of Nazareth: An Independent Historian's Account of his Life and Teachings*, London and New York: T&T Clark, forthcoming 2010.

Crossan, J.D., *The Historical Jesus: the Life of a Mediterranean Jewish Peasant*, New York: HarperCollins; Edinburgh: T&T Clark, 1991.

Journal for the Study of the Historical Jesus 3, 2005: an issue dedicated to Jesus' resurrection and responses to N.T. Wright.

Sanders, E.P., *The Historical Figure of Jesus*, London: Penguin, 1993.

Theissen G. and D. Winter, *The Quest for the Plausible Jesus: The Question of Criteria*, Louisville: WJK, 2002.

Vermes, G., *The Religion of Jesus the Jew*, London: SCM, 1993.

Wright, N.T., *The Resurrection of the Son of God*, London: SPCK, 2003.

Part Two

Revolutionary Origins of Christian Beliefs?

Chapter 6

The New Testament and the Origins of Major Christian Theological Ideas

This section will look at some of the key theological themes in the New Testament relating to the emergence of Christianity as a religion in its own right in distinction from Judaism and the pagan world at large. In many ways the distinctions were never clear cut on the ground because Christians belonged, like many other people in the ancient world, to different social groups and, as we saw in the previous section, this led to some questioning about how to behave in different settings and to a range of reactions. However, as we also saw, New Testament texts did try to construct a distinctive identity in the ancient world. This section will build on these questions but the focus will predominantly be on the general construction of Christianity emerging and splitting from Judaism, regularly labelled rightly or wrongly as 'the parting of the ways'. In particular this section will look at some of the main ways in which scholarship has looked at this shift. The first ways are fairly conventional, though I will try to tie these approaches in with the approaches of the previous section, and they are: Christology and issues of Law, faith and works. The third is becoming conventional, though here I will provide a particularly contemporary twist, and that involves Paul in relation to politics and Empire and the idea of Paul's 'revolutionary' ideas as some kind of blue print for 'western' culture. While this is increasingly a major issue in New Testament studies, I will look at this through the eyes of a parallel development which has taken place outside conventional New Testament studies and is now just starting to make its presence felt in mainstream New Testament studies, namely, Paul according to contemporary critical theorists and philosophers.

Christology, the New Testament and the Origins of Christianity

One of the most distinctive ways Christianity emerged as a religion in its own right was having Jesus made equal with God. The following are two classic and foundational definitions of Christian orthodoxy:

> We believe ... in one Lord Jesus Christ, the Son of God; begotten from the Father; only-begotten – that is, from the substance of the Father; God from God; light from light, true God from true God; begotten not made; of one substance with the Father ... who on account of us human beings and our salvation came down and took flesh, becoming a human being ...
>
> (Nicene Creed, 325 CE)

> ... we all with one voice confess our Lord Jesus Christ to be one and the same Son, perfect in divinity and humanity, truly God and truly human ... being of one substance with the Father in relation to his divinity, and being of one substance with us in relation to his humanity ...
>
> (Council of Chalcedon, 451 CE)[1]

With the possible exception of John's Gospel, much of this kind of elaborate theological language is not typically the New Testament, even in those passages where Jesus is described in elevated terms. Moreover, there is, of course, no mention of the word 'trinity' (the co-equality of Father, Son, and Holy Spirit) either. These important points have not stopped New Testament scholars from analysing the New Testament texts for related sentiments or the origins of such beliefs. Two major and distinctive approaches to the study of the presentation of the figure of Jesus/Christ ('Christology') in the New Testament in the past twenty years have been by Larry Hurtado and Maurice Casey, and in many ways both scholars are attempting to show how and why Christianity became distinct from Judaism and a distinctive religion in its own right.

According to Maurice Casey, Jesus was seen as a divine figure very shortly after his death.[2] But what might 'divine figure' mean? According to Casey, this does not mean Jesus was necessarily equated with the God of Israel in the strict orthodox sense, at least not in the first decades after Jesus' death. Casey, like many scholars of early Judaism, argues that early Jewish monotheism (one God only) ought to be defined as something like one God who rules everything but there are other 'supernatural' figures who serve God (e.g. angels, archangels) and who even share in the attributes of God but ultimately God must remain distinct. This even means that language used of God in the Hebrew Bible/Old Testament could be reapplied in early Judaism to the various elevated figures. For instance, look at the following passages from the Psalms:

> God (Hebrew: *Elohim*) has taken his place in the divine council [literally: 'council of *El*']; in the midst of the gods he holds judgement ...
>
> (Ps. 82.1)

> ... and over it take your seat on high, the Lord (Hebrew: *Yahweh*) will judge the peoples ...
>
> (Ps. 7.8–9)

Look at how these passages were used in the Dead Sea Scrolls:

> ... for it is the time for the year of grace of Melchizedek, and of his armies, the nation of the holy ones of God, of the rule of judgement, as is written about him in the songs of David [= Psalms], who said, 'Elohim has taken his place in the divine council; in the midst of the gods he holds judgement' [Psalm 82.1]. And about him he said, 'and over it take your seat on high, God (Hebrew: El) will judge the peoples' [Psalm 7.8–9].
>
> (11Q13 2.10–11)

The Hebrew words *El* and *Elohim* are used of God in the Hebrew Bible/Old Testament among many other names but it is not the actual name of God which is Yahweh. *Elohim* is a term which can be used to describe divinity or divine figures in Hebrew and in the Dead Sea Scrolls this language used of God is reapplied to the figure Melchizedek who is regarded as an elevated figure. Interestingly, 11Q13 has replaced the name of God, 'Yahweh', from Psalm 7.8–9 with the term '*El*' to refer to Melchizedek.

Casey sees similar things happening in New Testament texts. According to his sort of reading, divine language might be used of Jesus but it does not necessarily mean Jesus is co-equal with Yahweh. There are different ways of translating Romans 9.5 but for now let us go with the one which makes Jesus 'God': 'Messiah/Christ, who is God (Greek: *theos*) over all, blessed for ever.' According to a reading in line with Casey, this language of *theos* is the Greek equivalent of *Elohim* and could be used of other figures deemed elevated from angels to Moses, as in the following example from the first-century Jewish philosopher Philo:

> God honored him, and gave him instead the greatest and most perfect wealth; and this is the wealth of all the earth and sea, and of all the rivers, and of all the other elements, and all combinations whatever; for having judged him deserving of being made a partaker with himself in the portion which he had reserved for himself, he gave him the whole world as a possession suitable for his heir: therefore, every one of the elements obeyed him as its master, changing the power which it had by nature and submitting to his commands ... and if the prophet was truly called the friend of God, then it follows that he would naturally partake of God himself and of all his possessions as far as he had need; for God possesses everything and is in need of nothing; but the good man has nothing which is properly his own, no, not even himself; but he has a share granted to him of the treasures of God as far as he is able to partake of them. And this is natural enough; for he is a citizen of the world; on which account he is not spoken of as to be enrolled as a citizen of any particular city in the habitable world, since he very appropriately has for his inheritance not a portion of a district, but the whole world. What more shall I say? Has

he not also enjoyed an even greater communion with the Father and Creator of the universe, being thought unworthy of being called by the same appellation? For he also was called the god (Greek: *theos*) and king of the whole nation, and he is said to have entered into the darkness where God was; that is to say, into the invisible, and shapeless, and incorporeal world, the essence, which is the model of all existing things, where he beheld things invisible to mortal nature …

(Philo, *Life of Moses* 1.155–58)

According to a Casey-style reading, even the highly elevated language of Phil. 2.6–11 may push the figure of Jesus very close to being fully equal with God but still not quite there:

[Jesus Christ,] who, though he was in the form of God, did not regard equality with God as something to be exploited,[7] but emptied himself, taking the form of a slave, being born in human likeness. And being found in human form,[8] he humbled himself and became obedient to the point of death – even death on a cross.[9] Therefore God also highly exalted him and gave him the name that is above every name,[10] so that at the name of Jesus every knee should bend, in heaven and on earth and under the earth,[11] and every tongue should confess that Jesus Christ is Lord, to the glory of God the Father.

This may be some of the most highly elevated language about Jesus outside John's Gospel but it could still be argued that the language of being like God was known to be applied to other figures, notably the idea of Adam being 'like' God (Gen. 3.5, 22). Even the 'name that is above every name' with every knee bending on heaven and earth does not necessarily mean full equality with Yahweh in the strongest possible sense. We have already seen how Moses was extremely elevated and there are other texts where elevated figures are said to be given the divine name in the Bible and early Jewish literature (e.g. Exod. 23.20–21; Philo, *On the Confusion of Tongues* 146; *Apocalypse of Abraham* 10.9; 3 Enoch 12.2–5). As with Moses according to Philo, Moses remains distinct from God and this may also be the case with Jesus and God the Father in Philippians 2.11.

Philippians 2.6–11, it should be heavily stressed, is a controversial and much interpreted passage and the above is one possible reading of it. It is not difficult to see how people have read the idea of Jesus as fully equal with God in the strongest possible sense in light of Christian orthodox approaches to Christology. So how do we decide, according to a Casey-style reading, a reading of the figure of Christ which goes beyond anything in early Judaism? For Casey, the crucial moment when Jesus becomes equated with God in the strongest sense comes with John's Gospel. The people responsible for John's Gospel are in a fierce dispute with a local Jewish group over the nature of who Jesus was and is and this ultimately leads to the people responsible for John's Gospel taking on a 'gentile self-identification' and identifying themselves over against Jews and Judaism. A major reason for this is because Jesus is portrayed as equal with God in the strongest possible sense and in a way unacceptable and blasphemous for most Jews. Two crucial passages in this respect are found in John 5 and John 10:

> Therefore the Jews started persecuting Jesus, because he was doing such things on the Sabbath.[17] But Jesus answered them, 'My Father is still working, and I also am working.'[18] For this reason the Jews were seeking all the more to kill him, because he was not only breaking the Sabbath, but was also calling God his own Father, thereby making himself equal to God.
>
> (John 5.16–18)

> The Jews took up stones again to stone him.[32] Jesus replied, 'I have shown you many good works from the Father. For which of these are you going to stone me?'[33] The Jews answered, 'It is not for a good work that we are going to stone you, but for blasphemy, because you, though only a human being, are making yourself God.'
>
> (John 10.31–33)

Both passages have in common a generalised opponent in 'the Jews' and the big difference maker is the 'blasphemy' of Jesus making himself equal to God. For good measure, John 5 makes it clear that Jesus does not even advocate observance of the Sabbath anymore. Both texts are further important because they show that the idea of making Jesus equal with God is a deeply divisive issue and such conflict is a crucial way to show just how far Christians have gone in their elevation of Jesus. Clearly, this is a problem for Jewish monotheism, at least the understanding of Jewish monotheism of John's group 'the Jews'. Casey, it ought to be noticed, sees such a dispute as alien to the historical Jesus whose loyalty to Judaism meant he would never have said something so controversial as making himself equal to God. Instead, Casey argues, John 5 is a fiction created the community behind John's Gospel to explain why they were cast out of the synagogues and how they now viewed Jesus.

Larry Hurtado represents a notable alternative approach to Casey's.[3] He too sees early Jewish monotheism in more or less the same way as Casey but sees the difference between Jewish monotheism and Christian monotheism from a much earlier date, with evidence effectively stretching back to the first years after Jesus' death. Hurtado emphasises worship of Jesus or Christ devotion as a development of Jewish monotheism. In fact Hurtado goes one step further in arguing that Jesus was worshipped in the ways in which the Jewish God was worshipped and so this Christ devotion was a 'mutation' of Jewish devotional practice. There would be minimal difference from Casey's argument if it applied to John's Gospel alone but, Hurtado argues, Christ devotion was not only widespread in earliest Christianity but was present among the earliest post-resurrection communities.

But can we be as confident as Hurtado that Jesus was worshipped as Israel's God so early? Hurtado would certainly see something like Philippians 2.6–11 as reflecting intense Christ devotion but he also finds it in more subtle contexts such as the Gospel miracles. In the famous miracles where Jesus stills the wind and the sea while stunning the disciples (Mark 4.35–41) and the walking on the water (Mark 6.45–52), Hurtado sees indications of a presentation of Jesus as having godlike power and superiority over the elements. Here we might compare passages about God:

> Who shakes the earth out of its place, and its pillars tremble; who commands the sun, and it does not rise; who seals up the stars; who alone stretched out the heavens and trampled the waves of the Sea ...
>
> (Job 9.6–8)

> For he commanded and raised the stormy wind, which lifted up the waves of the sea ... Then they cried to the LORD in their trouble, and he brought them out from their distress; he made the storm be still, and the waves of the sea were hushed. Then they were glad because they had quiet, and he brought them to their desired haven.
>
> (Ps. 107.25, 28–30)

> Thus says the LORD, who makes a way in the sea, a path in the mighty waters ...
>
> (Isa. 43.6)

The feeding miracles (Mark 6.30–44; 8.1–9) similarly echoes God's miraculous provision from the Exodus story.

Yet could we not turn to the examples of figures such as Moses according to Philo (see above) and combine it with Casey's argument concerning the conflicts over Christology in John's Gospel being crucial for understanding the distinctively Christian view of Jesus? However, Hurtado would argue that there *were* disputes over Christology with Jewish opponents from before John's Gospel and, significantly for his argument, in the Gospels and hence the miraculous traditions remain part of the presentation of Christ as one worshipped in ways usually reserved for the God of Israel. He would see texts such as Mark 2.1–12 as evidence for earlier disputes and some of the conflicts in Acts. In the earliest years of the Christian movement according to Acts, Stephen became a martyr and this, according to a Hurtado-style reading was over Christ devotion:

> But filled with the Holy Spirit, he gazed into heaven and saw the glory of God and Jesus standing at the right hand of God.[56] 'Look,' he said, 'I see

the heavens opened and the Son of Man standing at the right hand of God!'[57] But they covered their ears, and with a loud shout all rushed together against him.[58] Then they dragged him out of the city and began to stone him; and the witnesses laid their coats at the feet of a young man named Saul.

(Acts 7.55–58)

This, of course, gets us into awkward questions not only about fair interpretation (could the above passage be about the source of authority rather than who Jesus precisely was?) but also about historicity. Unfortunately, Acts can sometimes be more difficult than the Gospels because of a lack of independent sources. Casey and Hurtado have hammered out their arguments in different contexts, often against each other, and readers can assess the respective arguments for themselves.[4]

Why Did Christology Happen?

What I want to do here is not say who is right and who is wrong but why did we get such speculation about the figure of Jesus that would eventually, whenever this may have been, make Jesus elevated in the strongest possible sense? How might we account for the rise of Christological speculation? One way might be to return to the issue of historical change and causality. If we recall the ideas of social upheaval in Galilee as Jesus was growing up as one way of explaining the rise of the Jesus movement at that time and place, we could develop this and apply it to the origins of Christology. When we looked at reactions to social upheaval in rural contexts, it was observed that this could include anything from restoration of the status quo to radical utopian idealism. In these kinds of contexts, figures have emerged making grand claims for themselves. Christopher Rowland has pointed out that his readings of radical millenarian contexts, such as the English Civil War, throw up figures making claims about the divine indwelling in themselves. This, Rowland suggests, may help us further understand the origins of Christology.[5] We know that Palestine in the time of Jesus witnessed a variety of prophetic and 'messianic' figures promising dramatic and even miraculous events so when combined with the more specific social upheavals in Galilee as Jesus was growing up we at least have context in which the potential for speculation about Jesus could begin, perhaps with Jesus himself!

But then, how secure, in terms of historical reconstruction, are the data about the historical Jesus and Christological in the Gospels? Many scholars would point out, and not without good reason, that the Gospels are full of Christian developments of the person of Jesus that have little to do with the historical Jesus' life and teaching. In the case of John's Gospel, all the dramatic claims made there such as equality with God are not made in the other canonical Gospels and so there is at least some weight to the traditional argument that the historical Jesus never made such claims of himself and nor did anyone in his lifetime, otherwise why would these views not be found in the other Gospels?

That said, the traditions about Jesus as healer and exorcist might get us somewhere. The Gospel exorcism stories have the authority of Jesus' exorcisms as a crucial component of the exorcist stories. The following is a well-known saying of Jesus: But if it is by the spirit of God [Luke: 'finger of God'] that I cast out demons, then the kingdom of God has come to you (Matt. 12.28//Luke 11.20). The issues of the kingdom and exorcism appear to have been typical of the historical Jesus so we may well be dealing with a saying which reflects the teaching of Jesus. Even Jesus' opponents accused him of having 'divine' power or authority, albeit of the very negative variety, when they accused him of being 'possessed by Beelzebul', and of casting out demons 'by the ruler of the demons'. Jesus' response in some ways assumes a greater authority or power but obviously much more positive:

> Truly I tell you, people will be forgiven for their sins and whatever blasphemies they utter;[29] but whoever blasphemes against the Holy Spirit can never have forgiveness, but is guilty of an eternal sin –[30] for they had said, 'He has an unclean spirit'.
>
> (Mark 3.28–30)

If these sort of claims do go back to the historical Jesus, then it is possible that this got the ball rolling for the Christological speculation that would follow. If Jesus has authority from God, has power but not from Beelzebul, casts out demons by the spirit or finger of God while proclaiming God's kingdom and claims authority on earth for healing, including healing in his name, then Jesus was making some elevated claims for himself. And what would happen if earliest followers recalled various Jewish texts about elevated figures in early Jewish thought, such as Wisdom, Moses, Enoch, or angels, figures who were also given divine authority? Would they not have seen some connection?

Maybe such connections would have been too tenuous if we only had the exorcisms and healings as a key feature of Jesus' influence. But we also have another very early continuation of Jesus' authority from God where he gets clearly elevated in the cosmic hierarchy because another important factor was, no doubt, the resurrection appearances. No matter what we make of the resurrection appearances in terms of whether Jesus really was bodily raised, scholars on all sides of the debate could say with some certainty that people believed they saw something and that this was perceived to be Jesus raised. This alone would have been enough to encourage further speculation on the figure of Jesus. Compare how Paul's vision is recalled in Acts:

> [3]Now as he was going along and approaching Damascus, suddenly a light from heaven flashed around him.[4] He fell to the ground and heard a voice

saying to him, "Saul, Saul, why do you persecute me?"[5] He asked, "Who are you, Lord?" The reply came, "I am Jesus, whom you are persecuting".

(Acts 9.3–5)

With Jesus now described in the context of a blinding light from heaven, presumably from this perspective he was no mere mortal human being.

We could further tie this in with broader socio-religious trends where the emergence of pagan monotheism seems loosely tied in with the development of empires and communication networks: one overarching God was always a helpful way of reflecting rule on earth. If we take a definition of monotheism in the sense both Casey and Hurtado do, namely with one overarching God ruling over all including other supernatural beings, then there are certainly trends in the ancient world outside Christianity and Judaism. Indeed, later critics of emerging Christianity noticed the strong similarities between Christian concepts of the divine and pagan concepts of the divine. The first critique is from Celsus and discussed by Origen and the second is an unknown philosopher and discussed by Macarius Magnes:

> ... their doctrine concerning heaven is not peculiar to them, but, to pass by all others, is one which has long ago been received by the Persians, as Herodotus somewhere mentions. 'For they have a custom,' he says, 'of going up to the tops of the mountains, and of offering sacrifices to Jupiter, giving the name of Jupiter to the whole circle of the heavens.' And I think, continues Celsus, that it makes no difference whether you call the highest being Zeus, or Zen, or Adonai, or Sabaoth, or Ammoun like the Egyptians, or Pappaeus like the Scythians.
>
> (Origen, *Contra Celsus* 5.41)

> At any rate, if you say that angels stand before God who are not subject to feeling and death, and immortal in their nature, whom we ourselves speak of as gods, because they are close to the Godhead, why do we dispute about a name? ... The difference therefore is not great, whether a man calls them gods or angels, since their divine nature bears witness to them ...
>
> (Macarius Magnes, *Monogenes* 4.21)

We could argue, then, that the broader ancient world was potentially receptive to monotheistic ideas.[6]

Indeed, we also know that non-Jews were interested in the monotheism of the Jewish tradition. The following example is from the Roman writer Juvenal:

> Some who have had a father who reveres the Sabbath, worship nothing but the clouds, *and the divinity of the heavens* [my italics], and see no difference between eating swine's flesh, from which their father abstained,

and that of man; and in time they take to circumcision. Having been wont
to flout the laws of Rome, they learn and practise and revere the Jewish
law, and all that Moses handed down in his secret tome, forbidding to
point out the way to any not worshipping the same rites, and conducting
none but the circumcised to the desired fountain. For all which the father
was to blame, who gave up every seventh day to idleness, keeping it apart
from all the concerns of life.

(Juvenal, *Satires* 14.96–106)

In this broad context, if Christianity was going to distinguish itself from
Judaism and the wider world, then its own form of monotheism would be
important. Of course, how far the earliest Christians went in speculating
about the figure of Jesus is the big question but we can at least suggest that there
are a range of factors underlying this speculation, no matter how we interpret it.

Summary

Two of the major approaches to the study of the earliest Christian elevation of
Jesus to the role of God have been those of Maurice Casey and Larry Hurtado.
Maurice Casey argues that shortly after Jesus' death, certain Christians saw
Jesus as a highly elevated figure, in the same way as other figures (such as
angels) were highly elevated in early Judaism. It was not until around the end
of the first century CE when the people responsible for John's Gospel were in a
bitter dispute with Jews over the figure of Jesus (among other things) that
something like the close identification of Jesus with the God of Israel was
made. In contrast, Larry Hurtado argues that devotion to Jesus, in a sense
previously reserved for the God of Israel alone, was present in the earliest
years after Jesus' death and was part of intense religious experiences. We also
saw different possible ways of explaining why such elevated views of Jesus
emerged on the historical scene, most notably the role of socio-economic
upheaval giving rise to dramatic claims about individuals.

Key Words

Christology: Literally, the study of Christ and used to describe the various
    theological descriptions of Christ.
El: Hebrew word used for 'God' and could be used more broadly to refer to
    other supernatural/divine figures.
Elohim: Hebrew word literally meaning 'gods' but is used in the Hebrew
    Bible/Old Testament to describe the God of Israel. The term could also be
    used more broadly to refer to other supernatural/divine figures.
Monotheism: Technically, the belief in one God who rules over all but can be
    qualified to incorporate the role of other supernatural subservient beings
    such as angels.

Theos: Greek word used for 'God' or a 'god' (depending on context) and could also be used to refer to other supernatural/divine figures.

Trinity: In the Western Christian theological tradition, the coequality of Father, Son, and Holy Spirit.

Further Reading

Bauckham, R., *Jesus and the God of Israel: God Crucified and Other Studies on the New Testament's Christology of Divine Identity*, Milton Keynes: Paternoster, 2008.

Casey, M., *From Jewish Prophet to Gentile God: The Origins and Development of New Testament Christology*, Louisville: WJK; Cambridge: James Clarke, 1991.

Crossley, J.G., 'Moses and Pagan Monotheism' in T. Römer (ed.), *La construction de la figure de Moïse*, Paris: Gabalda, 2007, pp. 319–39.

Fredriksen, P., *From Jesus to Christ: The Origins of the New Testament Images of Christ*, second edition, New Haven: Yale Nota Bene, 2000.

Hurtado, L.W., *Lord Jesus Christ: Devotion to Jesus in Earliest Christianity*, Grand Rapids: Eerdmans, 2003.

McGrath, J.F., *John's Apologetic Christology: Legitimation and Development in Johannine Christology*, Cambridge: CUP, 2001.

Stuckenbruck, L.T., and W.E.S. North, eds, Early Jewish and Christian Monotheism, London and New York: T&T Clark, 2004.

Chapter 7

Paul, the Law, Faith and Salvation

Old Perspectives, New Perspectives, Different Perspectives

If the divinity of Jesus is one way in which Christian splits from Judaism are analysed then it is perhaps the issue of salvation itself that has been arguably the other major area for understanding the 'parting of the ways'. More precisely, one of the most prominent controversies in the history of New Testament studies (modern and pre-modern) has been how to understand Paul's views on salvation and justification: does salvation and justification come through doing good works, through God's grace, or some kind of combination of the two?

Perspectives on Paul

Underlying contemporary discussions of salvation and justification are classic theological disputes, particularly the disputes over what the individual must do to be saved. The influence of the famous German theologian, Martin Luther (1483–1546), and his insistence that individuals are justified through faith alone, and through God's grace rather than through human works, has been profound, not least because Paul became a pivotal figure for Luther and Lutheranism. This influence was still massive in twentieth-century German scholarship, seen in the Pauline scholarship of major interpreters such as Rudolf Bultmann and Ernst Käsemann. Where the context for Luther was a dispute with the Catholic Church at the beginning of the sixteenth century, this was imposed on the first century where the fall guy was Judaism. To caricature the debate, Judaism was said to have an insistence on humans achieving salvation through observing the Law and performing good works while Paul and Christianity replaced this with concepts of God's grace and salvation through faith.

Predictably this meant that there were countless negative portrayals of Judaism as a cold, harsh and legalistic religion. However, these negative portrayals in scholarship on Paul were hit hard in E.P. Sanders' groundbreaking 1977 book, *Paul and Palestinian Judaism*. Sanders argued that Judaism could not be reduced to a religion of salvation by works but instead it was clear that there was a well-established concept of God's grace.[1] The general pattern of Jewish religion was then labelled 'covenantal nomism' and involved 'getting in', that is, God making a covenant with Israel after the graceful election of Israel, and 'staying in', that is, Israel maintaining this relationship by obeying the commandments. Within this system, God remained merciful to Israel and provided means of atoning for sin. For Sanders, Paul effectively swaps the Jewish model for a Christian one where participation in Christ becomes central. Sanders famously argued that Paul's logic moves backwards from solution to plight. Consequently, and to put it in blunt terminology, at the heart of Paul's disputes over salvation was whether or not the believer was to be a 'Christian'.

Sanders' views on Judaism were certainly controversial but also popular and were almost immediately picked up by New Testament scholars whose work was to become labelled the 'New Perspective' on Paul. While New Perspective scholars largely accepted Sanders' reading of early Judaism, there was much more dispute over Sanders' explanation of Paul. For instance, a prominent New Perspective scholar, James Dunn, argued for a less individualistic reading of Paul and argued that Paul critiqued the ways in which the Law functioned as a social boundary between Jew and Gentile and that the phrase 'works of the Law' referred to such 'badges' of the covenant as circumcision and food laws, a view he later developed more generally with reference to a critique of the Law functioning in a nationalistic manner.[2] But the 'Old Perspective' hardly gave up after the damaging critique of Sanders, with reactions ranging from fiercely critical to critically engaging, especially on the issue of the caricaturing of Judaism where Sanders has at least forced scholars to reassess the language used to describe Judaism. Today, the picture is not always so clear cut between Old Perspective and New Perspective and so scholars sometimes talk of being 'beyond' the New Perspective.[3]

So what are we to make of all this? Sanders was undoubtedly right and largely successful in challenging the anti-Judaism (and at times antisemitism) rife in New Testament scholarship but it may be the case that he has replaced the old Christianised categories imposed on Judaism (works versus grace) with new Christianised ones (different versions of grace and works). The different Jewish sources are anything but systematic and scholars can find with relative ease texts containing judgement for individual deeds and a heavy stress on God's grace. It is far from clear that one was emphasised more than the other in early Judaism. Whether these two issues are brought together in the ways Sanders suggests is also not clear. At the very least, we are lacking evidence of widespread attempts to bring the two together.

What might be the more plausible view is that when Paul has to deal with the issue of inclusion of gentiles not observing the Law or parts of the Law, the issue of how individuals are saved or justified *then* becomes sharply focused. Contexts where observance of the Law can be taken for granted (though certainly with disputes over which interpretations are correct) are significantly different from those contexts where its very validity is being undermined. Questions about what is to be done with these people not observing the Law (and this non-observance may have started to influence Jews associated with the new Christian movement) inevitably raise the issue of justification. What is Paul to do with people not circumcised, not observing the Law but attracted to the idea of Christ and Christianity? From one theological perspective, are these people attracted to the God of Israel not a sign of God's favour? In these sorts of contexts observance of the Law would presumably not work for the simple reason that too many Gentiles were not interested in things like circumcision, avoidance of pork and so on but theological traditions of God's grace would work extremely well in justifying such people. If God had saved and had justified people before and without obvious conditions attached, then why not again?

Was Paul consistent?

This is where Paul comes into his own as a serious thinker and theologian. Though to muddy the waters even more, Paul himself has some seemingly contradictory things to say on the Law, sometimes positive (e.g. Rom. 3.31), sometimes seemingly negative (e.g. Gal. 2.17–21; 3.10–13; 4.21–26), sometimes seemingly indifferent (e.g. Gal. 6.15; Rom. 14.1–8; 1 Cor. 7.19). One way to deal with the seeming inconsistency has been to suggest that Paul is simply just inconsistent, another to suggest that Paul developed his views between his writing of Galatians and Romans, or another to argue that Paul held different views on the Law and salvation for Jews and Gentiles, respectively. We could, alternatively, follow a fairly traditional line that Paul was in fact consistent and the differences between Galatians and Romans have more to do with tone and particular social setting rather than any significantly different theological development, though Paul's thought prior to the letters may well have developed significantly in reaction to more and more Gentiles included in the Christian movement.

So can we say that there are some areas of consistency in Pauline thought on issues of Law and salvation? A case can certainly be made. While it is true that Paul is far more aggressive in Galatians than he is in Romans, the issue of imposing the Law is crucial. For instance, in Galatians, Paul attempts to deal with differences on the issue of circumcision with some eye-watering polemic: 'I wish those who unsettle you would castrate themselves!' (Gal. 5.12). He is also clearly upset about Christians observing 'special days' (presumably including the Sabbath) and times (Gal. 4.9–11). In Romans, however, Paul is somewhat gentler when dealing with issues of believers observing the Law:

> Welcome those who are weak in faith, but not for the purpose of quarreling over opinions.[2] Some believe in eating anything, while the weak eat only vegetables.[3] Those who eat must not despise those who abstain, and those who abstain must not pass judgment on those who eat; for God has

welcomed them.[4] Who are you to pass judgment on servants of another? It is before their own lord that they stand or fall. And they will be upheld, for the Lord is able to make them stand.[5] Some judge one day to be better than another, while others judge all days to be alike. Let all be fully convinced in their own minds.[6] Those who observe the day, observe it in honor of the Lord. Also those who eat, eat in honor of the Lord, since they give thanks to God; while those who abstain, abstain in honor of the Lord and give thanks to God.[7] We do not live to ourselves, and we do not die to ourselves.[8] If we live, we live to the Lord, and if we die, we die to the Lord; so then, whether we live or whether we die, we are the Lord's.

(Rom. 14.1–8)

It is commonly believed that those eating vegetables are those still observing the food laws (by eating only vegetables food laws are effectively observed) and Paul accepts (in differing degrees) both those who abstain and those who do not. Likewise with those who observe special days, presumably including the Sabbath ('Some judge one day to be better than another') and those who do not. Notice, though, that Paul uses the phrase 'weak in faith' and everything is ultimately done for Christ. Justification of the individual clearly is still not through the Law.

While the tone in Galatians and Romans is obviously very different, there is some consistency in the line of thought: aspects of the Law such as circumcision, food laws, and holy days should not be imposed on believers. For Paul, 'neither circumcision nor uncircumcision is anything; but a new creation is everything!' (Gal. 6.15) which seems to be more or less the same sentiment as Romans 14.1–8. The polemic of Galatians might suggest that this was more of a pressing problem for Paul than it was when writing Romans but the general idea of Paul not wanting aspects of the Law *imposed* on believers seems clear enough (see e.g. Gal. 2.11–14; cf. Col. 2.16). If Paul believed observance was being imposed, he could react ferociously but if he believed there was no imposition he could accommodate people, such as those described in Romans 14.1–8.

The undermining of food, holy days and circumcision meant an undermining of the Law as a whole. If someone is to be circumcised, Paul argues, they will be obliged to obey the whole Law (Gal. 5.3). However, human beings are deluded to think they can do the impossible and obey the whole Law (Gal. 6.13) and so sin is inevitable (cf. Gal. 3.21–25). While the problem of Gentiles no doubt provoked the questioning of the role of the Law, Paul's logic seems to push the inability of keeping the Law and the inevitability of sin to all humanity, Jew and Gentile: 'for we have already charged that all, both Jews and Greeks, are under the power of sin, as it is written: "There is no one who is righteous, not even one; there is no one who has understanding, there is no one who seeks God."' (Rom. 3.9–11). Christ and faith are what is required (e.g. Gal. 3.24; 5.6; Rom. 3–4) and hence the famous Pauline phrase that has echoed through the ages, 'justification by faith'. Luther infamously added 'alone' to this formulation but did he not still get Paul right?

One of the logical conclusions that could, and has, been drawn from Paul's theology is that without the Law as a guide then anything is ethically permissible. Paul himself recognised this possibility and ruled it out (Rom. 6.15). Indeed, Paul has a notorious reputation for being morally conservative and 1 Corinthians 6 shows his concerns for correct behaviour. Paul's solution to the potential problem of boundless immorality is to bring in the Spirit:

> But you are not in the flesh; you are in the Spirit, since the Spirit of God dwells in you. Anyone who does not have the Spirit of Christ does not belong to him. But if Christ is in you, though the body is dead because of sin, the Spirit is life because of righteousness. If the Spirit of him who raised Jesus from the dead dwells in you, he who raised Christ from the dead will give life to your mortal bodies also through his Spirit that dwells in you.
>
> (Rom. 8.9–11; cf. Gal. 5.13–26)

From this perspective, those who manifest the 'works of the flesh', such as idolatry and drunkenness, will not inherit the kingdom while those who manifest the 'fruit of the spirit', such as love and goodness, will (Gal. 5.19–23). Through baptism and the death and resurrection of Christ, the believer avoids being a slave to sin (Rom. 6).

Paul's ideas of justification by faith and a human inability to keep the whole Law no doubt reflected social realities on the ground: certainly there would have been Gentiles not observing the Law. But perhaps there were Jews too. Acts has a lengthy section describing Peter's vision where he was told that food distinctions were no longer valid (Acts 10.1–11.18) and Paul himself claims,

> For though I am free with respect to all, I have made myself a slave to all, so that I might win more of them.[20] To the Jews I became as a Jew, in order to win Jews. To those under the law I became as one under the law (though I myself am not under the law) so that I might win those under the law.[21] To those outside the law I became as one outside the law (though I am not free from God's law but am under Christ's law) so that I might win those outside the law.[22] To the weak I became weak, so that I might win the weak. I have become all things to all people, that I might by all means save some.[23] I do it all for the sake of the gospel, so that I may share in its blessings.
>
> (1 Cor. 9.19–23)

Theologically speaking this suggests that the idea of observant Jewish Christians and non-observant gentile Christians starts to break down with the (Jewish) Paul and perhaps this reflects a wider blurring of the boundaries between the two. However, whether Jews associated with the Christian movement were openly not observing parts of the Law is difficult to establish. Even if we accept the historicity of Peter's vision in Acts (10–11.18), we still have no *explicit* evidence that he went out and ate whatever he wanted. If we accept that the dispute recorded in Galatians 2.11–15 concerns the food laws and Peter eating at the table with Gentiles who ate whatever they liked, we still have no *explicit* evidence that Peter ate pork, shellfish or whatever. For all we know, he, like other Jews associated with the Christian movement, simply might not have been able to stomach such food. Similarly with Paul's formula: in practice we cannot say for certain whether he was openly disregarding the Law. While in theory figures such as Paul and Peter might have been able to agree (sometimes ... Gal. 2.11–15) that Jews and Gentiles no longer had to observe the Law and were one in Christ, in practice habit may have made things look a little different. The lack of hard evidence for Jews associated with the Christian movement not observing the Law means we can only make educated guesses whether this was indeed the case.

Origins of Paul's Theology: Jesus?

Looking at the social realities underlying Paul's theology means we are now returning to issues of historical change and causality and here we might be able to contribute further explanations for the rise of Paul's theology. The emergence of Gentiles as numerically significant in the Christian movement has sometimes been traced back to Jewish thought about the end times because scholars have long noted that there was a well-established view that Gentiles, or those perceived to be righteous Gentiles, would share in Israel's blessings at end times. However, while these views would no doubt have been useful for the earliest Christians, looking at Jewish ideas on Gentile inclusion only gets us so far. After all, Christianity did become Gentile religion whereas Judaism, obviously, did not. So why was it the Christian faction which would become a Gentile religion?

We might turn to the historical Jesus. The historical Jesus, however, only seems to have had minimal interest in Gentiles (e.g. Mark 7.24–30; Matt. 10.5–6) – given the negative statements about Gentiles in the Gospel tradition this is less likely to have been an invention of the church and more likely something associated with the historical Jesus. However, Jesus' association with those deemed 'sinners' may well have provided an impetus. The term 'sinner' had a range of meanings but relatively stable ones, from centuries prior to Jesus to centuries after. The typical and overlapping meanings of the term 'sinner' include people who act as if there is no God, people who do not observe the Law (or certain interpretations of the Law), people who were effectively outside God's covenant with Israel, and people contrasted with 'the righteous'. Contrary to some common perceptions, those designated 'sinners' would not have been the poor masses because whenever the social status of those designated 'sinners' is mentioned they are rich people who oppress the poor and manipulate justice. These uses of the term 'sinner' are present in the Gospel tradition. The term can be used fairly generally (e.g. Mark 8.38; Luke 13.2), in contrast to the 'righteous' and possibly in the context of understandings and interpretations of the Law (Mark 2.15–17//Matt. 9.10–13//Luke 5.29–32; Luke 15.1–2). Given that 'sinners' like Zacchaeus (Luke 19.1–9) presumably did not observe commandments concerning social justice, and given that the Prodigal Son, in the context of a chapter about Jesus' association with 'sinners' (Luke 15), associates with pigs, there is a good chance that some 'sinners' were perceived as not observing major biblical commandments. It is clear in some contexts that 'sinners' are filthy rich and oppress, or have oppressed the poor and are associated with people notorious for being oppressive rich: tax collectors (Matt. 11.19//Luke 7.34; Luke 18.13; Luke 19.1–9; cf. Luke 7.36–50).

What is to be done with these 'sinners'? A consistent theme in Jewish literature is that they will face unpleasant judgement. Presumably Jesus and/or the Gospels thought similarly, particularly if Jesus had called them to repentance. In calling 'sinners' to repentance, Jesus was picking up on a strand of Jewish thought where it was hoped sinners might repent, most notably and influentially in the book of Ezekiel (e.g. Ezek. 33.7–9, 11, 19). As one text from before the time of Jesus put it:

> If you turn to him with all your heart and with all your soul, to do what is true before him, then he will turn to you and will no longer hide his face from you. So now see what he has done for you; acknowledge him at the top of your voice. Bless the Lord of righteousness, and exalt the King of the ages. In the land of my exile I acknowledge him, and show his power and majesty to a nation of sinners: 'Turn back, you sinners, and do what is right before him; perhaps he may look with favour upon you and show you mercy.'
>
> (Tobit 13.6)

However, there are plenty of texts whereby 'sinners' are strongly condemned with no discussion of repentance. Moreover, if people associated with such types then they would inevitably be corrupted. As the book of Sirach says, 'Who pities a snake charmer when he is bitten, or all those who go near wild animals? So no one pities a person who associates with a sinner and becomes involved in other's sins' (Sir. 12.13–14). Interestingly, Jesus is criticised for *associating* with such people. As the scribes of the Pharisees put it according to Mark 2.16, 'Why does he eat with tax collectors and sinners?' It is certainly possible individual passages are inventions of the early church but as the conflict over 'sinners' is multiply attested in sources and forms, as well as being culturally plausible in early Judaism, it could be suggested that we are at least dealing with an issue in the life of the historical Jesus.

Importantly, the range of meanings for the term 'sinner' meant that Gentiles became equated with the term: Gentiles were 'sinners' by definition were they not! In the literature where the term arises in conjunction with Gentiles, Gentiles were perceived as being rich, oppressive, law-less and beyond the covenant between God and Israel. We have a clear example of the latter in Galatians 2.15 when Paul says, 'We ourselves are Jews by birth and not Gentile sinners'. When the first Christians were active in synagogues, it seems as if they would have been in contact not only with Jews but interested Gentiles. This picture Acts paints of Gentiles attracted to synagogues where Christians were active (e.g. Acts 13.16, 26) is certainly plausible because we have some evidence of Gentiles interested in Judaism and interested in synagogues (e.g. *t. Meg.* 2.16; Aphrodisias 'god-fearer' inscription). Jesus' initial association of those Jewish 'sinners' deemed beyond the Law and God's covenant provided an impetus for the first Christians to engage with Gentile 'sinners'.

Social Origins of Paul's Theology

It might be reasonable enough to expect that in settings such as Jewish meetings any interested Gentile would inevitably observe Jewish laws, or at least not do anything offensive towards Jewish sensibilities. However, what happens when an interested Gentile goes off with Gentile friends? The social pressure to conform is obviously not as strong. And what if friends of friends of friends start to get interested to some degree? Is it not likely that more people interested in Christianity would have less concern for issues of Law?

This might seem a little speculative but in fact there is a lot of detailed work to support such suggestions. One of the most important works in this area, as we have already seen in Chapter 2, comes from the sociologist of modern religion, Rodney Stark.[4] Stark had worked extensively on conversion to new religious movements in the modern world and applied some of his arguments on, for instance, the rapid rise and spread of Mormonism to understanding the rapid rise and spread of earliest Christianity. One of Stark's key findings, and one which has been supported by other sociologists in their research, was that conversion to new religious movements typically involves friendship and work networks. The potential convert usually has a pre-existing affective tie (e.g. friendship) with a member or members of the religious movement. Conversion can often be a long, drawn out process with mixed levels of commitment to the movement among the interested or newly converted. As Josephus puts it with reference to conversion to Judaism (and remember the earliest converts to 'Christianity' would have been converts to a Jewish movement), 'The Greeks ... many of them have agreed to adopt our laws; of whom some have remained faithful, while others, lacking the necessary endurance, have again seceded' (*Apion* 2.123).

One reason why there are different levels of commitment among converts generally is because of powerful countervailing influences from family, partners, friends and a society, all lacking in a belief in the new movement. Josephus, among others, recalls the story of the conversion to Judaism of the king Izates and the house of Adiabene (*Ant.* 20.34–48) where several different countervailing influences are present. A Jewish merchant Ananias was said to have brought the women at the court of the king, including Izates' mother Helena, around to the worship of the Jewish god. Through these 'conversions' Ananias got to Izates himself. Izates took on more and more aspects of Judaism until he decided he wanted to be circumcised. Helena was against this because she thought the people would be angry at such a show of commitment to a foreign religion and Ananias agreed. On the other hand, a Galilean Jew called Eleazar believed Izates should be circumcised, the logic being it would be hypocritical to follow the easier parts of the Law. Eleazar's view won out but here we have an excellent example (and there are others) of different countervailing influences. We know (see also the Juvenal reference at the end of Chapter 6) how things such as avoidance of pork and avoidance of work on the Sabbath could be deemed peculiar outside Judaism and no doubt circumcision was always going to be a problem for men interested in Judaism. It is no surprise circumcision was a flashpoint in early Christianity.

We know family was one area of countervailing influences in the first century. Paul faces the problem of unbelieving partners in 1 Corinthians 7.12–16 and attempted to solve the problem by allowing the unbelieving partner to separate but also raising the possibility that if both stay together then, 'Wife, for all you know, you might save your husband. Husband, for all you know, you might save your wife' (1 Cor. 7.16). In 1 Corinthians 8 and 10, Paul has to deal with the issue of food dedicated to idols and offerings in pagan settings. Clearly this is because Christian converts still have connections with their previous ways and old friendship/family/work, etc. ties are still in place. More generally, we might suggest that given Paul's letters and other New Testament letters, and the amount of instruction and teaching they contain, people were in the process of understanding what is to be expected of them as Christians.

As scholars such as Wayne Meeks and Jack T. Sanders have shown, it is important to think of ancient networks with reference to households because, with the conversion of the head of the household the family and slaves would have to follow suit and then the different connections in the household could further perpetuate the Christian movement in different directions.[5] The New Testament gives several examples of the conversion of households. So, for instance, Paul writes, 'Now, brothers and sisters, you know that members of the household of Stephanas were the first converts in Achaia, and they have devoted themselves to the service of the saints' (1 Cor. 16. 15; see also John 4.46–54; Acts 10.2; 11.14; 16.14–15; 18.8; 1 Cor. 1.1; Phil. 4.22). If a household is going to be converted as a whole, irrespective of personal convictions, then it is reasonable to expect that not everyone would have had the same degree of commitment to the new movement. We have a clear example of a lesser degree of commitment among a household member in Philemon. Here Onesimus is the runaway slave of the Christian Philemon. While his previous Christian convictions were presumably not high, it seems that it took Paul to make Onesimus see the light: 'I am appealing to you for my child, Onesimus, whose father I have become during my imprisonment' (Philem. 10).

This general outline of different levels of commitment can be applied, as this author has tried, to the origins of non-observance of the Law in Christianity.[6] When the initial Gentile converts to Christianity were associated first with Jewish contexts (e.g. synagogue) then they would have been involved with at least superficially observing the Law. But such non-Jews would have faced a range of countervailing influences, from hostility to circumcision for males to puzzlement about the avoidance of pork, from dislike of Judaism to sheer indifference. With the conversion of households, would not fewer and fewer associated with Christianity have had the interest in the details of Jewish Law? Clearly, by the time we get to Romans, already in one context it looks as if Law-observant Christians, or at least those who observed Sabbath and food laws, are more under threat than those who did not (Rom. 14.1–8).

We can now see why some of the decisions made by the historical Jesus become important for understanding the emergence of Gentiles as a significant force in earliest Christianity. Jesus' controversial association with (Jewish) sinners provided a strong ideological justification for further association with non-Jewish sinners: both Jewish and gentile sinners are strongly overlapping categories. After Jesus' death, followers of Jesus went into synagogues and associations which would have involved consistent interactions between Jews and gentiles. The impetus given by association with people deemed beyond the Law and covenant (as gentile and Jewish sinners both were) meant that the Jesus movement could begin to spread outside Judaism.

It is worth mentioning some qualifications here because it seems some scholars have difficulties in understanding these sorts of understandings of the rise of non-observance of the Law. This does *not* mean that we have two defined camps of 'observant' and 'non-observant' camps in earliest Christianity. Already with Paul we have seen some people continued following the Law, or at least some aspects of it (e.g. Sabbath and food laws). Some Gentiles no doubt were observing the Law before, during, and after Paul. There were those identified as Christians who continued to observe Jewish festivals for some centuries after Paul. Around the time of the New Testament texts it is clear that some ethnically Jewish Christians may have seen no contradiction between Christ as the only way to salvation coupled with the Law (e.g. Gal. 2). The letter of James still seems to hold to a Law-observant view of Christianity as a crucial way for Christians to be justified:

> You do well if you really fulfill the royal law according to the scripture, "You shall love your neighbor as yourself."[9] But if you show partiality, you commit sin and are convicted by the law as transgressors.[10] For whoever keeps the whole law but fails in one point has become

accountable for all of it.[11] For the one who said, "You shall not commit adultery," also said, "You shall not murder." Now if you do not commit adultery but if you murder, you have become a transgressor of the law.[12] So speak and so act as those who are to be judged by the law of liberty.[13] For judgment will be without mercy to anyone who has shown no mercy; mercy triumphs over judgment.[14] What good is it, my brothers and sisters, if you say you have faith but do not have works? Can faith save you?[15] If a brother or sister is naked and lacks daily food,[16] and one of you says to them, "Go in peace; keep warm and eat your fill," and yet you do not supply their bodily needs, what is the good of that?[17] So faith by itself, if it has no works, is dead.

(James 2.8–17)

The point I am trying to introduce in this chapter is that we might be able to provide different explanations for the origins of non-observance in Christianity which would eventually become one of the ways Christians could define themselves in differentiation from Judaism.

There is inevitably a degree of speculation about the specifics of such a broad explanation but the general idea that more and more Gentiles would have led to a profound questioning of the role of the Law in earliest Christianity is clear enough. Then the question arises: what is to be done with all these people? One of the first major attempts to deal with this issue was the council at Jerusalem, around 50 CE (Acts 15; Gal. 2.1–10). According to Acts 15, the sheer number of Gentiles is seen as a blessing and the solution is written in a letter 'that you abstain from what has been sacrificed to idols and from blood and from what is strangled and from fornication' (Acts 15.29; cf. v. 20). In what looks to be a parallel retelling in Galatians 2.1–10, there is no mention of this letter, though it is possible that Paul did not think even these things ought to be imposed on Gentiles. According to Paul's account, there is little to be imposed it would seem (Gal. 2.1–10). In the long run, the most influential attempt to deal with the issue of Gentiles and the Law was, as we saw, Paul's letters and his idea of justification by faith without works of the Law. Paul's attempted solution was so influential that today even the world's most famous atheist thinkers still see him as a figure to be 'rescued' in that his thought and theology are now very much part of both a mainstream and radical intellectual tradition. It is to this we now turn.

Summary

Dominant views of Paul's theology traditionally stressed that Paul's theology of justification and grace was a reaction against a Judaism characterised as cold, harsh, and legalistic where the individual earned their salvation (the 'Old Perspective'). The 'New Perspective', inspired chiefly by E.P. Sanders, viewed Judaism as a religion with strong concepts of God's grace and that Paul's theology had to be worked out against this background. One feature of the 'New Perspective' is the idea of Paul reacting against a seemingly exclusive and nationalistic Judaism. Whichever view we take, it is clear that at least some parts of the Law were no longer required for Gentiles at least in Paul's thought. Different theological and social reasons might explain this, such as Jesus' association with people deemed 'sinners' and the role of Gentiles interested in the Law behaving differently in Jewish and Gentile contexts, including ways in which the Christian message might have spread in different social networks and among friends of friends of friends.

Key Words

Covenantal nomism: A term developed by E.P. Sanders to describe what he saw as the general pattern of early Jewish religion. 'Getting in' involved God's covenant with, and graceful election of, Israel, and 'staying in' involved Israel maintaining the relationship through observance of the commandments. God also provided means for atoning for sins within this system for when people inevitably fell short.

New Perspective: A reaction against the Old Perspective on Paul inspired chiefly by the work of E.P. Sanders. New Perspective scholars have tended to emphasise the role of grace in early Judaism and downplay the idea that Judaism was a religion whereby the individual earned their salvation. One feature of the New Perspective is the idea that Paul was reacting against an exclusive nationalism in early Judaism.

Old Perspective: A label typically given to scholarship on Paul influenced by Lutheranism which holds that Paul's theology was an alternative or reaction to a supposed emphasis on the individual earning their salvation. Paul instead stressed salvation or justification through faith (alone) and God's grace.

'Sinners': A phrase used in early Judaism and the New Testament to describe people deemed to be acting beyond the Law, beyond God's covenant with Israel, oppressive, rich, and the opposite of the 'righteous'. The term could also be used to describe non-Jews in general (Gentiles).

Social networks: In sociological terms, the human social connections (such as friendship, families, work, associations and so on) available to spread messages.

Further Reading

Boyarin, D., *A Radical Jew: Paul and the Politics of Identity*, Berkeley and Los Angeles: University of California Press, 1994.

Crossley, J.G., *Why Christianity Happened: A Sociohistorical Account of Christian Origins*, Louisville: WJK, 2006.

Dunn, J.D.G., *The Theology of Paul the Apostle*, Grand Rapids: Eerdmans; Edinburgh: T&T Clark, 1998.

Horrell, D.G., *An Introduction to the Study of Paul*, second edition, London & New York: Continuum, 2006.

Meeks, W.A., *The First Urban Christians: The Social World of the Apostle Paul*, second edition, New Haven and London: Yale UP, 2003.

Räisänen, H., *Paul and the Law*, second edition; Tübingen: Mohr Siebeck, 1987.

Sanders, E.P., *Paul and Palestinian Judaism: A Comparison of Patterns of Religion*, Philadelphia: Fortress; London: SCM, 1977.

Sanders, J.T., *Charisma, Converts, Competitors: Societal and Sociological Factors in the Success of Early Christianity*, London: SCM, 2000.

Chapter 8

Paul's Revolution for Our Times?

Paul and Continental Philosophy

In mainstream New Testament studies, scholars are starting to notice that in the past twenty years there has been a reappraisal of Paul (and Christianity) as part of the continental philosophical tradition. Paul has become a figure not only worthy of his place in intellectual history, but as someone worth listening to by those ordinarily outside the Christian tradition and outside academic biblical studies and theology, most notably in continental philosophical and political circles, and more specifically in the works of thinkers such as Jacob Taubes, Giorgio Agamben, Alain Badiou and Slavoj Žižek. Curiously, this interest in what is sometimes referred to as the 'political Paul' is mirrored in an intensified interest in Paul, politics and empire in New Testament studies. We will be returning to the reasons why this might be in the next section and readers might want to follow the merging of the key philosophical thinkers and biblical scholars in the recent book edited by John Caputo and Linda Martín Alcoff and in the work of the New Testament scholar Ward Blanton.[1] For now, the rest of this chapter will be dedicated to an attempt at summarising some (and only some) of the key points of the often highly complex and not-always-comprehensible views on Paul among the continental philosophers, with particular reference to issues relating to the more traditional question in New Testament studies of the 'parting of the ways'. The story of Paul among the continental philosophers has not often been told in New Testament studies and so hopefully this very basic chapter will provoke people to go and read the various thinkers, while becoming possibly intrigued, perhaps fascinated, and no doubt frustrated at this seemingly peculiar intellectual movement.

Jacob Taubes

The 'philosophical', 'political' and even 'atheistic' readings of Paul have a long intellectual history. We could, for instance, begin our story with Nietzsche at the end of the nineteenth century. Arguably the most immediate influence on the readings of Paul among contemporary theorists and philosophers has been the late Jacob Taubes, Professor of Hermenuetics at the Free University of Berlin, having also taught at Harvard and Columbia. In February 1987, Taubes was invited to present a series of lectures at the University of Heidelberg on Paul's letter to the Romans. At this time Taubes was also at the advanced stages of cancer – the lectures would be delivered just weeks before his death – and he even had to spend some of his time in intensive care. Clearly, then, delivering these lectures on Paul meant a great deal to him and, as the preface to the published version of the lectures by Aleida Assmann makes clear, this personal context provides a crucial interpretative framework for Taubes' reading of Romans.[2] Furthermore, Taubes relates his reading of Paul to conversations on Paul with influential figures in his personal life. Perhaps most important was a pressing correspondence and conversation on, and reading of, Romans 9–11 with the famous jurist Carl Schmitt, who himself was facing imminent death.

Taubes stressed that it was as a Jew, not as a professor, that he approached the text (though it ought to be noted that his anecdotes and references remain highly intellectualised) and he was convinced that he had a particular insight into Paul because the Pauline mindset was, so to speak, not Greek but Yiddish! Reading Romans was a deeply personal issue and a Jewish issue, not least because of the not infrequent hostility towards Paul in Jewish history, a figure representing a decline, perhaps, from the more loyalist Jew, Jesus. Taubes goes a step further in effectively bringing back Paul to the Jewish fold by attributing to him a particularly Jewish way of understanding crucial concepts such as 'law'. Taubes also makes a further crucial, and seemingly influential, move for the understanding of Paul in continental philosophy: the Bible and theology is needed (for Taubes at least) as the very basis for understanding and teaching *philosophy* no less! How about the following for an endorsement of academic biblical studies?

> I could have dedicated myself to this [biblical study], but by vanity and fate I became a philosopher. I thought it wasn't my calling. Today I see that a Bible lesson is more important than a lesson on Hegel. A little late. I can only suggest that you take your Bible lessons more seriously than all of philosophy.[3]

Throughout his book/lectures, Taubes brings both philosophy and biblical studies together by relating Paul to major modern thinkers such as Nietzsche, Benjamin, Freud and Adorno.

Arguably the most influential aspect of Taubes' reading for subsequent readings of Paul in certain circles has been what is seen in general terms as Taubes' politicisation of Paul's message, though often it does not seem so far removed from conventional theology and biblical studies. Using parallels from throughout Jewish history, Taubes suggests that Paul is tapping into a Jewish tradition whereby redemption is interpreted in light of catastrophe, of something that really should not have happened. In terms of Paul's thought, this involves the catastrophe of Jesus' shameful death on the cross whereby the values of shame are reversed: people now have faith in this crucified figure. The price demanded by Jesus, and by the examples from Jewish history, is so high that works are nothing in comparison.

Most crucially of all for the politicisation of Paul in continental philosophy, Taubes argued that when Paul critiques the Law he is critiquing a means of law and order accommodating Jews, Greeks and Romans, a widespread intellectual consensus, so Taubes believed, in the Mediterranean world under Roman rule. In contrast to this universalising consensus, the illiberal Paul makes an explosive challenge. The universalising law is turned on its head by having the one crucified by this law as the great ruler of all. In this light, Paul wants to establish a new people of God. This causes Paul great anguish – a type of anguish Taubes locates in Jewish tradition – because this new community does not require (Jewish) blood kinship but a kinship based on promise.

For Taubes, the key to understanding Romans is the opening (Rom. 1.1–7). With language of 'Son of God' and 'obedience of faith', Romans is a political declaration of war against the Emperor and the cult of the Emperor. Though certainly not a new view (as Taubes knew), this politicised interpretation anticipates the present scholarly preoccupation with Paul's attitude towards the Roman Empire, an issue to which we will return. Taubes also reads Paul's politics as a precursor of modern thinkers such as Nietzsche and Walter Benjamin and the idea of political development as a kind of nihilism. In language closer to Paul, the world and creation is in decay and working towards the end of the Roman Empire (cf. 1 Cor. 7.29–31). Compare Romans 8:

> I consider that the sufferings of this present time are not worth comparing with the glory about to be revealed to us.[19] For the creation waits with eager longing for the revealing of the children of God;[20] for the creation was subjected to futility, not of its own will but by the will of the one who subjected it, in hope[21] that the creation itself will be set free from its bondage to decay and will obtain the freedom of the glory of the children of God.[22] We know that the whole creation has been groaning in labour pains until now;[23] and not only the creation, but we ourselves, who have the first fruits of the Spirit, groan inwardly while we wait for adoption, the redemption of our bodies.[24] For in hope we were saved. Now hope that is seen is not hope. For who hopes for what is seen?[25] But if we hope for what we do not see, we wait for it with patience.[26] Likewise the Spirit helps us in our weakness; for we do not know how to pray as we ought, but that very Spirit intercedes with sighs too deep for words.[27] And God, who searches the heart, knows what is the mind of the Spirit, because the Spirit intercedes for the saints according to the will of God.[28] We know that all things work together for good for those who love God, who are called according to his purpose.[29] For those whom he

foreknew he also predestined to be conformed to the image of his Son, in order that he might be the firstborn within a large family [literally: 'brothers'].

(Rom. 8.18–29)

Verse 29 is important for Taubes because it is anything but a democratic image and is profoundly anti-Emperor. In a letter sent to the heart of the Roman Empire, the Emperor is *not* the first born among the brothers.

But for any revolutionary reading of Paul there is always the problematic passage of Romans 13.1–8:

Let every person be subject to the governing authorities; for there is no authority except from God, and those authorities that exist have been instituted by God.[2] Therefore whoever resists authority resists what God has appointed, and those who resist will incur judgment.[3] For rulers are not a terror to good conduct, but to bad. Do you wish to have no fear of the authority? Then do what is good, and you will receive its approval;[4] for it is God's servant for your good. But if you do what is wrong, you should be afraid, for the authority does not bear the sword in vain! It is the servant of God to execute wrath on the wrongdoer.[5] Therefore one must be subject, not only because of wrath but also because of conscience.[6] For the same reason you also pay taxes, for the authorities are God's servants, busy with this very thing.[7] Pay to all what is due them – taxes to whom taxes are due, revenue to whom revenue is due, respect to whom respect is due, honor to whom honor is due.[8] Owe no one anything, except to love one another; for the one who loves another has fulfilled the law.

Developing the ideas of the famous Swiss theologian, Karl Barth (1886–1968), one of the ways in which Taubes tried to overcome the common and forceful criticism that Romans 13 is not only a call to behave under the governing power but even an endorsement of governing power, was to turn to the end of the previous chapter in Romans (remember there was no such thing as chapter and verse divisions when Paul's letters were written): 'Do not be overcome by evil, but overcome evil with good' (Rom. 12.21). Taubes also looks to what follows Romans 13.1–7:

Owe no one anything, except to love one another; for the one who loves another has fulfilled the law.[9] The commandments, "You shall not commit adultery; You shall not murder; You shall not steal; You shall not covet"; and any other commandment, are summed up in this word, "Love your neighbour as yourself."[10] Love does no wrong to a neighbour; therefore, love is the fulfilling of the law.

(Rom. 13.8–10)

Taubes even pits Paul against Jesus here because Jesus endorses the *dual* commandment: honouring the Lord followed by loving your neighbour (Mark 12.28–34). With Paul, the Lord drops out and we are left with the neighbour and Taubes regards this as a highly revolutionary move because Paul must have known about Jesus and the dual commandment and so the stress is even greater on loving your neighbour as the only valid formation. This heavy stress on love means there is need and instead of 'I', and individual redemption, Paul goes for 'we' and the new people of God. This becomes doubly important with end times just around the corner, as Romans 13 moves on to say:

> Besides this, you know what time it is, how it is now the moment for you to wake from sleep. For salvation is nearer to us now than when we became believers;[12] the night is far gone, the day is near. Let us then lay aside the works of darkness and put on the armour of light;[13] let us live honourably as in the day, not in revelling and drunkenness, not in debauchery and licentiousness, not in quarrelling and jealousy.[14] Instead, put on the Lord Jesus Christ, and make no provision for the flesh, to gratify its desires.
>
> (Rom. 13.11–14)

For Taubes, this conclusion to Romans 13 is crucial for reading the rest of the chapter because it is effectively saying that there would be little point in revolution if 'the whole palaver, the whole swindle' were going to be over. The new movement has no political legitimation and if people were to behave in the ways criticised in 13.1–7 the movement would just stand out and be confused with some revolutionary movement.[4] Taubes draws the following analogy:

> Sure it's evil, but – what are you going to do. I know this sort of mentality. It's not at all foreign to me. I have a passport. But what do I have to do with my country beyond my passport? My president's name is Reagan. Do I strike you as very American?[5]

Alain Badiou and Slavoj Žižek

There is much more to Taubes than this brief summary but I have focused on what I think are his most influential arguments for those readings of Paul in continental philosophy outside biblical studies and those that cohere with those readings which, as we will see, have become prominent within New Testament studies. Arguably the other major influential figure on the 'political' and 'philosophical' readings outside the traditional walls of biblical studies and theology departments, and in line with the political reading of Taubes, has been the leading French thinker Alain Badiou.[6] While a number of other thinkers could have been added, the rest of this chapter will be largely devoted to Badiou's ideas and influence because Badiou's stress on universalism in Paul is a particularly helpful point of comparison with some of the things (especially postcolonial criticism) we have seen in previous chapters.

If Taubes focuses much of his analysis on the issue of Paul in relation to Jewish tradition, a concern for much of New Testament studies, Badiou focuses his analysis on issues of historical change, albeit in a highly abstract manner. Underlying Badiou's views on Paul are his philosophy of history. For Badiou, an 'event' is a dramatic disjunction with historical and cultural norms and establishes a new truth and new reality and demands fidelity even when everything seems to be going wrong in the post-'event' world. Such 'events' might include the French Revolution, the Russian Revolution or the social upheavals of 1968.

One such event, according to Badiou, was the resurrection of Jesus which is 'pure event, opening of an epoch'. Irrespective of whether the bodily resurrection really happened or not, this 'pure event' underlies Paul's view of Christianity and is the in-breaking of a new truth and historical reality. It follows from this that, for Badiou's reading of Paul, the resurrection is not falsifiable or demonstrable and Paul's discourse is fidelity to the possibility opened up by the event. Paul is not only an 'antiphilosopher', he is a militant, 'poet thinker of the event' who 'brings forth the entirely human connection ... between the general idea of a rupture, an overturning, and that of a thought-practice that is this rupture's subjective materiality.'[7] Even the very genre of Paul's letters points in this direction according to Badiou. They are not grand theological treaties but, typical of antiphilosophers, militant *interventions* sent to small groups of converts. Unsurprisingly perhaps, and echoing a generation of Bultmann-inspired New Testament scholars, proofs and signs (miraculous, logical or otherwise) of this shattering of reason and of this dramatic gift of grace are not going to be given by this militant antiphilosopher: 'But we have this treasure in clay jars, so that it may be made clear that this extraordinary power belongs to God and does not come from us' (2 Cor. 4.7).

Crucially for Badiou, Paul's conversion does not come through engagement with figures in the Church but a bolt from the blue which mimics the founding event: 'Just as the resurrection remains totally incalculable and it is from there that one must begin, Paul's faith is that from which he begins as a subject'.[8] The foundational resurrection and conversion also lead on to the idea that truth, for Badiou's Paul, cannot be done in degrees: either accept the truth or not and either accept the consequences of the foundational event or remain outside. This truth is a universal singularity and reliance on observances, rites, circumcision and so on, at least in the sense that opponents would make different degrees of belonging to the Christian movement, blocks the universal undertaking. Thus we get Paul recalling conflicts with echoes of a 'genuine fury' such as the recollection of the incident at Antioch (Gal. 2.11–14). Paul would not buckle and would not compromise when it came to fidelity to principles. Paul is not opposed to the Law as such but he is indifferent

('Circumcision is nothing, and uncircumcision is nothing' – 1 Cor. 7.19) which, Badiou believes, 'is worse'. This means (in contrast to Taubes?) the new universality 'bears no privileged relation to the Jewish community' even if Paul was very much part of Jewish culture and heavily uses the Old Testament. The 'truth effects', however, must function independently.[9]

Outside issues relating to Judaism, another of Paul's concerns is the Greek philosophical tradition. For Badiou, Paul would have found little success among the philosophers of Athens who no doubt would have found his views laughable (cf. Acts 17). Paul's problem from the perspective of the Athenian philosopher is the simple point that Paul is an antiphilosopher. While Paul opposes and critiques the 'Jewish discourse' of exception, he also opposes the 'Greek discourse', a cosmic discourse of totality and the fixed order of the world. Away from philosophy, in everyday reality Paul is active in the context of the 'military despotism' of the Roman Empire.[10] In all senses, Paul is at odds with the world as it was known.

There have been a variety of reactions to Badiou's work on Paul. Badiou has had a significant influence on one of the most famous and idiosyncratic contemporary thinkers, Slavoj Žižek. Žižek argues that Paul makes an important shift from the Jewish community by making the Christian community the true 'children of Abraham' and with the Jewish ethnic background replaced by faith in Christ. God still kept the promise to his chosen people but changed the identity of the chosen people in the process. While this sort of reading may need further nuance in light of a mass of scholarship on Paul, for present purposes it is important to see how this is a political move for Žižek's reading. This group is loyal to a 'Cause' and its 'key dimension' is a 'break with any form of communitarianism: his universe is no longer that of the multitude of groups that want to "find their voice," and assert their particular identity, their "way of life," but that of a fighting collective grounded in the reference to an unconditional universalism.' Indeed, Žižek typically casts this in the language of the revolutionary and how Christians live in the aftermath of the event, with obvious similarities with Badiou: *everything – the Big Thing – has already happened*, and that the 'truly difficult work' is not 'creating the conditions for the Event of the revolutionary explosion' but begins '*after* the Event ... drawing out the consequences ... of the new space opened up by the Event' (italics original).[11]

Žižek also sees the origins of a more modern view – something which, like Badiou, Žižek has taken up elsewhere – and that is how we see the kernel of atheistic ideas in Paul and Christian origins. There is, according to Žižek, just 'a tiny nuance, an almost imperceptible shift in perspective, that distinguishes Christ's sacrifice from the atheist's assertion of a life which needs no sacrifice.' This is close to one of the distinctive features of Žižek's reading of the seemingly revolutionary and subversive message at the heart of Christianity: desires can be indulged without having to pay the price because Christ took the price upon himself. It may be significant that Paul comes close to reining in this logical outworking in a not unrelated context (Rom. 6.15). Žižek might add, however, that the Christian can betray desire (e.g. renounce marriage) in a fake sacrifice because you are then welcome to all the trivial pleasures so wished![12]

Paul among the Marxists

At this point it is perhaps worth raising the question: why are atheistic Marxists such as Badiou and Žižek so keen on Paul and Christianity? One factor is presumably the need for a credible figure for Marxist thinkers after the not-particularly-credible Marxism associated with the Stalin and Mao. The potential for Paul's message to be read as anti-Rome would have potential appeal for Marxist thinkers. But the old allegation that Marxism is another form of religion has something in it, as thinkers such as Žižek accept and endorse.[13] To caricature for a moment, both have tendencies to believe that a collection of documents can serve as a basis for understanding the world through careful application, both have traditions which look to the transformation of the present world, and both their respective histories entertain seemingly contradictory tendencies, both towards freedom and justice, on the one hand, and totalitarianism, on the other. At the very least, there is the potential for mutual attraction.

The adoption of the suggestion/allegation of similarity between Christianity and Marxism is important because it is in many ways a traditional form of Christian readings of Paul where we find significant similarities with some of the philosophical readings. More precisely, the philosophical readings of Paul have a striking similarity with the Old Perspective on Paul, itself a product of centuries of orthodox Christian readings. If we think of the Old Perspective of Paul in terms of a dramatic upheaval of Jewish dedication to Torah observance required for salvation in favour of an effectively brand new system of grace and justification through faith (alone), then we might think of the arguments of Badiou and Žižek as complementary, in the abstract least, with one line of Protestant scholarly thought (minus belief in God of course!).

On the other hand, we could compare some of the New Perspective thought with the continental philosophical debates, most notably the communal aspect of the New Perspective. Dunn's argument on Paul critiquing the supposed nationalism of Judaism and the of the Torah has clear affinities with the portraits of Paul in continental philosophy, but mostly with Taubes perhaps given that there is a strong concern in New Perspective circles to stress the 'Jewishness' and Jewish origins of Paul's thought. N.T. Wright has been the most prominent exponent of the New Perspective pushing that line of thought in the direction of Paul being a revolutionary anti-imperialist thinker, a trend which has become firmly 'mainstream' in recent New Testament scholarship.

Given the heightened sensitivities concerning anti-Judaism and antisemitism in New Testament studies since the 1970s, it is perhaps no surprise that continental philosophical readings of Paul would encounter similar allegations, notwithstanding the explicitly Jewish emphasis of the influential Taubes. In a scathing analysis of Paul according to continental philosophers, Mark Lilla makes some strong allegations about the apparent anti-Jewish implications of Badiou's work, in that Jewish particularism has to go in the face of revolutionary Pauline universalism. Lilla adds,

> Here there is an important difference between Badiou's and Taubes's readings of Saint Paul. For Taubes, Paul universalized the messianic promise first given to the Hebrews, he did not abolish it. Thanks to him, we are all children of Sinai. For Badiou, Paul's militant universalism gives us a foretaste of what Kant, in a regrettable phrase, once called 'the euthanasia of Judaism.'[14]

This sort of criticism can be, and has been, developed further by noting that there could be problems when viewing 'Jewish works' as the negative foil, or even the counter-revolutionary tendency, which needed to be resisted in light of the event. The overlapping of religious and political categories, between the Old Perspective and the philosophical Paul, is clear. These sorts of criticisms aimed at the philosophical Paul are further unsurprising given the above comparison between Badiou and the Old Perspective because they are the kinds of criticisms which have been increasingly levelled at the Old Perspective since Sanders' devastating critique in 1977 (see Chapter 7). In some ways it became almost an 'anti-Jewish' reading to emphasise the role of works and particularity in Judaism, at least if dressed in negative language and contrasted with the apparently superior message of Christianity.

This, however, raises another issue: what if Paul really was being as revolutionary, at least in relation to Judaism, as both the Old Perspective and those readings from continental philosophy suggest? It is one thing to say Judaism is a second rate religion but is it not possible to keep the judgmental attitude to one side and accept that the reading of Paul as trying to transcend, or at least struggle with the idea of transcending, his Jewish background is a fair reading? In terms of the Old Perspective, we could theoretically suggest that there is nothing necessarily good or bad about 'works', or at least show some detachment from value judgements, and it just so happens that Paul is now representing something perceived to be very different from much of Judaism. In a slightly different way we could turn to Daniel Boyarin who refers to the work of Stephen Westerholm as 'A neo-Lutheran reading which is not anti-Judaic' because it effectively keeps the radical Lutheran reading of Paul without slandering rabbinic Judaism and without accepting that everything negative in Paul represents Judaism.[15] If we follow this sort of logic, it could still be possible to keep the radical break on Pauline terms while accepting that if we want to understand Jewish views on (say) universalism, Law, grace and so on, we ought to turn to Jewish texts. These are all difficult moral and interpretative questions, and I do not profess to have an adequate answer, but anyone working on such material will inevitably be faced with these and similar problems.

Similarly, the 'philosophical' reading of Paul does not have to be 'anti-Jewish'. For a start, recourse to Taubes could always help (and indeed others such as Agamben) but Taubes still has Paul moving 'beyond' Israel as an ethnic group. Žižek is, in fact, aware of the contemporary scholarly debates surrounding the 'Jewish Jesus' and the 'Jewish Paul'.[16] Indeed he claims that Paul has only just recently been seen positively because of his Jewish roots, though he does add that Paul was different in key respects. This is not simply passing from Judaism to a different position but, in a move similar to that of Taubes, something that had been done with Judaism itself. Žižek also turns to Nietzsche to explain the role of Christ in 'the passage from Judaism to Christianity' and the role of the Law, more specifically using the term 'High Noon'. The Nietzschean 'High Noon' becomes the thin edge between 'Before and After, the Old and the New ... ' As such he is both simultaneously, at the 'extreme end of the Old' and the culmination of the logic of sacrifice but also the overcoming of the old.[17] Whether this is ethically, exegetically or philosophically helpful can be further debated, but there certainly is an attempt to understand sympathetically the shift from Judaism to Christianity.

However, once the ideas of a 'shift from', and 'transformation of', are in place, irrespective of whether this comes from Paul or his interpreters, placing the language of Jews and Judaism in the negative becomes all too easy, as it has in the Christian tradition. Terry Eagelton, a fan of Badiou's work on Paul, and recent defender of Christianity against its critics, makes uncomfortable claims such as the following in relation to Paul's transformation of the 'old':

> It is this overturning of the Satanic or super-egoic image of God in Jesus that offers to unlock the lethal deadlock between Law and desire, or what Jacques Lacan calls the Real. It is a condition in which we come to fall morbidly in love with the Law itself, and with the oppressed, unhappy state to which it reduces us, desiring nothing more than to punish ourselves for our guilt even unto death. This is why Saint Paul describes the Law as cursed. It is this urge to do away with ourselves as so much waste and garbage to which Freud gives the name of the death drive, the opposite of which is an unconditionally accepting love. As Paul writes, the Law, and the sin or guilt which it generates, is what brings death into the world. The choice is between a life liberated from this pathological deadlock, which is known to the Gospel as eternal life, and that grisly caricature of eternal life which is the ghastly pseudo-immortality of the death drive. It is a state in which we prevent ourselves from dying for real by clinging desperately to our morbid pleasure in death as a way of affirming that we are alive ... This is the hell ... of those who are stuck fast in their masochistic delight in the Law, and spit in the face of those

who offer to relieve them of this torture. ... To be unburdened of their guilt is to be deprived of the very sickness which keeps them going. This, one might claim, is the primary masochism known as religion.[18]

It is not difficult to notice that language associated with the Law, some of which is Pauline, some of which comes from Eagleton and his more recent intellectual sources: morbidly, death drive, pathological deadlock, ghastly pseudo-immortality, masochistic, torture, sickness, hell, and even religion. In contrast, Christianity is represented by language such as: love, liberated, eternal life and so on. Given the contrast is with the Law, we are extremely close to a contrast with 'Judaism', and certainly elsewhere in Eagleton's work groups such as Pharisees and Zealots are portrayed in negative terms and in sharp contrast to Jesus.[19] There is a hint here of a previous generation of New Testament scholars who once spoke about the 'Jew' as merely a symbol of all things wrong with religion. It could be argued that Eagleton is just trying to represent Pauline thought, and to some extent this would be true. However, the context in which Eagleton is writing is explicitly a *modern* one. More precisely, this particular work is in many ways a defence of Christianity against the hardened atheists, Richard Dawkins and Christopher Hitchens, where Christianity is a belief system representative of something more palatable than the liberalism of Dawkins and Hitchens (reduced to 'Ditchkins' by Eagelton!):

> Jesus does not seem to be any sort of liberal, which is no doubt one grudge Ditchkins holds against him. He would not make a good committee man. Neither would he go down well on Wall Street, just as he did not go down well among the money changers of the Jerusalem Temple.[20]

On the other hand, we could also point out that by its very definition a revolutionary Marxism, such as that underlying the work Badiou and Žižek (as well as Eagleton), almost by definition requires the social, cultural, political, economic and general ideological contexts to be transcended or replaced or overthrown. While, for Žižek, Paul needs to be read from within Jewish tradition to show just how radical he was in his break by undermining Judaism from within, it is the break itself that is important for Žižek. In readings from continental philosophy, Judaism happens to be one of the key contexts, as does the Roman Empire, and if they are in the way of the revolution then, according to this logic, they must be overthrown ... as must *everything*.

Paul the Totalitarian?

This brings us on to another prominent issue raised in relation to these readings of Paul: the scholarly politics. In many ways these continental philosophical readings of Paul have done to Paul what Žižek claims Paul did to Jesus, namely, reducing Paul to his fundamentals. Paul was not part of the 'inner circle', namely, those who might have shared the final Passover/Last Supper. On Žižek's reading, Paul even symbolically takes the place of Judas among the apostles by 'betraying' Christ in more or less ignoring the details of his life and teaching, and reducing Christ to the fundamentals.[21] By doing a similar thing to Paul, thinkers like Žižek are able to reclaim Paul for the revolutionary Marxist tradition. In fact, some of the rhetoric might seem somewhat alarming to those used to conventional New Testament studies. Žižek frequently uses analogies and comparisons relating to none other than Soviet Russia! Here is one of the more mild ones:

> Paul goes on to his true Leninist business, that of organizing the new party called the Christian community. Paul as a Leninist: was not Paul, like Lenin, the great 'institutionalizer,' and, as such, reviled by the partisans of 'original' Marxism-Christianity? Does not the Pauline temporality 'already, but not yet' also designate Lenin's situation in between two revolutions, between February and October 1917? Revolution is already behind us, the old regime is out, freedom is here – *but* the hard work still lies ahead.[22]

From this perspective, it is perhaps no surprise that Jesus replaces, or is compared with, Marx. As Badiou puts it, 'I am not the first to risk the comparison that makes of him [Paul] a Lenin for whom Christ will have been the equivocal Marx.'[23]

Whether this is a problem depends on your perspective. Mark Lilla is deeply concerned about the reduction to the basics and the Leninist spin:

> Reading stuff like this must give an armchair frisson to assistant professors too young or clueless to know just what the names Lenin and Mao conjure up to millions of people around the globe. And since they seem not to know anything about Saint Paul, either, they apparently find it unobjectionable that the worst butchers of the twentieth century are now being presented as heirs of the same man who could write "and now faith, hope, and love abide, these three; and the greatest of these is love" (1 Corinthians 13:13) ... There is not a hint of love to be found in the new pomo [postmodernist] Paul, just hope for a miraculous secular transformation of the human condition and faith that it can be brought about through political revolution, violent if necessary.[24]

But has Lilla missed the point here? On the issue of love, Lilla is not being entirely fair. For continental philosophical readings of Paul, a key passage is from 1 Corinthians 7.20, 29–31:

Let each of you remain in the condition in which you were called ...
I mean, brothers and sisters, the appointed time has grown short; from
now on, let even those who have wives be as though they had none,[30] and
those who mourn as though they were not mourning, and those who
rejoice as though they were not rejoicing, and those who buy as though
they had no possessions,[31] and those who deal with the world as
though they had no dealings with it. For the present form of this world is
passing away.

For Žižek (see also Taubes) this passage does not legitimate existing power
relations by keeping some kind of disengaged distance. Paul, according to this
reading, and notice the politicised language, 'is a thoroughly engaged fighter
who ignores distinctions that are not relevant to the struggle' and is not bound
by those symbolic obligations. As part of the engaged position of Paul, Žižek
brings in a contemporary concept of *love* to help understand (or perhaps, we
should say, *Paul* helps understand a contemporary concept of love), alongside,
and with the help of Agamben and Taubes' famous interlocutor, Carl Schmitt,
the idea of a 'state of emergency/exception'. Žižek speculates whether love is
like the state of exception/emergency whereby the person's emotional life is
suspended. So, when someone falls passionately in love, everything changes,
the daily life is shattered. As Žižek puts it, 'To paraphrase Paul, when we are
in love, "we buy as though we have no possessions, we deal with the world as
though we have no dealings with it," since all that matters is love.'[25]

However, Lilla's critique of the turn to Lenin has something in it, though it
is not always clear just how seriously Žižek is taking some of his own ideas.
On one level, many of us would no doubt agree that a turn to Lenin and the
seizure of power and governance by a revolutionary (or better: intellectual)
clique has been a disaster for millions but this does not make the reduction to
a transformation of human conditions a necessarily wrong reading of Paul.
Indeed, the 'revolutionary' reading can be used against Lilla and at least some
of the readings of Paul in continental philosophy in that Paul and these continental philosophical readings implicitly buy in to the rhetoric of totalitarian
power. An early critic of Marx, Mikhail Bakunin (1814–76), prophetically saw
one potential future of Marxism as a 'red bureaucracy'. In one scathing criticism of the implications of Marxism, he added:

The reasoning of Marx ends in absolute contradiction. Taking into
account only the economic question, he insists that only the most
advanced countries ... are most capable of making social revolution ...
This revolution will expropriate either by peaceful, gradual or violent
means, the present property owners and capitalists. To appropriate all the
landed property and capital, and to carry out its extensive economic and
political programs, the revolutionary State will have to be very powerful
and highly centralized. The State will administer and direct the cultivation

of the land, by means of salaried officials commanding armies of rural workers organized and disciplined for that purpose. At the same time, on the ruins of existing banks, it will establish a single state bank which will finance all labour and national commerce ... For the proletariat this will, in reality, be nothing but a barracks: a regime, where regimented work-ingmen and women will sleep, wake, work, and live to the beat of a drum; where the shrewd and educated will be granted government privileges ... There will be slavery within this state, and abroad there will be war without truce, at least until the 'inferior' races, Latin and Slav, tired of bourgeois civilisation, no longer resign themselves to the subjection of the State, which will be even more despotic than the former State, although it calls itself a People's State.[26]

And this *before* the rise of the Soviet Union!

Could we not make equivalent criticisms of certain readings of Paul in continental philosophy and by implication in Lilla's slightly twee reading of Paul? If we recall the postcolonial readings of Mark and Revelation in Chapter 2 whereby a text can be transformed from an anti-imperial text to a text of imperial power by absorbing the language and structures of power, can we not say the same of Paul? Whereas the imposition of Marxism *did* become a Red Bureaucracy, did not Paul's letters and Christian theology become Empire? The radical transformation of the past, the shaking off of particular identities, the idea of neither Jew nor Greek, male nor female, slave nor free *in Christ*, meant that everyone could now be placed under the umbrella of a Christian Empire. Rome effectively developed, rightly or wrongly, these ideas and Christianity became central to a theocracy. If we take this one step further and follow Badiou's line of fidelity to the 'event', are we not on the slippery slope to the defences of Stalin's mass murders or the Inquisition, both in the name of fidelity to the event despite things not quite working out as they seemed? What we can also say is that whereas continental philosophical readings of Paul do have a dangerous element of dominant power, Lilla's reading underestimates this potential danger in Paul by focusing on what he dislikes about certain continental philosophers and providing his more twee reading of Paul. Is not Paul much more dangerous than all that?

Not least in light of what we have seen, it would be fair to say that such philosophical readings of Paul have modern concerns predominantly in mind and never did set out to be primarily historical readings in the sense of simply trying to understand the texts in their ancient contexts. Badiou is quite expli-cit: 'My intention, clearly, is neither historicizing nor exegetical. It is subjective through and through.'[27] This brings us, then, to the final section of this book and, superficially at least, a different kind of history: a history of the reception of the New Testament, the ways in which the New Testament has been read in historical contexts after the time in which the documents were written.

Summary

In continental philosophy, the figure of Paul has become of some interest in recent decades. In the work of thinkers such as Jacob Taubes, Alain Badiou and Slavoj Žižek, Paul is a major political thinker of Western tradition in the sense that he constructs the idea of an overarching universal to replace the particularities of Jewish Law and the broader views of Greek and Roman thought. There are close connections with Marxism and comparisons between Jesus and Paul, on the one hand, and Marx and Lenin, on the other, are made regularly enough. This can be developed with reference to, among other things, postcolonial criticism. Where one strand of Marxism contributed to the rise of the totalitarian Soviet Union, one strand of Pauline-influenced thought contributed to rise of the Christianised Roman Empire. In addition to the renewed interest in Paul and Empire in more conventional New Testament scholarship, there are notable parallels with Old and New Perspective scholars of Paul among different continental philosophers. There are also the problems concerning anti-Judaism among New Testament scholars and continental philosophers alike.

Key Words

Alain Badiou (b. 1937): Prominent French Marxist thinker and was Professor of Philosophy at the École Normale Supérieure. Badiou is known for, among other things, his ideas on being, event and truth.

Event: According to Alain Badiou, a dramatic disjunction with historical and cultural norms whereby a new truth is established and fidelity to the 'event' is demanded at all costs.

Jacob Taubes (1923–87): Prominent Jewish thinker and was Professor of Hermeneutics at the Free University of Berlin with interests in the religious studies and Judaism. Taubes also taught in the US at Harvard and Columbia.

Slavoj Žižek (b. 1949): Prominent and popular Slovenian Marxist and Lacanian psychoanalytical thinker, covering a range of diverse topics from popular cinema to the war on terror. A visiting professor at a number of international institutions but his best known affiliation is the University of Ljubljana.

Universalism: In general terms, ideas believed to apply to and concern everyone and/or all things.

Further Reading

Agamben, G., *The Time that Remains: A Commentary on the Letter to the Romans*, Stanford: Stanford University Press, 2005.

Badiou, A., *Saint Paul: The Foundation of Universalism*, Stanford: California, 2003.

Caputo J.D., and L.M. Alcoff, eds, *St Paul among the Philosophers*, Bloomington & Indianapolis: Indiana University Press, 2009.

Eagleton, T., *Reason, Faith, and Revolution: Reflections on the God Debate*, New Haven and London: Yale University Press, 2009.

Taubes, J., *The Political Theology of Paul*, Stanford: Stanford University Press, 2004.

Žižek, S., *The Puppet and the Dwarf: The Perverse Core of Christianity*, Cambridge, Mass.: MIT Press, 2003.

Part Three

Reception

Chapter 9

What is 'Reception History'?

A typical introduction to New Testament studies might, like this book, introduce the various 'criticisms': source criticism, form criticism, redaction criticism, literary criticism, social-scientific criticism and so on. One that may well become a popular addition in years to come involves 'reception' (actually 'reception history' is a more common term) and this generally involves the ways in which biblical texts have been used through the ages, the 'afterlives' of the biblical texts. Noticeably, despite the centre of scholarly power moving to North America in the past few decades, scholars in the English-speaking world have not lost their love of using a related German term, in this instance, *Wirkungsgeschichte*, or literally 'impact history'.

Reception history is becoming the next big thing in New Testament studies and perhaps not before time. The New Testament and the Bible have been used to support the Iraq war, oppose the Iraq war, endorse slavery, oppose slavery, legitimate imperialism, resist imperialism, promote gay rights, contest gay rights and so on, and not to mention the various positions in between. Reception history may also be the future of New Testament studies for the following simple reason: how much interpretation of the same small collection of texts can be done without coming close to exhausting the options or be doomed to repeating old arguments over and over, with only highly specialist analysis of the smallest detail being left? Dale Allison has chastised aspects of modern scholarship for acting as if there were no significant work on the historical Jesus between Albert Schweitzer at the beginning of the twentieth century and Ernst Käsemann in the middle of the twentieth century. Not only does Allison point out the range of historical Jesus scholarship in this period but he also adds that those who fail 'to learn the exegetical past condemn themselves to repeating that past, to needlessly recapitulating older debates unknowingly'.[1] Similarly Allison fires at the common view that post-1980 historical Jesus scholarship witnessed something new and distinctive, such as an interest in non-canonical sources, Jesus in relation to Judaism, and a reaction against apocalyptic eschatology, all of which, Allison points out, are prominent scholarly traits to be found in post- and pre-1980s scholarship. Perhaps the application of the latest approaches in the humanities to old questions might be a way to produce something innovative, but even if Allison is largely right, then does it not follow that the historical study of Jesus (and by extension the rest of the New Testament) is running out of new things to say?

Perhaps the idea of exhausting all the possibilities of reading the New Testament in its original contexts is going too far (there is a lot of work still to be done on Aramaic reconstructions of gospel passages, for instance) but it is probably fair to suggest that it is increasingly difficult for people to say too many new things. The major advantage reception history has is that there are masses and masses of material waiting to be exploited, researched, analysed, collected, compared and so on. Christianity has spread across the globe and so the Bible is found and read in a wide array of different historical and cultural contexts. Given the use of the Bible as a foundational text in many cultures, its influence and language have not died out even if the overtly religious settings have. Use of the Bible can be found in poetry, music, film, philosophy, law, literature, popular culture ... anything!

Reception History and Historical Theology

We could make convenient sub-categories of reception history. A first sub-category could be classed as a more church-inspired and overtly theological approach. Here we might look at the views of the major theologians. How did famous theologians such as Augustine, Aquinas, Luther, Calvin, or Barth interpret this or that passage? This, in fact, is not particularly new and in many ways is what the discipline of historical theology is all about: how theologians and believers have interpreted scripture. But in terms of the classic genre of the scholarly biblical commentary, this history of theological reception has become increasingly prominent. Probably the most prominent example is the commentary on Matthew by Ulrich Luz. Luz is quite explicit in his choices to include in his commentary on the posthistory of Matthew:

> In the commentary I have favored especially influential biblical texts, in particular those whose later influence paradigmatically form and illumi-nate the present situation of churches, confessions, and Christians ... I have preferred interpretations that influenced the Catholic and Protestant churches as confessions ...[2]

A major commentary influenced by the approach of Luz is Anthony Thiselton's commentary on 1 Corinthians. Thiselton likewise wants to 'identify those effects which have held particular influence in theology in the history of the daily life of the church, or more broadly in the history of ideas'.[3] Both Luz and Thiselton lay out their sections on the post-history of Matthew and 1 Corinthians, respectively, with classical chronological-theological categories 'The Apostolic Fathers', 'The Patristic Era', 'Medieval and Reformation', and (in the case of Thiselton especially) 'The Modern Period'.

Reception History: An Aid to 'Correct Interpretation'?

A second sub-category might be reception history as an aid to 'correct interpretation', including assistance in understanding the original context. On a very general level, approaching a work of art or cinema might even raise the most basic questions interpreters do not always ask: what colour were the clothes people wore? What did it all really look like? Even if the artist, sculptor or director makes historical mistakes or makes interpretative decisions that say more about their own times, they are at least forced to raise these sorts of questions. Similarly, reception of the biblical texts could help traditional historical interpretation. Luz is quite explicit that reception history (or, rather, *Wirkungsgeschichte*) is a crucial addition to traditional historical-critical approaches and claims, 'I have favored interpretations that I think can offer corrections for us, especially when they approach the original sense of the text in a changed situation.'[4] Similarly Thiselton: 'A flood of light is shed in both directions – back onto the text and forward into the world.'[5]

An example of how later interpreters apparently show insight is given by Thiselton in his commentary on the following passage from 1 Corinthians 2.10–16 and the background of those professing spiritual gifts at Corinth:

> ... these things God has revealed to us through the Spirit; for the Spirit searches everything, even the depths of God.[11] For what human being knows what is truly human except the human spirit that is within? So also no one comprehends what is truly God's except the Spirit of God.[12] Now we have received not the spirit of the world, but the Spirit that is from God, so that we may understand the gifts bestowed on us by God.[13] And we speak of these things in words not taught by human wisdom but taught by the Spirit, interpreting spiritual things to those who are spiritual.[14] Those who are unspiritual do not receive the gifts of God's Spirit, for they are foolishness to them, and they are unable to understand them because they are spiritually discerned.[15] Those who are spiritual discern all things, and they are themselves subject to no one else's scrutiny.[16] "For who has known the mind of the Lord so as to instruct him?" But we have the mind of Christ.

Thiselton turns to the ideas of Martin Luther (1483–1546) and when Luther was confronted with figures such as the Thomas Müntzer use of Reformation ideas, figures who 'were found carrying them to extremes ... [and] inspired radicalism in politics, theology, and liturgy'. Part of this carrying of ideas to extremes involved a radical turn to scripture without the authority of major theologians of the past and an emphasis on the role of the Holy Spirit. According to Thiselton, connections can be made with the not dissimilar situation faced by Paul: 'By 1522 the excesses of the "enthusiasts" had much in common with "the people of the spirit" at Corinth.' Thiselton then develops this in more theological terms, using Luther's contrast between a theology emphasising God's revelation in the suffering of Christ on the cross (theology of the cross/*theologica crucis*) with a theology stressing God's power and glory as apparently revealed in the world around us (theology of glory/*theologica gloriae*), to argue that Luther provides some sort of echo of the original setting of 1 Corinthians: 'Luther's contrast between a *theologica crucis* and a *theologica gloriae* resonates both with his own attack on the "fanatics" and their claims about the Spirit and with Paul's formulation of a theology of the cross against what Horsley calls "the language of exalted religious status and spiritual perfection" found among some at Corinth.'[6]

Whether this is a fair interpretation, or whether this reading might be importing later judgements, I leave open. The main point for now is that the example of Thiselton shows a trend in reception historical scholarship whereby a later interpreter is said to provide an insight into the 'original context' of a given New Testament text. A less conventional theological example of how a later interpreter can provide insight is given by Markus Bockmuehl, though Bockmuehl is careful to place greater emphasis on *earlier* reception for questions of its use in historical reconstruction of the first century.[7] Bockmuehl provides a picture of a sixteenth-century icon from the Chapel of St Athanasios at Mount Athos where Peter and Paul embrace and notes how the artistic juxtaposition of the two dates back to the fourth century and the embrace image continues after and elsewhere. Bockmuehl provides an interpretation of the icon showing how Peter and Paul are both distinct, are not looking directly at one another, and have a complex and uneasy relationship with one another. Yet the embrace is the dominating image and they are ultimately united in Christian ideals.

Bockmuehl uses this image to challenge a major view in historical-critical approaches to the New Testament over the past 200 years, namely, that Peter and Paul represent two opposing wings of early Christianity. Bockmuehl points out that the historical evidence from the earliest Christian centuries shows that the visual interpretation in fact represents and maintains a mainstream Christian view from the first century onward, with only Marcionites (anti-Peter) and Ebionites (anti-Paul) representing the extreme view. Martyrdoms and sufferings of Peter and Paul were remembered together since the first and second centuries and jointly laying the foundations of churches in Antioch and Rome (1 *Clement* 5.1–6; Ignatius, *To the Romans* 4.3; Irenaeus, *Against Heresies* 3.1.1; 3.3.2). In terms of the New Testament, Bockmuehl points out that Acts of the Apostles portrays many similarities between Peter and Paul: both work for the same gospel, both receive a vision, both preach great sermons, both work great healings, and both face persecutions and dangers with deliverance and open-ended conclusions. 2 Peter refers to Paul as a 'beloved brother' whose writings must be respected highly (2 Pet. 3.15–16). Of course there are tensions (Gal. 2) but there is a significant broad tendency in the New Testament to bring both together serving the same quest.

But does this mean theological traditions always get interpretation 'correct'? Clearly not in absolute terms if the long and bloody history of opposing Christian interpretations are anything to go by. And what do we make of the long and bloody history of church hierarchies using the New Testament texts to persecute Jews or the long and bloody history of the use of the New Testament as a tool of colonial domination? What about those biblical interpreters who feel compelled by the Spirit but ostracised by mainstream church views? This sort of questioning means that my kind of definitions of reception history, as with any definition in the humanities, cannot be hard and fast because now we start looking beyond the orthodoxy and beyond any 'official' theological history.

A clear example of looking at the reception of the Bible beyond the conventional theological mainstream is Christopher Rowland and Jonathan Roberts, *The Bible for Sinners*.[8] Rowland and Roberts explicitly see their work as not necessarily in opposition to more official Church/Anglican 'tradition' but certainly providing 'alternative resources' for controversial debates (e.g. same-sex relationships) based on the guidance of the Spirit and attention to the specifics and experiences of a given situation. These interpretations can be based from 'below', from those deemed 'sinners' and 'nobodies', rather than from 'above', from church hierarchies, experts, and moral and religious 'betters'. In doing this they make regular appeal to Jesus who is portrayed at odds with the religious authorities of his day. Among other things, Rowland and Roberts turn to the examples of interpreters on the fringes of mainstream Christianity who have claimed inspiration from the Spirit, drawn on their experience, and were deemed subversive.

One such figure discussed by Rowland and Roberts is William Stringfellow (1929–85), in many ways a product of the US civil rights movement and the reactions to the horrors of Vietnam, including the notorious My Lai massacre.[9] While he had a privileged education, and had served in the US army, Stringfellow decided to provide legal services for the poorest in Harlem where he also lived. For Stringfellow, America was to be understood in terms of the Bible not the Bible in terms of America. In particular, the book of Revelation provides a means not so much of understanding the future but more in anticipation of end times, a means of interpreting the present and the issues raised by the present. Babylon and Jerusalem in Revelation represent two different types of community. Babylon describes every city and represents the condition of death upon which apocalyptic judgement is made. In direct contrast, Jerusalem represents human freedom from the bondage of death. My Lai was the outworking of the forces of death embedded in US society.

This is not necessarily the interpretation of any 'official' churches yet it is still interpretation concerned with theological understanding and a resource for Christians. Rowland and Roberts engage with figures such as Stringfellow and different perspectives on same-sex relationships (among other things) not as an attempt 'to assess the truth value of particular acts of biblical interpretation' but rather to 'reflect on different types of interpretative strategy'. The authors add,

> This book does not ... provide prepared answers that can be taken away
> on any of its key topics. Instead, each chapter provides a different heuristic
> (illustrative) discussion as a means to thinking about interpretation, and
> attempts to illuminate the key differences between open-endedness and
> closure in acts of interpretation.[10]

Rowland and Roberts open the way for any kind of Christian to show ways of understanding the Bible in a given social context and so while being attached to church-based readings, their book is not restricted by orthodox theology and is a kind of bridge to a third sub-category which might be defined as 'anything goes', that is, analysis of anything else that is out there, irrespective of the 'correct interpretation' of the biblical texts and theological orthodoxy, and how biblical texts influence, are used and are influenced in those diverse areas mentioned above: film, music, television, politics, literature, popular culture and so on. We will look at various examples which might be classified as 'anything goes' throughout this chapter and section but we might mention that biblical language, allusions and interpretation have been looked at from Johnny Cash to *Battlestar Galactica*, from American presidents to Hollywood epics, from Philip Pullman to Harry Potter.

Reception History: Anything Goes?

One thing that might strike people is just how broad reception history is and, superficially at least, just how different biblical studies and New Testament studies might look if reception history continues to become popular. What could the potential popularity of reception history mean, then, for the future of biblical and New Testament studies? If we take our sub-categories, the first (mainstream theological history) would mean we are not dealing with anything too different from traditional theology and this sort of approach will no doubt continue to thrive in church-based contexts and theology departments. The second sub-category (helping us understand 'correct' interpretations) would similarly be part of the conventional make-up of New Testament studies and a further tool in the interpretative quest.

The third sub-category ('anything goes') has the potential to make biblical and New Testament studies look very different. Perhaps church-based contexts would want a place for the ways in which society uses the Bible, but the ways in which such an approach might survive in a university-based context throws up some interesting questions. Here some speculation about the future might help us understand what is happening in the present with reception history. What if in twenty years (say), reception history of the anything goes variety was the dominant approach to biblical and New Testament studies? Would this not mean such biblical study became a branch of cultural studies? Or might it mean that New Testament/biblical scholars became scattered around different departments such as French, History, English, and so on?

Perhaps. But what this speculation does is to take us to the heart of what Biblical Studies is as a discipline and these questions are hardly new. Traditional approaches to the Bible also face the same issue: some people prefer history, some literature, some archaeology, and some linguistics but typically biblical and New Testament studies remains a major area in its own right in departments of theology, religion, biblical studies and Jewish studies. What this further tells is that the study of the Bible and the New Testament is firmly entrenched in intellectual society at least. There are, of course, historic reasons for this (notably the role of the church in the formation of universities), organisational reasons (the Society of Biblical Literature can boast an annual conference where over 5000 biblical scholars attend) and related cultural reasons, especially the ways in which the Bible continues to be a major cultural resource in contemporary 'Western' societies (the Qur'an, of course, has a comparative role in societies where Islam has been the more dominant religion). There is obviously no collection of literature so deeply rooted and continually influential, or at least continually used, than the Bible in 'the West', not even the ever popular Shakespeare (and even in 'the West' Shakespeare's influence has its limits).

There is perhaps no better example of the cultural importance of the reception of the Bible than its use in US politics where it has been employed in the rhetoric of the past three presidents and used in contexts of massive national and international importance. The use of the Bible in contemporary American politics is part of what Yvonne Sherwood surprisingly but accurately calls the 'Liberal Bible', an interpretative tradition developing since the sixteenth and seventeenth centuries.[11] The Liberal Bible is a Bible supportive of 'freedom of conscience', 'rights', law, and consensus, and marks a shift from the Absolute Monarchist's Bible where decisions made by the monarch were to be seen as proof of divine power. The Liberal Bible has also produced the (mistaken) assumption that the Bible is the foundation, and consonant with the principles, of Western democracies without acknowledging that such a view of the Bible has its roots in sixteenth- and seventeenth-century Europe. It usually follows from this (mistaken) perspective that the Bible and Jesus are more representative of democracy than the Qur'an and Muhammad. Sherwood points to the example of Roy Moore, former chief Justice of the Supreme Court of Alabama, who contrasted the Christian tradition and the Bible with Islam and bought into the idea of the Christian Bible as the Bible of democracy. She wryly remarks,

> He has no idea that the Christian Bible he describes is only a few centuries old and thoroughly fused with secularized, modern notions. The idea that the God of the Christian scriptures holds freedom of conscience among his

most cherished principles is rather like those recoveries of the true story of creation and the flood that incorporate dinosaurs and fossils while claiming to restore the pure biblical text.[12]

Perhaps because of the non-explicit link with the details and specifics of modern democracy in the Bible, and functioning as a way of concealing its early modern origins, another significant development of the Liberal Bible is that the 'liberal' reading is continually vague. In this context, Sherwood is able to use that most unlikely of descriptions to describe George W. Bush's use of the Bible, 'liberal'. Bush is particularly deft in referencing the Bible just enough to attract key electoral support from Protestant Christians, with the specifics of faith left ambiguous. and significantly the Liberal Bible is able to endorse actions against its constructed opposite: the undemocratic, tyranny, and terror.

In his analysis of the Bible in the run-up to the 2008 US presidential elections, Jacques Berlinerblau picks up on the importance of vague uses of the Bible by looking at what makes a 'good' (defined as electorally successful or not damaging) and 'bad' (defined as electorally unsuccessful or damaging) use of the Bible in American political speeches and language.[13] In 'good' political speeches, Berlinerblau argues, biblical citations ought to be sparse and measured. They must also be positive in the sense of not using it to attack a particular social subgroup but used instead in the interests of societal unity supporting uncontroversial values deemed American, such as freedom and care for others. Of course, the Bible itself is hardly backward in coming forward when it comes to attacking different groups. John the Baptist is said to have called his opponents a 'brood of vipers' (Matt. 3.7; Luke 3.7), Jesus is said to have called his opponents various things such as 'blind guides' and 'blind fools' (Matt. 23) and is remembered as talking of an unforgivable sin (Mark 3.27), while Paul even floats the idea of his opponents castrating them-selves (Gal. 5.12)! This sort of polemic, however, is irrelevant, Berlinerblau argues, because it simply would not work for political speeches. Vagueness is also important because no one *really* uses the Bible for key policy decisions and the main function of using the Bible is to signal to the electorate that the politician is a decent God-fearing person. References to chapter and verse are typically best avoided because it may well lead to unfortunate and otherwise avoidable debates about the church/state distinction, a backlash from the liberal media, on the one hand, and dedicated-to-interpretation fundamental-ists, on the other. Scriptural references need to be inconspicuously merged into the address.

Berlinerblau's examples of 'the bad' include Joe Lieberman and John Kerry. In the 2000 election, the Democrats were badly scarred by Lieberman explicitly playing the 'religious card' with heavily scripture-drenched speeches and Democrats were nervous come the 2004 election where Kerry was regarded as an awkward and insincere performer in religious contexts. Berlinerblau notes that his biblical references were forced and too direct, with attacks on opponents and a lack of unity. So, for instance, in a church speech on 28 March 2004, he cited complete sentences from James 1.22 ('Be doers of the word and not hearers only') and James 2.14 ('What does it profit my brethren if some say he has faith but does not have works?') which are not only 'too much' according to Berlinerblau's criteria but are clear attacks on opponents with the potential to ostracise. And, of course, such verses inevitably lead to differing interpretations. Furthermore, Berlinerblau points out, figures such as Liebermann, Kerry and Howard Dean lack the perception of religious credibility (was citing the New Testament by Liebermann, an Orthodox Jew, really ever going to work?), and indeed the southern, Midwestern and mountain region background, so their use looks forced, especially with quotation-heavy language that is not part of most people's day-to-day speech. To Bill Clinton, a Baptist from Arkansas, in addition to being media savvy, the credible use of calm allusion came naturally. Likewise, George W. Bush, who despite an elite schooling and upbringing, was effectively marketed to a certain audience to appear a 'natural' with his not unhelpful additional Texan accent and cowboy image.

Unsurprisingly, then, examples of the 'good' for Berlinerblau are George W. Bush, Bill Clinton and Barak Obama, all of whom have scored notable electoral victories. The use of biblical language may have reached new levels when Barak Obama, the unity candidate par excellence, effectively became Obama the Messiah (or even God) among his followers. It is notable that his opponents went for the aggressive negative angle by making Obama the anti-Christ, perhaps not surprising for certain followers of the preceding president whose favourite philosopher is Jesus. While this does *not* mean, of course, that use of the Bible wins or loses elections, what it does mean is that each was successful in establishing their religious credentials and not ruining their electoral chances through misuse.

In his inaugural and State of the Union addresses, Bush made few allusions to the Bible and observed Berlinerblau's 'rules'. So, for instance, in his 2004 State of the Union Address, Bush talked about marriage and how 'the same moral tradition' also 'teaches us that each individual has dignity and value in God's sight'. The phrase 'God's sight' is found occasionally but Bush appears to be alluding to 1 Peter 3.4: 'let your adornment be the inner self with the lasting beauty of a gentle and quiet spirit, which is very precious in God's sight'. But, in the aftermath of September 11, Bush did quote biblical verses. On September 14, at the National Cathedral in Washington, he made direct reference to Romans 8.38–39: 'As we have been assured, neither death nor life, nor angels nor principalities, nor powers, nor things present nor things to come, nor height nor depth can separate us from God's love'. It is noticeable that here the verse is not completed because Paul adds, '... that is in Christ Jesus our Lord'. Berlinerblau argues that it is important for speakers to be not too 'Christey' and we may add to this that it serves the function of not excluding other religious groups and, indeed, avoids the implication of a

specifically Christian crusade against the Muslim world, a highly charged
subject in the aftermath of September 11. Yet, at the same time, this type of
vague biblical allusion crucially nods, or perhaps we should say winks, in the
direction of Christian Americans. Indeed, there is a dual function of biblical
allusions where they are as vague as that from 1 Peter 3.4: they play to a
variety of audiences. When Bush talked about 'freedom' both religious and
secular listeners could agree that freedom in general is a good thing and part
of their tradition. Or, perhaps more to the point, Bush could nod/wink to his
Christian base, with many non-believers, including anti-religious non-believers,
noting precious little.

Let us develop Berlinerblau's argument in a slightly different direction with
reference to one of the 'good' examples of the uses of the Bible in political
speech making, Barak Obama. On 4 June 2009, Obama gave a highly antici-
pated speech in Cairo where he addressed America's relationship with Arabs
and Muslims past and present and used not only biblical language but also
language from Jewish and, especially but perhaps unsurprisingly given his
context, Muslim traditions and his own Muslim heritage, the latter so conspicuously avoided in his presidential campaign. Obama referenced the 'Holy
Koran' several times in his speech (balanced, incidentally, with the 'Holy
Bible') and brought together Christianity, Islam and Judaism under the
umbrella of peace and with reference to quotations from the different traditions and effortlessly harmonising the three under the term 'God':

> We have the power to make the world we seek, but only if we have the
> courage to make a new beginning, keeping in mind what has been written.
>
> The Holy Koran tells us, "O mankind! We have created you male and a
> female; and we have made you into nations and tribes so that you may
> know one another."
>
> The Talmud tells us: "The whole of the Torah is for the purpose of
> promoting peace."
>
> The Holy Bible tells us, "Blessed are the peacemakers, for they shall be
> called sons of God." [Matt. 5.9]
>
> The people of the world can live together in peace. We know that is
> God's vision. Now, that must be our work here on Earth. Thank you.
> And may God's peace be upon you.

Just prior to this Obama spoke of 'one rule that lies at the heart of every
religion' that 'we do unto others as we would have them do unto us' (cf. Matt.
7.12; Luke 6.31). 'This truth', he adds, 'transcends nations and peoples –
a belief that isn't new; that isn't black or white or brown; that isn't Christian,
or Muslim or Jew.' When Obama referred to 'do unto others as we would
have them do unto us', he vaguely interpreted the admittedly vague saying and
sentiment as 'a faith in other people', adding it was 'what brought me here
today'. We might respond, 'Faith in other people to do … what?' Well, in the

same context, Obama mentioned that 'we should choose the right path, not just the easy path' the former presumably being the path Obama's administration choose. When we look at the political context of this speech – for politics and religion are explicitly integrated in this speech – the sentiments may have a steelier edge. Before that, it is worth looking at some analytical remarks made on the use of the religion in American political rhetoric.

Berlinerblau's argument is one based on the brutal values of electoral success. We can play with this here and point out that this measurement of success also, of course, points to ways in which power works. What we see here is how vague and 'liberal' approaches to scriptures and traditions functioned and appeared to be effective. As analysts from Chomsky to Žižek have argued, it is frequently in liberal rhetoric and liberal circles where real power lies and is credibly maintained (and in this instance supported by some positive reporting of the speech in the mass media). One of the ways in which this can be done with reference to the Bible is by deflecting the details of policy with the simplistic biblical allusion. In a different but related context, Michelle Krejci points out that the 'message that Obama is not Jesus is more efficient at refuting those unaired details than making the point with an analysis of the philosophy'.[14] Alice Bach makes a related point with reference to 'Bush's Bible' in the aftermath of Hurricane Katrina where Bush spoke in terms of a natural disaster in the hands of God. God, Bush claimed in a speech to the National Cathedral in New Orleans, works in mysterious ways, suffering is mysterious, God's purposes are sometimes impossible to know but God will always care. Bach points out that a lack of human preparedness was a major problem in the flooding of the streets and Bush said nothing about the government's inaction and contribution to human suffering.[15] Resort to God, it seems, means blame can be shifted to a broad generalisation with which orthodox believers at least would not disagree in the abstract.

Similarly, it is more efficient, or perhaps ideologically effective, to cover over the details and intentions of US foreign policy with broad biblical allusions and generalisations. The Obama speech in Cairo has little to say on specifics and on some of the central issues such as the Israel–Palestine problem, and it did not deviate from standard US positions on the Middle East in recent years. Instead, like the allusions and quotations from the different traditions, much of the speech is couched in generalisations. 'America', Obama further claims, 'respects the right of all peaceful and law-abiding voices to be heard around the world, even if we disagree with them. And we will welcome all elected, peaceful governments – provided they govern with respect for all their people.' The phrasing may well sound different from the Bush-era (and Obama certainly did not make favourable remarks about the Iraq war and Guantánamo) but it was sufficiently general. After all, who decides what are 'peaceful governments', governing 'with respect'? Obama was, we might add, the guest of the Egyptian head of state, President Mubarak, who effectively runs a police state with torture widespread, with political imprisonments, with a recently renewed state of emergency for a further two years, and with presidential election figures in 1999 reaching 93.79%, hardly a government that could be described as peaceful and respectful by most common definitions.[16] In many ways Obama's speech is obviously designed to get Muslims in the Middle East on side. But, realistically, does this not merely mean Muslims agreeable with American foreign policy? As we will note with reference to Christian 'fundamentalists' and US foreign policy, there is little chance of influencing foreign policy in any substantive way. In terms of US interests, is there really so much difference from the famous Bushism, 'you're either with us or against us', albeit with a kindlier face? It was still the case that the Obama speech defended the actions in Afghanistan and of the pursuit of violent extremists he mentions the international support received and, in this context, how 'the enduring faith of over a billion people is so much bigger than the narrow hatred of a few. Islam is not part of the problem in combating violent extremism – it is an important part of promoting peace'. Are we that far away from the Bushism, the 'coalition of the willing'?

What this deliberately vague use of the Bible also suggests is that we are dealing more with rhetoric than political substance. A notable recent concern was that certain conservative evangelicals with an obsession with end times and Israel were influencing US foreign policy under George W. Bush. In contrast to this, Berlinerblau points out the important distinction between rhetoric and policy: while Bush may have used grand religious rhetoric of good versus evil, there is no evidence that the high-level decision-making behind the Iraq war was taking into consideration various beliefs from certain conservative evangelical thought concerned with Israel and end times.[17] This present writer and plenty of other scholars have pushed for a complementary argument, namely, that a complex mix of geopolitics and elite interests are the primary influences on foreign policy, while certain conservative evangelical belief, along with various secular views and party political views, reflect broader supportive ideological trends in contemporary culture.[18]

A Fear of Ancient History?

The very fact that reference to the Bible comes up in foreign policy issues means that we are still dealing with the role of the Bible in questions of huge international significance. Yet, while the example of American politics illustrates the importance of studying the reception of the Bible, one criticism of reception history that I have encountered, and one that might even be fair to some extent, is that reception history is a safe place to work and avoid all the tricky questions of historical accuracy, problematic interpretations of earliest Christianity, and anything a traditional reading with the potential to challenge faith might produce. Put another way, questions such as 'did the historical Jesus really think he was God?', 'was Jesus really bodily raised from the dead?', or 'did the historical Paul not really mean what this or that theological tradition claim he meant?' have been some of the most bitter and controversial debates in New Testament studies and issues that really do matter to people. The avoidance of such questions may well (partly) account for the rise of reception history. However, it is equally worth stressing that the idea of reception history as a refuge for the frightened is not necessarily a good or bad thing in itself. On one level, so what if people are frightened of the earliest history? If such people can do good things in reception history is it not for the better? Could it not be for the better if people were doing good work in reception history rather than potentially compromising intellectual integrity when studying earliest Christian history?

Yet pious fear of controversial questions in Christian origins can only partially explain the rise of reception history. There are prominent scholarly examples of reception history from non-believers. In terms of what we have just seen, some of the scholars mentioned are openly atheist. Prior to his work on the Bible in presidential politics, Jacques Berlinerblau, an openly atheist biblical scholar, wrote a book called *The Secular Bible* where he tried to develop secular interpretative methods. Michelle Krejci self-identified as an atheist in her article, 'An Atheist's Dilemma: Should We Bend the Bible for Justice?'[19] It is obviously difficult to try and dismiss Berlinerblau and Krejci as being scared of answers the texts may give. Indeed, one of Berlinerblau's points in *The Secular Bible* was a willingness to accept whatever answer emerges from interpretation, irrespective of whether the answer coheres with personal theological and ideological views. Both, significantly perhaps, are Americans and both have worked on the Bible in American political rhetoric. The reason why this point may be significant is that the sheer importance of the Bible in American national and international politics is obviously clear to both these atheists and should warn us that questions about the reception of the Bible in this context at least are questions which believers and non-believers (not to mention agnostics) will almost inevitably have been pondering for some time.

Summary

The history of interpretation of the biblical texts ('reception history') is one of the fastest growing areas of contemporary biblical studies. Some forms of reception history are traditional approaches to biblical texts, most notably historical theology and the ways in which different theological thinkers have interpreted the texts. A related approach is to see how the history of the reception of the texts is an aid to 'correct interpretation', in some ways an addition to traditional historical criticism. A different approach to reception history is, however, the 'anything goes' approach which has little concern for historical theology or 'correct interpretation' but looks at the ways in which biblical texts function in different cultural contexts, anything from party politics to pop music.

Key Words

Liberal Bible: Term developed by Yvonne Sherwood to describe a tradition of interpreting the Bible which gained momentum from the sixteenth and seventeenth centuries onward and views the Bible as a text of liberty, freedom, rights, law, consensus, and democracy.

Reception history: General term in biblical studies to describe the interpretation and use of biblical texts.

***Wirkungsgeschichte*/impact history/effective history**: Often synonymous with 'reception history' but can be used more precisely to describe the effects and influence of the biblical texts on people, culture and/or history.

Further Reading

Berlinerblau, J., *Thumpin' It: The Use and Abuse of the Bible in Today's Presidential Politics*, Louisville: WJK, 2008.

Bockmuehl, M., *Seeing the Word: Refocusing New Testament Study*, Baker Academic: Grand Rapids, Michigan, 2006.

Kovacs, J.L. and C. Rowland, *Revelation: The Apocalypse of Jesus Christ*, Blackwell Bible Commentaries; Oxford: Blackwell, 2004.

Luz, U., *Matthew 1–7: A Commentary*, Minneapolis: Fortress, 2007.

Rowland, C. and J. Roberts, *The Bible for Sinners: Interpretation in the Present Time*, London: SPCK, 2008.

Sherwood, Y., 'Bush's Bible as a Liberal Bible (Strange though that Might Seem)', *Postscripts* 2 (2006), pp. 47–58.

Thiselton, A.C., *The First Epistle to the Corinthians: A Commentary on the Greek Text*, Grand Rapids: Eerdmans, 2000.

Chapter 10

Methods and Questions in Reception History

With the sheer mass of material available for research, how can we go about analysis of reception history? In terms of a classic verse-by-verse commentary, those interested in mainstream and orthodox Christian theology have life a little easier in that the boundaries are relatively clear: a scholar can simply look at the ways major theologians in Christian history have interpreted a given verse. Then, as we saw above with the examples from Thiselton and Bockmuehl, it is possible to move on the questions of why a certain interpretative decision was made by a given theologian, whether that verse or passage has been interpreted 'accurately' and 'fairly', and whether a particular insight has been missed by traditional historical critical approaches.

Those who want to write a commentary with a more 'anything goes' attitude to reception history do not have such clear boundaries. Selecting evidence is a problem at the best of times but selecting evidence for a reception-historical commentary of the 'anything goes' variety is even more difficult. Ultimately, how does a reception-historical commentary of a more open variety avoid the problem of seeming random? Luz recognised this problem even though his boundaries were relatively fixed:

> Making choices was unavoidable ... While it is relatively easy to gain an overview of the most important Matthew commentaries in church history, the material in other theological and nontheological texts and even more in art, the history of piety, literature, and so on, is nearly infinite.[1]

It is worth raising moral questions too. Could a reception-historical study of John's Gospel leave out the repeated criticisms of 'the Jews' and the allegation that 'the Jews' are from the devil and carry out his desires (John 8.44)? Could a reception-historical study of Matthew's Gospel really leave out the infamous Matthew 27.25, 'Then the people as a whole answered, "His blood be on us and on our children!"'?

Theoretically, a perfectly competent commentary on John or Matthew could leave out such debates but clearly there would be moral pressures (on some at least) to incorporate such a discussion. Even so, the issues of inclusion and morality easily descend in to highly subjective choices. One way to guide such a commentary might be to take some inspiration from those inspired by Christian orthodoxy and instead look at other ideological traditions such as feminist, party political, Marxist, popular movements, colonial/postcolonial criticism and so on, and see how biblical texts have been used in these contexts, notwithstanding the masses of material still requiring selection issues. But without some guiding principle, there is a danger that reception-historical work ends up being little more than cataloguing. In other words, this novel, pop singer, work of art or film, references this, that or the other biblical verse. This does not have to be all bad: an analogy with the traditional historical criticisms might suggest that hefty works of reference to biblical allusions and quotations in (say) popular music, literature, art collections, film and so on would be an extremely helpful resource in the same way that works of reference, lexicons and dictionaries are in traditional historical criticism.

Reception History and Historical Criticism

Of course, there is no reason why those using a reception-historical approach need to follow the traditional biblical studies and theology route of the biblical commentary. And there are countless ways to tackle the reception of the Bible, from choosing the use of a text or texts by an individual or group to the use of a text or texts in any given cultural and geographical context. The analogy with traditional historical criticism is important because in many ways the methodology is not really different. In a paper delivered to the British New Testament Conference at Durham University in 2008, W. John Lyons points out that some of the methods of classic historical criticism such as redaction criticism already have traits associated with reception history.[2] Redaction criticism will, for instance look at how Mark has been received by Matthew. Paul was a notably creative reader of the Old Testament/Hebrew Bible. Methodologically, then, there is little difference between this kind of historical criticism and reception history as both try to analyse ways texts have been read, heard and digested. Lyons notes that a key difference between what we define as 'historical criticism' and 'reception history' is simply one of packaging: both are allocated different time frames. To put it in a way Lyons did not, and picking up on what was discussed above, historical criticism typically gets first and maybe second century; reception history gets, well, the rest!

Lyons was primarily concerned with audiences and we might similarly add that there are links with literary criticisms we discussed in Chapter 2 where we mentioned the turn to reader- and audience-orientated approaches. In many ways, reception history is simply one logical outworking of reader-response criticism and the roles of reading communities in creating meaning. Postcolonial criticism is a very good example of the merging of literary and historical approaches we saw in Chapter 2 and it too has important things to say on reception history. One of the notable developments in postcolonial criticism, inspired by Homi Bhabha, is the ways in which the coloniser–colonised relationship is not simply one of brutal imposition of power (though it certainly includes this) but also one of ambivalence, ambiguity, allure, mimicry, and so on, on both sides. The reception of the Bible is an excellent example of this. As has long been recognised (but not always remembered in certain recent readings of biblical texts as anti-Empire), the Bible was a central document of European colonialism. But it is also clear that the Bible and Christianity have been taken up (and resisted) in different and creative ways by a range of colonised people and one example shows all the hallmarks of ambivalence, ambiguity, allure and mimicry.

Mary Huie-Jolly argues that after the Anglo-Maori wars of the 1860s and early 1870s some indigenous Maori in New Zealand's Bay of Plenty region started to identify themselves with 'the Jews' of John 5, the hostile enemy of Jesus, and by association Christianity. In earlier missionary activity, while some people would profess Christianity, others identified themselves as 'Jews' or 'unbelievers' and similar reactions were found later among those previously deemed converted.[3] This was done as a response to colonial practices which undermined traditional ways of life and land rights. This also led to another aspect of the identifying with 'the Jews' because of the connotations of Israelites as the real chosen people entitled to the land over against the Caananite settlers, that is, the European settlers. According to Huie-Jolly's postcolonial reading, John 'constructs a dominating Christology which has affinities with the universalizing claims of later colonist Christianity'. While originally John 5 may have been designed to give the group's authority to the Son in the context of a split from synagogue authority, John 5, in the context of a politically dominant Christianity, can be used to make claims of cultural and religious superiority. Note the shift in John 5 from Jesus as one 'the Jews' sought to kill (5.18) to the all-powerful judge (5.19–23). In the context of the colonisation of New Zealand, the decision to identify with 'the Jews' of John 5 was part of 'a decision to "leave the way of the Son" and to resist colonial domination'.[4]

Reception History: Historical Change and Cultural Contexts

This analogy with traditional biblical criticisms means that scholars will have to make similar interdisciplinary moves to those who have worked in traditional criticism, assuming they have not already done so. If someone works on the reception of the Bible in art then it would no doubt be a good thing to be well read in methods in art history and the historical and cultural context of the given work of art to explain why certain interpretative decisions were made in context, in addition to contexts in the history of ideas. Likewise, film studies, music studies, literary studies or whatever. This seems an obvious enough point and may seem banal to those trained in traditional historical criticism but I have been to enough reception historical papers presented by academics at conferences to know that such contextual study of historical and cultural contexts is sometimes avoided.

Another area which brings us back to traditional historical criticism involves the issues of causality mentioned in Chapters 5 and 6. Put another way, what brings about different interpretations in different contexts? Given that the Bible is deeply embedded in Western culture, how do long-established interpretative traditions influence readings? How do different and changing social and economic circumstances influence interpretations? How have the narratives, ideas and arguments of the Bible influenced social contexts and individuals?

One culturally prominent example of the ways in which social context and biblical interpretation overlap and intertwine would be the current controversies in the Anglican Church over homosexuality. On one level there is a debate over interpretation of the key biblical verses (Lev. 18.22; 20.13; Rom. 1:26–28; 1 Cor. 6.9–11; 1 Tim. 1.8–10) and if it could be said that they are fairly explicitly anti-homosexual practice then the Bible is having an influence. But again, why now? Why not 150 years ago? Well the obvious reason is that more liberal views towards homosexuality have developed in the past forty years and so it becomes an issue, with the Bible dormant, so to speak, on the issue, just waiting to be woken. So it starts to become a bit 'chicken and egg' and we are seeing an example of how broader cultural trends spring the Bible into action but with the influence of the Bible always lurking and perhaps its sheer presence always influencing and only now being endorsed or bringing forth a particular reaction.

A clearer example of how social changes have affected biblical interpretation is the use of the Bible in the alternative rock/pop scene in Manchester (UK) between 1976 and 1994.[5] Alternative rock/pop scene may not seem the most obvious place to look for uses of biblical and religious language but in Easter 2006 the BBC broadcast the Manchester Passion, a public re-enactment of the gospel story, featuring music written by some of the more prominent Manchester alternative musicians, culminating in the Stone Roses' song, 'I Am the Resurrection', and featuring some of the personalities from the Manchester music scene.

The period under question (1976–94) in Manchester is distinctive for the construction of a very particular Manchester identity in music, from accents to fashion. What is clear in this period is that there was a distinct shift in the use of biblical and religious language from the late 1970s to the early 1990s. At the beginning of our period there is clear evidence that biblical and religious language was being used in the name of dark introspection, cynical observation, nihilism and pessimism. By the end of our period such language was being used in the name of self-congratulation, self-importance, hedonism, and (largely misguided) optimism. One clear example at the beginning of our period is Ian Curtis, the lead singer of the band Joy Division, who committed suicide in 1980. In the 1979 song 'Wilderness' Curtis sings about a vision of travelling far and wide 'through many different times' seeing various destructive scenes relating to Christianity and the Bible. As with Curtis' more personalised reflections, there is no redemption in his vision. Christ's blood is nothing more than innocent blood unfairly shed and the power and glory of sin rules and, unlike the argument of Paul, there is no glorious countering of sin. Saints do nothing more than destroy all knowledge while unnamed martyrs unfairly die and without even their names remembered and with tears in their eyes. Religion is little more than the suffering of the innocents and the sheer dominance of sin. Other musicians of the time are not as extreme but the use of the Bible, including texts such as the book of Revelation, constantly portrays a cityscape of fear, decay, helplessness and 'apocalyptic' disaster. For instance, in their song, 'Lay of the Land', The Fall describe a physical and cultural world in a state of decay and decline and in the midst of this 'apocalyptic' cityscape stands, 'the good book of John/Surrounds the son'.

However, by the end of the 1980s there is a clear tendency for hedonistic manifestoes and self-confidence. An example of the latter is the Stone Roses in the not-so-subtle song from 1989, 'I Am the Resurrection', which effectively uses one grand narrative of the Bible, namely, from the punishment of the Israelites to the availability of repentance in Jesus, to describe a standard love relationship. The singer is placed in the position of God/Christ with the distinctly second placed partner begging the divine superior and using explicit allusions to Luke's passages about begging and pleading for acceptance (Luke 11.5–10; 13.23–27). The song sings about how the inferior lover has been given plenty of chances to repent and turn to the truth and really should not be accepted back into the fold. Finally, the singer can accept and exclaims triumphantly, 'I am the resurrection and I am the life/I couldn't ever bring myself/To hate you.' Little wonder people accused the singer Ian Brown of having a Messiah complex! Again, there are plenty of examples to support the idea of egotistical and hedonistic tendencies at the end of our period.

Of course, documenting this is one thing but then what do we do with the data? How do we explain the shift in biblical interpretation? Such changes can be explained by a range of social and cultural upheavals. The changing Manchester cityscape is one key reason. In many ways, the city had a long cultural history of being portrayed as the archetypical dour working class city from black and white British films such as *Love on the Dole* and *A Taste of Honey* to Ewan MacColl's famous 1949 song 'Dirty Old Town', written about the Salford district of Manchester. In the harsh reality on the ground, by the 1970s Manchester was an industrial city that had witnessed massive decline and this was being noticed at the time in relation to the emerging music scene in the music press. Broader social trends are, therefore, of obvious significance and here we cannot avoid the impact of Margaret Thatcher, the British Prime Minister of the 1980s and the ideological soul-mate of Ronald Reagan. Under Thatcher, unemployment reached extremely high levels (3 million) and the

Manchester musicians of the late 1980s explicitly talked about music as a way out.

However, music was not the only way out: narcotics accompanied. Of course drug use itself is hardly news in the music world but the *types* of drugs used or name-checked explain a lot. One of the major drugs of choice, and one that makes its way into the music of the 1970s bands, was amphetamine. Amphetamine is a stimulant but one of its notable side effects is paranoia, again reflected in the songs of groups such as The Fall and Joy Division, and something more conducive to the darker use of biblical language. Other typical drugs of choice were tranquilisers, again hardly the kind of things that will lead to upbeat egotism. Yet by the late 1980s things had changed dramatically when the euphoria-inducing drug 'ecstasy' became massively popular in youth culture. In the context of new dance music developments of the late 1980s, which were consciously adopted by the Manchester bands, ecstasy made lots of dance-shy young men dance all night. Ecstasy was cheap and became centre of the new dance music culture and was adopted by the main Manchester musicians of the late 1980s.

Yet, the music of the late 1980s was also as much a part of Thatcher's England as a reaction against it. While the dance and ecstasy culture may well have had a strong communal tendency it is difficult to ignore the serious commercial aspect of the rave scene and related music-based youth movements of the late 1980s/early 1990s. In broad terms, such movements were as much a part of late Thatcherism as they were a reaction against it. Hand-in-hand with an ecstasy-fuelled youth movement was a massive interest in designer and labelled clothes and a serious poseur culture. Part of the common uniforms among participants could include expensive labels that became synonymous with the dance music scene of the late 1980s and early 1990s. We are now seeing, then, not only how particular issues such as fashion can be intertwined with interpretation but how interpretation (and indeed fashion) is intertwined with broader international trends, in this case the rapid rise of economic liberalism associated with Thatcher and Reagan.

Reception History: National and International Contexts

I have mentioned 'the West' on several occasions and this can obscure differences. If we look more carefully at different contexts we can see just how different social contexts lead to different readings. Let us make a division between the US and UK and take the issue of the Bible in party politics. In the UK it is difficult to see how the use of the Bible can make a serious impact on politics in the way it can in the US. Certainly some British politicians are motivated by faith and the Bible and leading politicians (e.g. Tony Blair, Margaret Thatcher and Gordon Brown) have hardly hidden their faith and have not always shied away from biblical allusions. Most explicitly, Margaret Thatcher famously claimed that no one would remember the Good Samaritan if he only had good intentions and so he needed the money to carry them out. However, in the UK there is not at present a significant Bible-belt style vote to be won and references to faith and the Bible make British politicians nervous. It was not without reason that Tony Blair's leading spin doctor, Alistair Campbell, famously said 'We don't do God'.

In US party politics, of course, the issue of God and the Bible are seriously important and have been profoundly significant in American political thinking since the Pilgrims and Puritans of the seventeenth century, though, with the ever problematic separation of church and state, and strengthened by the rise of secularism and sixties counter-culture, it was not until the great evangelical revival of the 1970s that the Bible was brought ever closer to the mainstream of American politics.[6] This was famously recognised in the 2004 election when Karl Rove saw the millions of white evangelicals as the party's 'base' and potential major players in electoral success.

While, as we have seen, there is no denying that the Bible is a major issue in US politics, the issues surrounding causality and influence are hardly straight-forward. Let us take the example of Christian Zionism in the US, a particular brand of biblical interpretation which dramatically rose to prominence after 1967 and has become associated with views such as imminent end times, the Rapture, the Jewish restoration of Israel, staunch support for land claims made by the state of Israel, the rebuilding of the Third Temple in Jerusalem, and the Bible providing clear prophetic guidance to events in the contemporary Middle East and world politics. 1967 was a turning point due to the 'Six Day War' which Israel overwhelmingly won and gained religiously significant increases in territory (Sinai Peninsula, Golan Heights, West Bank, Gaza and East Jerusalem). From the perspective of Christian Zionism, biblical - prophecies about the restoration of Israel were emphatically being fulfilled. At the same time, outside evangelical circles, US culture and politics saw a dramatic shift in attitudes towards Israel, from indifference to staunch sup-port, and even great admiration at the ways in which Israel had defeated their enemies in contrast to the ongoing difficulties the US was having in Vietnam.[7]

A landmark publication in Christian Zionist circles was Hal Lindsey's multi-million selling *The Late Great Planet Earth* (1970). This book effectively marks the shift for Christian Zionism, from being a sort of conservative evangelical Christian fringe movement to a significant cultural and political force. *The Late Great Planet Earth* turns to biblical prophecies to show how events in Israel were predicted in the days of old and how the rapture, the second coming, rise of the antichrist, and so on, are imminent. Lindsey devotes much space to the political details of the events surrounding 1967 and the role of Egypt under President Nasser. After giving numerous biblical quotations, Lindsey adds, 'Current events in the Middle East have prepared the stage for Egypt's last act in the great drama which will climax with the finale, Christ's personal return to earth.'[8]

Lindsey's book was a major influence on Jerry Jenkins and Timothy LaHaye's best selling *Left Behind* novels and computer games. Their website uses a prophecy from Luke's gospel which historical critical biblical scholars, conservative and liberal, typically argue refers to the fall of Jerusalem in 70 CE (though whether a genuine prediction or a prediction written after the event does split scholars), and is not self-evidently about the events of the twentieth century, to refer to what has been happening in Israel in 1967:

> Did you know the Bible is full of prophecies that have already come true? When Jesus Christ was born in Bethlehem, he fulfilled a prophecy. The fact that his mother was a virgin fulfilled another prediction. Later when Jesus healed the blind and the crippled and fed the hungry, his actions fulfilled more prophecies. When Jesus died on the Cross, it fulfilled a prophecy. More prophecies were likely fulfilled in 1948 when Israel became an Independent nation and in 1967 when Israel regained control of Jerusalem from Jordan in the Six Day War.
>
> 'They will be brutally killed by the sword or sent away as captives to all the nations of the world. And Jerusalem will be conquered and tramped down by the Gentiles until the age of the Gentiles comes to an end'
>
> (Luke 21:24)[9]

Since 1967, figures and groups linked with Christian Zionism have become household names, such as Pat Robertson, Jerry Falwell, the Christian Coalition and the Moral Majority. A variety of pressure groups and pro-Israel church networks have emerged, such as Christians' Israel Public Action Campaign, Christian Friends of Israel, Christians United for Israel, the International Fellowship of Christians and Jews/Stand for Israel, and The Friends of Israel Gospel Ministry, Inc.

What Christian Zionism shows us is how a major interpretative tradition emerged after a major historical and intellectual upheaval post-1967. It was sustained politically to some extent by the rise of Christian fundamentalism in the US, itself sustained in the following decades where wages and family incomes stagnated or declined with working hours and indebtedness rising and social benefits declining. The political mobilisation of such people became important for the rise of political neoliberalism because if issues of gay rights and evolution are of utmost importance, the issues of economic power can remain in the realm of the corporate world with less fear of popular opposition.[10] While the social, economic and historical factors play a role in the emergence of such a tradition, we must not forget the role of ideas and the role of the Bible. Christian Zionism became very much an American tradition and one way it became credible was because its established interpretation of biblical prophecies really did seem to be coming to fulfilment. Here we have a good example of the overlapping and intertwining ways in which interpretation and social context influence reception. While it is unlikely Christian Zionism would have been a big hit if Israel had not become established as a central feature of US foreign policy, it still needed the interpretative tradition to at least appear credibly fulfilled. It is not so easy, then, to make division in terms of primary influence and say just how much the Bible and biblical interpretation play a role and how much interpretation itself was a product of historical events. But if we think of the way historians might work out causes we might just do that standard thing and lay out the social, economic, religious, and intellectual causes behind the emergence of Christian Zionist interpretation, just as we might lay out such causes for the emergence of a given issue in the historical study of Christian origins.

Reception History and Individual Influence

Among all this we should not rule out the influence of the individual in interpretation. In our brief discussion of the changes in biblical interpretation in the Manchester music scene, we noted how broad social changes played a major role in the shift from dark, introspective readings to hedonistic and egotistical readings between 1976 and 1994. However, we can also add the role of the individual here. At the beginning of the period, Ian Curtis suffered from epilepsy, and was poorly treated, which contributed to his depression, which in turn contributed to his suicide in 1980. It is difficult to see how these factors did not play at least some role in the dark nature of his lyrics and use of biblical texts, as well as, perhaps, influencing the lyrics of others in the Manchester music scene.

A comical example of personal influence on a distinctive biblical reading is the disgraced British politician Jeffrey Archer. In 2007 Archer published the fictional *The Gospel According to Judas by Benjamin Iscariot* with the assistance of the New Testament scholar Francis J. Maloney.[11] The physical features of this fictional Gospel are made to look like a mini-family Bible with a mock-leather Bible cover, an attached tassel, gold-coloured page edges and red letters for Jesus' words. Naturally, the book is also written in chapter and verse. In this account, Judas' son, Benjamin, gives his father's side of the story and clears his father's name because Judas was unfairly smeared. Judas was only really mistaken in thinking Jesus to be a more nationalistic, anti-Roman Messiah. Judas may have had his doubts but other disciples, including Peter, did not have his fierce loyalty and only Judas could save Jesus and Israel by getting Jesus out of Jerusalem safely. However, poor Judas was manipulated by a scribe who was not really helping Judas but rather trying to get Judas to give away Jesus' location. The scribe betrayed Judas and Judas became known as the betrayer. A heartbroken Judas retired to Qumran, home of the Dead Sea Scrolls.

Rehabilitations of Judas are nothing new. In 2006 there was a prominent example with the publication of the ancient *Gospel of Judas* which may well have provided Archer with an immediate source of inspiration. While April DeConick has since argued that the ancient Gospel of Judas does not portray Judas as a positive figure, the media unanimously agreed Judas was innocent.[12] For instance, the BBC headline read 'Judas "Helped Jesus Save Mankind"'.[13] Yet the various cultural rehabilitations of Judas only provide the template: Archer's own life is clearly the primary influence on his retelling of the Judas story.

Outside the UK Archer is little known apart, perhaps, as a bestselling novelist so it is worth recalling a few general details. In the UK, Archer has a notorious reputation as a disgraced politician. He has been embroiled in various financial scandals and has been shown to have invented various details about his past. One of the most infamous episodes was when he initially won a court case against a British tabloid in 1987 about allegations over dealings with a prostitute. However, by 2000 Archer was charged with perjury and perverting the course of justice and in 2001 he was imprisoned. Throughout his career, Archer was repeatedly criticised by certain journalists and it was they, at least in terms of the legal outcome, who were proven to be correct. Archer, on the other hand, continued to stress in his prison diaries that he was not given a fair trial, that numerous allegations were simply false, and that many of his former colleagues in the Conservative party abandoned him. This apparent lack of justice, supposed misunderstanding and betrayal by former colleagues are major themes in his prison diaries.

Archer's post-imprisonment *The Gospel According to Judas by Benjamin Iscariot* is quite obviously autobiographical. Could it really not be autobiographical when the opening section makes claims such as the following?

> Indeed, they have blackened my father's name to the point where he is now thought of as the most infamous of all Jesus' followers. He has been branded a traitor, a thief and a man willing to accept bribes. ... The Christians continue to spread the word throughout Galilee that Judas was a man of violence, a hanger-on and someone who could not be trusted. Despite contrary evidence, these libels are still abroad and often repeated by the followers of Jesus, even to this present day.[14]

There are some more specific indications of (misunderstood) Judas-as-Archer. Money predictably arises and Judas is the treasurer of the Jesus movement. Despite making sure everyone gets fed, clothed and sheltered, Judas is suspected (wrongly) of financial irregularities.[15] And we should never forget that, with Archer's bitter enemies in the printed media in mind, the real manipulative enemy in *The Gospel According to Judas by Benjamin Iscariot* is none other than a *scribe* ...

In *The Gospel According to Judas by Benjamin Iscariot*, Archer also hammers home issues of forgiveness and warnings against hypocrisy (e.g. Chapter 9). It is Judas who asks Jesus how to pray with Jesus then telling his followers about the Lord's Prayer which of course contains the words, 'Forgive us our sins, as we forgive the sins of others'. This is probably not reading too much into the delivery of the Lord's Prayer because immediately prior Judas poignantly wept when Jesus preached, 'It is always easy to love those who love you, but it is far more difficult to bring compassion and unity where there is division. Be merciful, even as your Father in heaven is merciful'. Jesus continued by telling people not to condemn 'their fellow men, as there was no one among them who was not guilty of some offence'. After all, 'Who are we to set ourselves up to judge others?' To hit the point home, Archer's Judas will pass these words on to those not present, no doubt with a nod to the reading audience. If there is any remaining doubt of autobiographical influence, when Jesus then speaks of the problems of being judgemental (Luke 6.41; Matt. 7.3), Archer's Judas can only endorse: 'such wise and compassionate words, showing how good and full of authority Jesus' ministry was'.[16]

The 'Effects' of New Testament Texts and New Testament Narratives

These issues of influences from social change to individual idiosyncrasies bring us on to questions of 'effective history'. Perhaps more than any other contemporary scholar, Heikki Räisänen has raised the problems defining and understanding the 'effective history' of biblical texts.[17] How do the biblical texts bring about change? *Can* biblical texts really bring about historical and social changes? Or are biblical texts simply used to justify pre-existing views? How much stress should we place on cultural contexts and biblical influence? Is it so easy to separate textual influence from cultural influence? Building on Räisänen's work, Kenneth Newport has recently argued that the book of Revelation can 'be seen to have been instrumental in inspiring, or at least being conducive to, acts of Apocalyptic self-destruction'.[18] Newport gives the example of the Branch Davidians of Waco, Texas, whose headquarters were burned down in 1993 with the loss of over eighty lives. The leader of the Branch Davidians, David Koresh, saw himself as an angel or messenger from God based on Revelation 10.7, along with various other parts of Revelation being idiosyncratically interpreted by Koresh. Most notably in terms of the final results of the Waco deaths, Newport argues that the burning was 'not a random act of desperation' but rather the time had come to be 'faithful unto death' (cf. Rev. 2.10). In terms of influence, Newport adds:

> ... it was rather a quite exceptionally dramatic act of faith, the necessity of which had long been anticipated and planned for. In the spring of 1993 it was plain to the Branch Davidians that they were facing desperate times. The great beast of Revelation 13 was about them and it was clear that the time had come for action.[19]

Of course, as Newport is aware, there are a whole host of short-, medium-
and long-term social and economic factors which would have to be factored in
but issues of deeply held interpretative convictions play no small part.

Newport also analysed the importance of the interpretative traditions of the
Branch Davidians. Interpretative tradition is another important factor in
understanding the 'effects' of biblical texts. In addition to the influence of the
text itself, it is worth discussing the influence of an interpretative tradition.
We saw above how the interpretative tradition of what Sherwood called the
Liberal Bible has had a profound influence on the use of the Bible in American
politics. It can be helpful to distinguish between the types of effects of the text
itself. Luz discusses a telling definitional issue around the concept of influence
of the text itself:

> Instead of *Wirkungsgeschichte* I could have said *Rezeptionsgeschichte* ...
> I did not do so, because *Rezeptionsgeschichte* connotes for me primarily
> the people who receive the text, while *Wirkungsgeschichte* suggests for me
> the effective power of the texts themselves. For me that is what is basic. ...
> The history of the interpretation and influence of the texts shows what we
> have become because of them ... Studying the history of the text's influ-
> ence is designed to call attention to the power of the texts that precedes
> our interpreting. ... to help us understand how the specific interpreters are
> formed by their texts ... [20]

A more negative reading of the effects of the New Testament is by Burton
Mack and his controversial book, *A Myth of Innocence*. For Mack, the gospel
of Mark, and its insistence on the death of an innocent in Jesus, laid the
foundations for a powerful and influential idea in Western thought. Mack
outlines the basics of this 'myth':

> And so it is that a single event, composite and complex, has haunted the
> Christian imagination for nearly two thousand years. That event is the
> manifestation of divine authority and power breaking into human history,
> coming to a violent climax in the crucifixion of God's Son. His vindication
> by resurrection, then, envisages the radical transformation of the perfectly
> just and peaceable kingdom. ... The mission of this new community is
> also determined by the event. That mission is to re-present in the world
> the power of the event to change the world. Under mandate and destiny to
> expand until the whole world has been transformed, the church calls upon
> the world to receive its redemption.[21]

Other (now canonical) gospels may have modified Mark but the fundamental
plot was not altered and so the Markan logic continued, even though Mark
was not particularly popular in the early Christian centuries, and martyrdom
continued as an important theme. A major change came when the Roman

Emperor Constantine converted to Christianity and so the Christian story became part of the Empire and Christianity a religion of power. This meant the Gospels would be read differently, with the myth of innocence enduring in this radically different context and the Gospels would from that time on be central in Western cultural understanding. As part of the Christian mission, and indeed at 'every level of human experience', there is the expectation that those outside the fold convert and, according to Mack's reading, this means passing through the 'event of transformation, the moment of judgment upon the past and its forgiveness', in order to gain social acceptance.[22] The symbols of transformation are, according to Mack, deeply embedded in Western culture to the extent that they appear self-evident.

In America especially, according to Mack, popular culture and this Christian mythology have combined to provide a more secularised sense of identity with ideas of a new people, a new land, and an egalitarian divine mandate, with the promises of Christian origins finally being fulfilled. Yet in post-war America came a loss of innocence due in part to America seemingly not able to solve the world's problems and an apocalyptic mentality took grip, with blame levelled at all sorts of institutions and enemies. So, for all the different proposed solutions, there was an agreement that something was wrong with the world and this something needed to be destroyed or transformed for the peaceable kingdom. America has become the innocent redeemer of the world with a Messianic mission. National mission has replaced the religious human transformation and to avoid failure victims may be sacrificed, just as martyrs and punishment of the wicked function in the apocalyptic scheme as a means of bringing forth a new creation. In more concrete terms, borders have to be crossed because America has a 'right to be there' and, from Vietnam to Latin America, this can involve violence to save the world but violence in the hands of a 'pure' leader, someone akin to the Markan saviour.

But, Mack argues, this influential idea has led to a series of tragic consequences. This includes the damnation of the Jews in the Gospel through the miserable history of Christian attitudes towards Jews and Judaism, including the Nazi Holocaust where the rationale was Christian, he argues. It is no surprise, then, that Mack sees the Markan myth, its 'remarkably pitiful' condemnation of the world and its legacy as a bad thing. He ends his book as follows: 'A future for the world can hardly be imagined any longer, if its redemption rests in the hands of Mark's innocent son of God.'[23]

With Mack, then, we have what would be a profound example of 'effective history'. But if we read Mack as giving Mark some degree of influence over the darker side of Western and American history, is this a fair reading of the influence of Mark on society? In this case it is worth going back to reading Mark in its historical context. As it happens, Mack's reading of Mark has not been widely accepted. Normally an appeal to consensus is not much of an argument and often merely tells us what lots of people think rather than any historical truth but in this case it *may* show that the myth is not so all-pervasive if scholars are not regularly finding it in their readings of Mark. It could be suggested that Mark is not quite so condemning of the Jews as *the* great opponents as Mack reading might imply. A leader, Joseph of Arimathea, is not treated negatively (Mark 15.42–46) and there are general positive statements about Jesus throughout Mark. Crowds gather around his home in Capernaum (2.1–3), Jews spread their cloaks for him in the triumphal entry, the chief priests and scribes cannot kill him because of the (Jewish) crowd (11.18), the large crowd were listening to him with delight (12.37), and Simon the Leper and the women of Mark 14 were no doubt Jewish. However, it could be argued that Mark's criticisms of Jewish authorities and opponents become crystallised and developed as representative of Jews or Judaism, hence in Matthew we get the infamous, 'His blood be on us and on our children!' (Matt. 27.25), and in John's Gospel 'the Jews' are notable opponents of Jesus believed to be sons of the devil (John 8.44).

Back to our earlier questions of influence and causes, even if we assume Mack's reading of the Markan myth is correct, is there not a case to be made that Mack has placed too much emphasis on the influence of the narrative? The idea of empires behaving as Mack shows the present American empire behaving is surely older than Mark, and the implied 'us versus them' mentality is hardly unique to Christianity. Violence and imperialism have always been justified in some way with reference to the divine, from the Persian Empire through the Roman to the British, or to the divine equivalent (and suitably capitalised) History and inevitable historical progress in the atheistic Soviet Empire. Superpowers behave the way they do and if they can fit an underlying religious narrative in along the way, so much the better. Though he does not quite push it, Mack's outline seems to place a heavy emphasis on the Gospel narrative playing a major role in many prominent tragedies in human history without giving due attention or reference to a massive range of social historical features. If this is the case, or if Mack is to be developed like this, is it perhaps better to say that the Gospel myth or narrative has been employed by the powerful to give their actions a distinctive gloss rather than any profound influence in terms of framing social attitudes and beliefs? Does this not tip the scales back in favour of the social context of readers making the Bible read the way it reads, at least in this major instance?

Perhaps. But would not the history of antisemitism have been radically different if the New Testament texts and Christianity had not placed such emphasis on the split from Judaism? On the other hand, Christians and Jews have managed to get along cordially in different historical periods and places so presumably early Christian hostilities towards Jews do not always have a powerful rhetorical impact. To be fair, much of this is a question of emphasis, and Mack is clear that such views become embedded in society, but even so, what this development of Mack's ideas shows is just how difficult it is to ascribe degrees of influence to the Bible and to social context. Perhaps we might rethink the question another way. It may be more useful to speak of the Bible, as Jacques Berlinerblau does, in terms of 'raw power'. The Bible is not, Berlinerblau recalls, a senior unnamed academic's argument given to other academics in a pub, inherently good or evil. The Bible can be used for both, and it can, and has, been used to support anything and everything.[24] It is the rhetorical links to the Bible itself that potentially give different views credibility, even to the extent of being a potential election winner. In this sense, the Bible is 'raw power'.

Mack's argument points more to the narrative logic rather than the odd verse as a primary influence and here we might nuance or qualify our discussion by talking about how certain texts *resonate* with certain social, cultural, social and historical changes. The postcolonial readings we saw earlier in this book provide a potentially helpful example of the ways in which the logic of a fiercely anti-imperial text, such as the book of Revelation, was useful in establishing Christianity as the religion of Empire, not least because of the reversal of power and the role Jesus plays as ruler of all. Of course, this logic of reversal and universal rule does not have to be anti-Empire in origins: it could alternatively be said of different claims to Christian superiority which are re-read in contexts of colonial power as we saw in Mary Huie-Jolly's study of the Maori receptions of John 5 discussed above. Indeed, Huie-Jolly writes of the 'polarizing structure' of John 5.16–47, pointing out that the passage has explicit stark difference and forensic language maintaining a difference between insiders and outsiders. In the language of John's Gospel the insiders are those who honour the Son as God and those refusing to honour him, cast as 'the Jews' in John 5 and those who are judged by the Son.[25] On the one hand, there is a world of difference between a marginal group making the judgement of John 5 and the 'Son equals the Father' idea being used in the context of imperialism; on the other hand, the structural difference is in place and, when transferred into different contexts, the invitation to interpret this stark difference has an obvious potential to polarise.

Perhaps there been no greater influence on Western thought than Paul. By looking at Western *thought*, we are on slightly different ground to the influence on historical changes because we have people reading Paul and thinking about ideas where Paul's thought has been used. Mark Lilla points out that 'Paul continues to breed strange enthusiasms' and has been the subject of numerous 'mistaken' yet hugely influential readings across the centuries, from Augustine to Calvin, from Luther to Kierkegaard, not to mention a range of radical and 'heretical' views. Yet Lilla is interested in these 'misreadings' and 'why a certain kind of mind is drawn to Paul, and to the Epistle to the Romans in particular'. Is it perhaps significant that there are a range of stark and radical sounding statements, such as justification by faith apart from works of the law (Rom. 3.28), the Lord is Lord of all and so there is no distinction between Jew and Greek (Rom. 10.12), and if God is for us who is against us (Rom. 8.30–31)? Do not such sentiments, Lilla asks, imply that 'interior' faith trumps all law, Jewish, Greek or Roman, does not the universality of the religious movement imply the abolition of those that preceded them, and does not this new movement want to bring universal truth too all irrespective of opposition?[26]

However, Lilla goes on to make scathing criticisms of the 'political' and 'philosophical' Paul of the continental philosophers we saw in Chapter 8. He locates this reading, 'and probably many of their readers', as belonging to 'the cult of political romanticism' and that this political romanticism

> ... longs to live life on more dramatic terms than those offered by bourgeois society, to break out and feel the hot pulse of passion, to upset the petty laws and conventions that crush the human spirit. We recognize this longing and know how it has shaped modern consciousness and politics, often at great cost. But its patron saint is not Paul of Tarsus. It is Emma Bovary.[27]

Much of Lilla's review descends into a bit of a rant about the politics of Badiou and others but if we cut through this we can point to the more useful comments made. Perhaps it is fair to take Lilla's first comments on the 'misreadings' of Paul more seriously than his second on the location of the 'political romanticism' of those readings Lilla does not like. For a start, patron saints are what people make them and so while we may not agree with readings it does not mean there is no connection between the misreading and the misread text. As Lilla rightly points out, Paul *does* seem to inspire the most radical ideas because it seems that in Paul's very arguments there is an inbuilt stark change and radical transformation. And is not this stark change and radical transformation precisely what makes Paul so attractive for the 'political readings' of Paul, whether such readings are right, wrong, incomprehensible, anachronistic or whatever? Is this not one of the reasons why Paul has been central in support of radical transformation, whether Luther's reading of Paul and the Reformation or the twentieth century, Luther-inspired, scholarly readings where Judaism was placed in such a negative light?

Of course, these readings tie in with major social upheavals, whether the sixteenth-century Reformation or the alarming rise of Nazism in 1920s and 1930s Germany, but it is notable that Paul 'works' in these contexts. Similar things could be said for the 'political' and 'philosophical' readings of Paul in continental philosophy. Stalin, totalitarianism, Soviet Russia and the end of the Cold War saw Marxism and many of its key thinkers, rightly or wrongly, thoroughly discredited and in decline since the 1970s. As Marxism declined, religion has returned as a topic of serious cultural interest, from the rise of Christian fundamentalism in the US to its reaction in pop cultural figures such as Richard Dawkins and Christopher Hitchens. The prominence of Islam has also been significant, from radical Islam filling the void of the decline of secular nationalism in many countries with a high Muslim population, to Muslim immigration becoming an increasingly discussed topic. And, of course, in this general context ideas of a 'clash of civilisations' emerged, a clash typically deemed to be between Islam and the West and a thesis which has echoes in contemporary New Testament scholarship (see Chapter 11).

With this context in mind, the figure of Paul, often deemed the founder of Christianity and perhaps even Western culture, and someone long discussed in the history of philosophy, becomes a thoroughly credible figure. While the 'philosophical' readers of Paul tend to come from the radical left, have been hostile to treatment of Muslim immigrants (especially Badiou), and have been critical of the proponents of the 'clash of civilisations' thesis, it is still fair to say that we are broadly dealing with a diluted form of the thesis in the sense that Paul is seen as a figure worth reclaiming for 'our' cultural heritage, though certainly with the implication that Paul can undermine the more liberal-minded views of the biblical texts. Giorgio Agamben opened his book on Paul in notably dramatic terms: 'First and foremost, this seminar proposes to restore Paul's letters to the status of fundamental messianic text for the Western tradition.'[28]

There are, of course, more specific and localised reasons for the different continental philosophical readings of Paul and the Pauline idea of a radical transformation of the past (and present). In the case of the influential Badiou, French politics and French intellectual culture colour his reading. Like many French intellectuals, the social and political radicalism of 1968 constantly hovers in the background and Badiou brings this and French political traditions into play in his polemical book concerning the French President Nicolas Sarkozy.[29] Indeed, in a similar way, Badiou contextualises his study of Paul with reference to modern France, including the French nationalist right. Badiou is scathing of the question effectively posed in contemporary France – What is a French person? – and its counterpart – 'French for the French'.[30] One result has been a targeting of people living in France who do not come up to standard, most famously the recent controversy over Muslim schoolgirls wearing headscarves. This leads to distinct groupings: the truly French, integrated foreigners, and non-integrated foreigners. Subsets of the population are defined by their special status. This identity-based national model, Badiou argues, is devoid of any real principle and is little more than police monitoring and not so far removed from the French state as the servant of the Nazi occupiers. In this context what are we to make of that famous verse from Galatians, 'There is no longer Jew or Greek, there is no longer slave or free, there is no longer male and female; for all of you are one in Christ Jesus' (Gal. 3.28)? For Badiou this is a 'genuinely stupefying statement' which is particularly appropriate for those who replace God 'by this or that truth'. After all, Paul also says, God shows no partiality (Rom. 2.10).

Yet there is no problem accommodating French particularism when it comes to human beings, and its localised 'persecutions', with the universality of global market. With the global market, there is also, Badiou points out, a range of fragmented identities with endless potential for investment, groups demanding recognition (e.g. women, homosexuals) and groups that can be endlessly fragmented and qualified (black homosexuals, ecologist yuppies) and so along come the specialist magazines, improved shopping malls, targeted advertising, public debates at peak viewing times, and so on. Identities effectively push to be exposed to the market. Consequently no truth can be maintained to cover the whole expansion of capital. Also present in this system is the idea that only a particular subset can understand its own: only a homosexual can understand a homosexual, only a woman can understand a woman and so on. Paul would never allow the Good News to be determined by the available generalities which in the ancient world would have been state driven (Roman Law and Roman citizenship) and ideological (Greek philosophy and morality), or their equivalents in Jewish Law. Paul may well have been proud of his Roman citizenship but Roman legal categories cannot identify the Christian subject and so slaves, women, people of different nationalities are accepted without restriction. What ultimately matters for Paul (and for today) is a universal singularity against all this.

Summary

In many ways, the methodological approaches used in reception history are no different from the approaches used in more traditional historical criticism. Instead, it is simply the historical contexts which are different. Reception history, like historical criticism, still concerns itself with close readings of texts or paintings or films (or whatever), with readers and audience, with historical change and cultural context, with national and international politics, with the influence of ideas and the individual, and, more recently, with postcolonial criticism. One, perhaps superficial, difference is that we are now dealing with the 'effects' of the very texts themselves.

Key Words

See Chapter 9.

Further Reading

Dube, M.W. and J.L. Staley, eds., *John and Postcolonialism: Travel, Space and Power*, London: T&T Clark, 2002.

Lyons W.J. and J. Økland, eds., *The Way the World Ends? The Apocalypse of John in Culture and Ideology*, Sheffield: Sheffield Phoenix Press, 2009.

Mack, B., *The Myth of Innocence: Mark and Christian Origins*, Philadelphia: Fortress, 1988.

Northcott, M., *An Angel Directs the Storm: Apocalyptic Religion and American Empire*, London & New York: I. B. Tauris, 2004.

Prothero, S., *American Jesus: How the Son of God became a National Icon*, New York: Farrar, Straus and Giroux, 2003.

Räisänen, H., 'The "Effective History" of the Bible: A Challenge to Biblical Scholarship', in H. Räisänen, ed., *Challenges to Biblical Interpretation: Collected Essays 1991–2001*, Leiden: Brill, 2001, pp. 263–82.

Chapter 11

How to Read New Testament Scholarship

One notable impact of reception history is that it might start to blur the intellectual boundaries between Old Testament/Hebrew Bible and New Testament because the area of historical and cultural specialism is no longer rooted in the original audiences of the different texts. Of course, this already assumes a context where Christian culture has been dominant and no doubt many Jewish scholars will be more interested in the reception of the Hebrew Bible, though we have already seen ways in which issues relating to the reception of the New Testament or New Testament texts might also be of interest. Furthermore, there is nothing stopping the scholar studying the reception of the New Testament as New Testament in distinction from the Old Testament/Hebrew Bible. However, in this chapter, and keeping in line with the subject matter of this book, the New Testament will be the primary focus. There is further reason to look more specifically at the New Testament and one that brings us to another important contribution made by reception history: reception history can help us understand the often unchecked cultural assumptions of New Testament scholars who may well be unintentionally repeating a variety of theological and cultural views which have come before them. Returning to his analysis of reception history discussed earlier in the previous chapter, W. John Lyons stresses that the modern study of the Bible has always been dominated by audiences and this includes *contemporary historical critical scholarship*.[1] It is to the reception of the New Testament in contemporary scholarship we now turn.

New Testament Scholarship and the 'Great Man' View of History

There are countless examples of the ways in which the history of interpretation has influenced historical scholarship. In Chapter 7 we saw how the Lutheran and anti-Jewish traditions has had a profound influence on the 'Old Perspective' on Paul. In fact there is increasing awareness in contemporary scholarship of the ways in which deep-rooted ideas are influencing contemporary scholarship itself. One is the old but still popular 'Great Man' view of history where great figures, typically at the expense of wider trends and more popular movements, are deemed to be the most significant factors in bringing historical change and are usually the focuses of numerous scholarly biographies. One of the pioneering figures in the quest for the historical Jesus was Friedrich Schleiermacher (1768–1834). Halvor Moxnes has shown how Schleiermacher's work on the historical Jesus is in many ways typical in the sense that there is great interest in developing the idea of a biography of Jesus.[2] The general development of 'biography' was a major form in nineteenth-century bourgeois Germany. The function of the nineteenth-century biography was to describe 'great men' who were tied in with new bourgeois values and distinct from the more traditional power structures. This meant that the individual was discussed with reference to concepts of nation, land, and the people. Indeed, the nineteenth century was an important period in the development of particularly European concepts of nation and nationalism, alongside the Great Man view of history. Biographies of Jesus engaged with and used such concepts of nation and land, and Schleiermacher's Jesus, Moxnes shows, becomes the ultimate ideal Great Man, the ideal figure for European nationalism, especially that he was deemed to have influenced all people and all ages.

Some nineteenth-century lives of Jesus developed in this context with Jesus the archetypal liberal statesman-like figure. These are typically referred to as the 'liberal lives of Jesus' in scholarly literature. Jesus' proclamation of the kingdom of God was interpreted in moral and spiritualised terms. One of the most famous of all the nineteenth-century Jesus scholars, Ernest Renan (1823–92), exclaimed,

> But still more happy, Jesus would say to us, is he who, freed from illusion, shall produce in himself the celestial vision, and, with no millenarian dream, no chimerical paradise, no signs in the heavens, but, by the uprightness of his will and the poetry of his soul, shall be able to create anew in his heart the true kingdom of God![3]

One of the great changes in New Testament scholarship came with Albert Schweitzer's book at the turn of the twentieth century, *The Quest of the Historical Jesus* (1906), where Jesus was firmly placed in the context of first-century Jewish apocalyptic thought. Schweitzer's Jesus was a tragic failure, preaching the imminent end which never came, though this Jesus did succeed in discrediting the more pleasant liberal lives of Jesus in the eyes of many scholars. Yet in turn, as Ward Blanton has shown, Schweitzer's apocalyptic Jesus, along with Schweitzer's analysis of mysticism in Paul, are part of his nineteenth-century philosophical training and a broader reaction to the narrative of the progress of human reason, liberalism, technology, and industrialisation, a reaction against what is commonly known as 'modernity'.[4]

But one thing Schweitzer's work did not do was to halt the Great Man view of history in its general sense. Schweitzer's Jesus was still, after all, a tragic hero worthy of emulation. As it happens, the importance of the Great Man view of history has never left New Testament scholarship, though 'great people' might be more accurate given the occasional prominence of women in scholarly histories. This should probably come as no surprise given how culturally prominent the idea of the great individual remains. How many times do we hear that we need a resolute Commander-in-Chief in times of war who ought not to be replaced, or a strong Prime Minister in times of recession? Irrespective of the rights and wrongs of whether we *need* such leadership, it is an idea that has not left us. Indeed, Dieter Giorgi has shown that the view that Jesus had been 'a genius of sorts' became 'the dominant view in the late eighteenth, nineteenth, and twentieth centuries, not only in Germany but also in western Europe and North America, among both Protestants and Catholics'.[5]

There are numerous famous portraits of Jesus the great individual vying for attention: Jesus the Cynic-like philosopher, Jesus the charismatic holy man, Jesus the prophet of end times, Jesus the great rabbi, Jesus the revolutionary, Jesus the social critic and so on. Jesus is typically seen as the figure who effectively started Christianity, or better, the figure in whom the seeds of the parting of the ways were planted. The idea of a biography of the great individual is still significant. One of the most celebrated writers on the historical Jesus, E.P. Sanders, opens his life of Jesus by placing the book in the context of biographies of other great figures (and notice how Jesus is still being compared to major figures of state and empire):

I shall discuss Jesus the human being, who lived in a particular time and place, and I shall search for evidence and propose explanations just as does any historian when writing about history ... Jesus' own theology and the theologies of his first followers are historical questions, which are to be explored in the same way as one studies what Jefferson thought about liberty, what Churchill thought about the labour movement and the strikes of 1910 and 1911, what Alexander the Great thought about the union of Greek and Persian in one empire, and what their contemporaries thought about these great men while they still lived ... The historian who studies a great human being, and reports fully on his or her findings, will almost certainly write at least a few things that some admirers would rather not read. People whose image of Jefferson has been created by imagining the character of the author of the Declaration of Independence may be shocked by a study of his love life and consumption of alcohol ... This is not a warning that I am going to 'expose' something truly shocking about Jesus, such as sexual promiscuity ... I shall not only write about how nice he was, nor shall I ignore the aspects of his life and thought that many of his most ardent admirers wish would go away.[6]

Other major scholars likewise mould their lives of Jesus the great individual in biographical form and so the term 'biography' or 'life' regularly occurs in subtitles (e.g. Crossan's, *Jesus: A Revolutionary Biography*, Wright's *The Original Jesus: The Life and Vision of a Revolutionary*, Chilton's *Rabbi Jesus: An Intimate Biography*). Similar remarks could be made about Paul. If the seeds of the new religion are to be found in Jesus then it was Paul who was the other great figure whose genius found 'something wrong' with Judaism and effectively created a Gentile religion. Maybe that is a little unfair but it certainly is fair to say that the study of the historical Jesus and Paul is overwhelmingly concerned with fact finding, description and descriptive interpretation, theology, and so on, with much less concern for questions such as *why* the Jesus movement and Pauline mission emerged when and where they did and *why* this movement subsequently led to a new religion. As we saw in Chapter 2, even the use of social sciences has tended to be static, another aid to understanding the world of Jesus and Paul and their respective theologies.

Whether this is all right or wrong is, in one sense, another question (one also addressed in Chapter 2); the point is that New Testament studies has a heavy concentration on the role of the individual in history. This continued interest can partially be explained with reference to the nineteenth-century Great Man view of history in New Testament scholarship but not entirely. The discipline of history was likewise influenced by the Great Man view of history in the nineteenth century but has since managed to have major historians looking at a range of broad social, economic, political, and cultural trends in historical change, with the individual one factor among many. So why does the individual remain such a prominent feature? For a start, individualism is a major cultural feature of British and American capitalism at least, perhaps best summed up in the infamous words of the British Prime Minister of the 1980s, Margaret Thatcher, 'There's no such thing as society.' But this just shows that focus on the individual is a prominent cultural option and the example of the discipline of history shows other cultural options are available. Here we can bring in the idea of faith. Jesus and Paul are the central figures of orthodox Christian faith and theology and most scholars and students of the New Testament are, unsurprisingly enough, Christians, practising or lapsed. With these reasons we can thus explain why there is such a major influence on the great individual in contemporary New Testament studies.

Race, Ethnicity and Judaism in New Testament Scholarship

Disturbingly, some of the racial categories of the nineteenth century still haunt contemporary scholarship. In the history of modern scholarship, key categories for understanding the emergence of early Christianity involved concepts for identifying the degree of assimilation and the categories 'Palestinian Judaism' and 'Hellenistic Judaism'. Caroline Vander Stichele and Todd Penner have pointed out how these categories were being vigorously developed in the context of nineteenth-century debates over nation and nationalism, in particular the idea of 'the Jewish problem'.[7] Jews were required to assimilate and were marked from their surrounding context in racial terms. Similarly, Shawn Kelley has argued that contemporary biblical scholarship has inherited some disturbing perspectives which derive from nineteenth- and early twentieth-century Germany and are profoundly racialised, reaching their most notorious low point with the racialised politics of German fascism. These categories include authenticity, lapsing into conventionality, and pure origins.

Kelley argues that the philosopher Martin Heidegger was a major influence, brought into biblical studies through the hugely influential New Testament scholar Rudolf Bultmann. According to Bultmann's Heidegger-inspired reading of the New Testament texts, 'inauthentic existence' involves human beings relying on and justifying themselves for salvation rather than God whereas 'authentic existence' involves human beings placing their faith in God who has given the gift of justification to human beings. For Bultmann, Judaism was effectively representative of inauthenticity, Paul represented the existential encounter, and Luke-Acts and the Catholic Epistles represented the fall and lapse into conventionality. Kelley points out that these categories became transferred into the liberal scholarship of the later twentieth-century scholars, Robert Funk and John Dominic Crossan, where original and apparently playful and open-ended parables of Jesus replace Paul in this scheme and the reinterpretation of the parables and the writing up of the Gospel tradition replace Luke-Acts. Furthermore, these general patterns of original, great moment and existential encounter play into racialised categories where the (positive) original great moment representing Western, authentic and individualised encounter is replaced by the Eastern (/Jewish) and inauthentic. The pure, pristine original, according to this scheme, is betrayed, distorted and hidden. As Kelley puts it, 'The purging of the inauthentic to make possible authenticity, which has structured much of the twentieth-century's most respected biblical scholarship, necessarily means identifying and shattering the forces of Jewification to better create a racially pure West.'[8]

Kelley makes a crucial point about contemporary scholarship and the perpetuation of a racialised discourse: it is highly unlikely that most contemporary scholars accept racist views such as white supremacy and anti-semitism, and in many cases (Crossan and Funk included) are openly opposed to racism and are openly supportive of liberal and civil rights agendas. The point is that scholarship functions in a context whereby racialised ideas have been unconsciously perpetuated. Others, including myself, have developed a related and complementary argument that scholars work in a broader cultural context and can unwittingly perpetuate widely used cultural stereotypes and unpleasant ideas. A good example of the significance of broad cultural influence can be seen in a comparison between Nazi German scholars and non-Nazi German scholars. Antisemitism was rife in late nineteenth-century and early twentieth-century Germany, ultimately leading to the rise of the Nazi party and the Holocaust. In this context openly Nazi and respectable New Testament scholars emerged. These included Walter Grundmann (a member of the Nazi party and supporting member of the SS), who argued that it was more likely Jesus would have been racially Aryan rather than Jewish. In Grundmann's case few would dispute that his committed antisemitism directly contributed to a reading that would rightly appear absurd today.

However, there were plenty of non-Nazi and anti-Nazi scholars of the time. Yet famous scholars such as Rudolf Bultmann and Ernst Käsemann were still talking about Judaism in negative terms as a religion of cold, harsh legalism and using 'the Jew' as a negative symbol. Even in the 1960s Käsemann was claiming that Paul was firing at 'the hidden Jew in all of us, at the man who validates rights and demands over against God on the basis of God's past dealings with him and to this extent is serving not God but an illusion'.[9] Here we have the broad cultural tradition of central European anti-Judaism still influencing scholars who were certainly not committed Nazis. Notably, in this context, German form criticism developed which, despite its major claims, had little interest in the life setting of the Gospel traditions, presumably because this would have involved locating these traditions within the everyday social setting of Palestinian and Diaspora Judaism (see Chapter 2).

In the 1970s the more overtly negative views of Jews and Judaism were undermined by the work of scholars such as Geza Vermes and E.P. Sanders. Vermes published the book *Jesus the Jew* in 1973 where he vigorously argued that the teaching of Jesus was to be located squarely within Jewish thought, most famously the thought and actions of charismatic holy men of the time. In 1977, E.P. Sanders published his hugely influential *Paul and Palestinian Judaism*, the bulk of which demolished the idea that Judaism was a cold, graceless religion. Scholars have since debated the details of the works of Vermes and Sanders but the *overtly* anti-Jewish sentiments of scholarship were in decline. One of the notable developments was a repeated stress on Jesus' 'Jewishness' and his relationship with Judaism. William Arnal has noted that there have been plenty of allegations of a 'non-Jewish Jesus' aimed at certain scholars who do not stress Jesus' religious identity. Arnal points out that this is unfair because no one these days denies Jesus was Jewish and that Jewish identity according to much scholarship is fixed and unchanging. Why couldn't a Jew in the ancient world stress (as certain Jews did) things about their identity other than certain 'religious' observances (e.g. Sabbath, circumcision, food laws) scholars have deemed to be normative for Judaism (see Chapter 3)? Two of Arnal's key reasons for the scholarly stress on fixed Jewish identity are a reaction against pre-1970s German scholarship and attempts to distance Christianity from the Holocaust, alongside socio-economic instability since the 1970s, fractured cultural identities, and globalisation. Scholarly descriptions of a fixed Jewish identity, Arnal argues, cannot be removed from such global trends.[10]

The present author has made complementary arguments about the rise of the stress on Jesus the Jew since the 1970s, developing from the 1967 Six Day War where Israel comprehensively dealt with her Arab enemies. The Six Day War brought about important strategic change and geographical accumulation in the area associated with Christian origins and Christian memory. This also brought about a marked attitude change, particularly in the US and the UK, heavily favouring Israel in the Middle East, combined with a marked rise in the *rhetoric* of philo-Semitism and vigorous interest in the Holocaust. This has been well documented in areas of popular culture, higher education, intellectual thought (including the New Left), popular evangelical thought (especially the spectacular rise of Christian Zionism), mass media, and politics, transcending the traditional party political divide(s), initially as a peculiarly American obsession with the ways in which Israel dealt with her enemies with relative ease in 1967 compared to America's ongoing problems in Vietnam (see Chapter 10).

Yet for all the scholarly emphasis on Jesus as Jewish, he is regularly reconstructed as something *better* than his background in 'Judaism' ('Judaism', of course, as defined by scholarship) or overrides one of the symbols constructed by scholarship to be central to defining Judaism (e.g. Sabbath, food, etc.). John Meier's multi-volume work on the historical Jesus, for instance, has a heavy stress on Jesus' 'Jewish context' but his Jesus remains, as the title of his series of books puts it, *A Marginal Jew*. I have argued that 'Jesus the Jew' is happily stressed in the sense that Jesus must be explicable in his Jewish context yet with the regular qualification that Jesus must also be in someway *different from* his Jewish context as constructed by scholarship. This approach is what I slightly polemically called a 'Jewish ... but not *that* Jewish' approach. Or as N.T. Wright, one of the worst offenders, describes his Jesus: 'a very Jewish Jesus who was nevertheless opposed to some high-profile features of first-century Judaism'.[11] For instance, Wright claims Jesus' views on family (e.g. Mark 3.21, 31–35; Matt. 8.21–22//Luke 9.59–60; Luke 14.26//Matt. 10.37) are extremely radical in comparison to early Jewish views yet, for all his praise about generalisations of Jewish family and ethnicity, he never refers to parallel Jewish texts which might contradict his theory (e.g. *Ant.* 3.87) but rather stays at the level of generalisation (e.g. family and ethnicity were very important in early Judaism) or refers to scholarly views with their roots in pre-1970s scholarship where Judaism was typically seen in negative terms![12]

A similar pattern, I argued, is found in different works on different New Testament texts and figures. This approach does not rule out the idea that the texts themselves did not or could not contain constructions over against Judaism (they certainly did – after all, Christianity did become a different religion) but rather this process is regularly carried out without proper attention paid to readily available parallel Jewish texts or imposed on texts where no evidence for construction over against Judaism is obviously present.

On the other hand, as with the discussion of reception history outside conventional scholarship, we do not necessarily have to think in terms of rights and wrongs of interpretation, or indeed moral rights and wrongs, but instead we could say that scholarship reflects dominant cultural trends which the strange stress on 'Jewishness' certainly does. On the issue of the implicit superiority of Jesus and/or Christianity in the studies of the New Testament, when we turn to the broader cultural context, at least in Anglo-American popular and political culture, I pointed out that we find that Jews, Judaism and Israel are also regularly portrayed as somehow inferior. For all the apparent love, Israel and Jews will have to convert or die according to certain Christian Zionist arguments while Israel is being used for political expediency in the case of political love. It seems New Testament scholarship is deeply embedded in the broader trends of its cultural context.

'The Arab World' in New Testament Scholarship

Kelley points out that 'racialization ... has a nasty habit of reasserting itself in the most unlikely of places – even in the work of those who are self-consciously opposed to racism and its effects'.[13] Perhaps no better example of this is that of the use of social sciences in contemporary scholarship where much of the agenda has been inspired by liberal-left politics and the avoidance of 'ethnocentrism', yet has ended up making some of the most unfortunate stereotypes about 'the Arab', 'the Middle East' and 'the Mediterranean'. In Chapter 2 we looked at the rise of social sciences since the 1970s; in this chapter we can now start explaining why social sciences have become increasingly popular.

Between approximately the 1930s and the 1970s, social scientific scholarship was largely absent from New Testament scholarship. This is best explained by the close association of Marxism and social sciences and the even closer association of Marxism and the rise of the atheist Soviet Union. Social sciences were, understandably enough, made less appealing to the Western Christian academic, and New Testament studies has had a long history of battles with Marxism, with some of the earlier pre-1930s proponents of investigating the social context of Christian origins (e.g. Adolf Deissmann) in open intellectual battle with Marxist scholars of Christianity (e.g. Karl Kautsky) over both the New Testament texts and the hearts and souls of the German working class.[14]

Why did social sciences return in such a major way in the 1970s? There are several reasons, such as protest movements in the 1960s, the expansion of sociology in higher education, declining church attendance numbers, perception of secularisation, and the emergence of prominent non-Marxist anthropological approaches to history. There are further reasons. Probably the most influential use of social sciences since 1980, and in particular cultural and social anthropology, has been that of Bruce Malina and the Context Group, an international (though largely North American) group of scholars dedicated to using models, such as those relating to honour and shame, to understand the social world of the New Testament (see Chapter 2). The emergence of this group of scholars, is part of a broader cultural shift in the 1970s whereby 'the Arab', 'the Middle East', and/or 'the Persian' became the object of intense scrutiny, particularly after oil crises, well-publicised hostage and hijacking crises, the Iranian Revolution and so on. It has been well documented that this cultural shift is to be found in party politics, mass media, popular culture, and higher education, gaining academic credibility in the work of Samuel Huntington and his famous 'clash of civilisations' thesis (typically 'the West' versus 'Islam') to explain the new post-Cold War global politics and emboldened in the 'war on terror'.

In this general context it is important to observe that Malina and many Context Group members describe the area of interest for understanding the New Testament as 'the Mediterranean' where evidence from the twentieth century can almost be readily used as much as evidence from the first century to describe the apparently shared features of the Mediterranean. Significantly, it is not difficult to find examples in the work of Malina and some Context Group members where 'the Mediterranean' notably overlaps with the designation 'the Middle East' (and this includes the *modern* Middle East). Notice the following example from Malina: 'since in Mediterranean perspective all Americans form an undifferentiated ethnic ego mass, it would be impossible for a Middle Easterner to view the kidnapping of a single American as a random act ... any group member equally well represents the whole group'.[15] Here Malina drifts from 'Mediterranean perspective' to 'Middle Easterner' when effectively talking about the same group (and not to mention the stereotypical image of the hostage taker). Other notable features of related work include outlining the differences between the Mediterranean and North America, between the apparently collective culture or the Mediterranean and the apparently individual culture of North America. As this may imply, it becomes too easy to descend into unfortunate generalisations about Arabs and the Middle East. A clear example of New Testament scholarship echoing cultural trends is when Malina positively quotes the work of older scholars of the Arab world, Raphael Patai and Hans Tütsch, on *contemporary* Arabs to analyse *ancient* Mediterraneans. The following is from Malina's book on Jesus and the Gospels:

> ... personalization of problems goes so far in the Arab countries that even material, technical difficulties accompanying the adoption of elements of Western civilization are considered as resulting from human malevolence and felt to be a *humiliation* ... Where the Arab encounters an obstacle he imagines that an enemy is hidden. Proud peoples with a weak 'ego structure' tend to interpret difficulties on their life path as personal humiliations and get entangled in *endless lawsuits* or throw themselves into the arms of *extremist political movements*. *A defeat in elections*, a risk that every politician must face in a democracy, appears to be such a

humiliation that an Arab can thereby be induced without further ceremony to take up arms against the victor and the legal government ... [16]
[italics original]

Notice how issues of democracy and themes which came to further prominence in the 'war on terror' are never far from the surface ... in a book on
Jesus and the Gospels!

A more subtle example of how such concerns have had an impact on interpretation is Context Group member Richard Rohrbaugh's interpretation of the
famous parable of the prodigal son (Luke 15.11–32). Rohrbaugh gives his
standard criticism that Individualist/Western/American culture is different
from Collective/Mediterranean/Middle Eastern culture, and dismisses the use
of modern psychology, apparently dominant in 'Western biblical exegesis'. On
the parable itself, we find an argument grounded in grand differences of 'civilisations' and an ignoring of possible local diversities and 'backgrounds' and
textual detail. Rohrbaugh fires at the 'traditional' interpretation of the parable
as a parable about repentance. This supposed misunderstanding is, according
to Rohrbaugh, 'due to the usual preunderstandings of Western soteriology
[views of salvation]'.[17]

Yet, against Rohrbaugh, this criticism simply ignores crucial points through
its sweeping generalisations about different cultures. For instance, the parable
itself is preceded by two parables explicitly concerning repentance, a theme
picked up in the parable of the prodigal son. Whoever was responsible for this
clear connection with the theme of repentance shows that *someone* in the
ancient world did and someone who could not be guilty of Western biblical
exegesis. Given that this parable is located in what might reasonably be
deemed a Jewish setting, and given Rohrbaugh's own concern for the socio-
cultural setting, it might be expected that Jewish views should be investigated.
Rohrbaugh does not do this but, in addition to repentance being a theme in
Jewish literature from the Hebrew Bible/Old Testament onward, there is a
well-known parallel to the parable of the prodigal son in rabbinic literature. In
this parallel, a son returns to a king and the message is explicitly said to concern repentance (*Deut. R.* 2.24). Interestingly, in there are plenty of Jewish
texts whereby repentance is described as 'returning', precisely what the boy
does with his father in the parable of the prodigal son. Rohrbaugh's polarising
'us' and 'them' method excludes this evidence almost by definition and all this
evidence is not modern Western imposition but ancient evidence of direct
relevance.

Are New Testament Scholars a Threat to Anyone?

These sorts of critiques of modern scholarship are in line with arguments
inside and outside of biblical studies whereby scholarship and higher education
play a supportive role in state and private power.[18] It could be argued, however,

that New Testament studies produces work profoundly critical of Empire and profoundly critical of the present dominant superpower, the US. There are, after all, books and articles by N.T. Wright, Ched Myers, Richard Horsley, John Dominic Crossan, Warren Carter, among others, all critical of imperialism and often not too subtly critical of the US government. One of the most famous recent debates at the major annual meeting of the Society of Biblical Literature, and available online,[19] was between Wright and John Barclay as part of the Paul and Empire group. Barclay, not unlike Badiou (to whom he refers), and not necessarily in stark contrast to Wright, argued that Paul was subversive not through coded critiques of Rome itself but through indifference, with Rome as nothing more than a bit player in a grander cosmic drama. Wright, however, pushed his well-known anti-imperial and anti-Roman reading through reference to, among other things, competing titles and terms such as 'Son of God', 'Saviour' and 'Good News', and Christ as a counter to, and parody of, the idea of the Emperor as deity. Wright's published work is a goldmine of quotations on issues relating to radicalism and power in New Testament studies. On writing about Jesus' bodily resurrection, Wright claims that 'in the real world ... the tyrants and bullies (including intellectual and cultural tyrants and bullies) try to rule by force, only to discover that in order to do so they have to quash all rumours of resurrection, rumours that would imply that their greatest weapons, death and deconstruction, are not after all omnipotent'.[20]

Surely the discipline allows criticism of the powerful! Well, yes and no. Criticism there certainly is but at the same time the radicalism is neutralised and tamed. Is an English bishop (Wright is the present Bishop of Durham) writing on the resurrection really a threat to any tyrant? Do tyrants really care? Even though his books sell extremely well, it seems unlikely, does it not? Is a radical Paul or a radical Jesus really a threat to imperialism *now*? It seems unlikely, at least in the sense of academics writing about such matters in learned books. Noam Chomsky spoke similarly of what is perceived as the radical left in universities. He argued that it is possible to enter academia and be radical as long as the questions asked remain at least relatively incomprehensible or the dangerous questions of contemporary politics are not systematically addressed head on and clearly. The scholar may feel like they are not selling out by acting as, for instance, a Marxist economist, but in reality the individual has been neutralised and can keep working without being much of a danger to anyone.[21] This seems to be a similar process to what is happening with the radical Paul and Jesus scholarship. By pushing criticism of imperialism back to the days of the Romans, the effectiveness of criticism of the present is almost nullified.

Where there is a danger is when people follow their convictions. Liberation Theology is the most obvious example. Liberation Theology can describe the liberation of any oppressed group but it has become associated with Latin American theologians (especially, but not exclusively, Catholic) who put their theology into practice by siding with workers and destitute people against the powers of oppression. Liberation theologians have been controversial figures within the Catholic Church hierarchy but also dangerous figures for those in power, including a number of figures being assassinated. As Chomsky puts it,

> In the 1980s, the United States fought a vicious war in Central America primarily against the Catholic Church – and that means European priests, not just priests from indigenous origins – because the Church had started working for what they called 'the preferential option for the poor,' there-fore they had to go. In fact, when Americas Watch did their wrap up study on the 1980s, they pointed out that it was a decade framed by the murder of the Archbishop in 1980 and the murder of six Jesuit intellec-tuals in 1989, both in El Salvador ... the Catholic Church became the main target of the U.S. attacks in Central America because there was a radical and very conscious change in critically important sectors of the Church (including dominant elements among the Latin American bishops) who recognized that for hundreds of years it had been a Church of the rich and the oppressors ... they decided to finally become a Church in part devoted to the liberation of the poor – and they immediately fell under attack.[22]

Final Remarks

The above includes just some (again, only some) of the ways we can now read New Testament scholars and scholarship. Of course, sometimes political, historical and social contexts can interfere too much with scholarship, as we saw most obviously in the cases of the Nazi Jesus and an obsession with 'the Arab' and 'the Middle East' in certain scholarly quarters. But perspective and historical context does not automatically make readings wrong and can pro-vide insights. For a start, it is difficult to see the emphasis on Jesus as a Jew as a bad thing, especially in contrast to some of the views of Judaism coming out of scholarship prior to the 1970s, and even if this emphasis has been abused. We also do not have to force the moral question: reading the history of scho-larship could be like reading earliest Christian history, that is, trying to explain why certain intellectual and theological trends happened when and where they did.

This does not mean, of course, that any of us are immune from cultural, religious, political, etc. influences (on the contrary!), though it may not be so easy to analyse ourselves. But it is worth finishing this chapter by at least trying to turn some of this analysis on the author. In Chapter 4, the approach of cultural historian Robert Darnton was developed in reading the death of John the Baptist in Mark 6.17–29. Is the approach developed from Darnton concerning the understanding of alien cultures helpful? Does this approach also over-emphasise the cultural difference between 'them' and 'us' rather than help us understand shared values? And are there contemporary political and cultural ramifications on over-emphasising the differences between 'them' and 'us'? Alternatively, could we suggest that analysis of the ancient cultural context does in fact give us insight into our own culture, particularly the stereotyping of women as nagging wives and capable of misleading men with sexual charm? Are they not common enough contemporary themes? Or again is there a danger in emphasising shared 'negatives'? None of these questions makes a Darnton-inspired reading historically right or wrong but these questions are worth asking if we are interested in the impact of our interpretations. Supposedly 'right' readings can be dangerous too.

Summary

Reception history can, of course, include analyses of the reception of the biblical texts among biblical scholars and the historical and cultural influences on scholarship. Some of these have long been noted, most famously the influence of nineteenth-century nationalism on the quest for the historical Jesus. Increasingly, there is awareness of the ways in which ideas of race and antisemitism, alongside the rise of Nazism and fascism in the early twentieth century, had disturbing influences on New Testament scholarship. Other more recent historical contexts are now being seen as significant influences on the history of scholarship, from the Cold War onward. The turn towards more rhetorically positive views of Judaism is also to be seen as part of a broader cultural turn to Israel and a more open concern for the Holocaust since 1967. Similarly, the strange emergence of 'the Arab world' in New Testament scholarship is part of an American and European interest since the 1970s. It seems as if New Testament scholarship finds it difficult to break away from the language of power and, despite protests to the contrary, it seems as if scholarship only becomes a threat to power when it breaks free from its institutionalised settings and becomes active in the world.

Key Words

Clash of Civilisations: A view which has become associated with the American political thinker Samuel Huntington which views the post-Cold War world as being characterised by potentially violent culture clashes between major civilisations, especially, Huntington argued, between the West and Islam.

'Great Man' view of history: An approach to history which emphasises the importance of the great individual (traditionally a man) in bringing about historical change and/or representative of a given culture or nation. This emphasis is usually carried out at the expense of broader historical and social trends.

Liberation Theology: A theological tradition which has emphasised the role of siding with the oppressed and has become associated with active support in class and colonial conflicts in Latin America but has also become associated more generally with other liberation movements such as feminism.

Further Reading

Blanton, W., *Displacing Christian Origins: Philosophy, Secularity, and the New Testament*, Chicago: Chicago University Press, 2007.

Crossley, J.G., *Jesus in an Age of Terror: Scholarly Projects for a New American Century*, London and Oakville: Equinox, 2008.

Georgi, D., 'The Interest in Life of Jesus Theology as a Paradigm to the Social History of Biblical Criticism', *Harvard Theological Review* 85 (1992), pp. 51–83.

Kelley, S., *Racializing Jesus: Race, Ideology and the Formation of Modern Biblical Scholarship*, London and New York: Routledge, 2002.

Moxnes, H., 'The Historical Jesus: From Master Narrative to Cultural Context', *Biblical Theology Bulletin* 28, 1998, pp. 135–49.

Moxnes, H., W. Blanton and J.G. Crossley, eds, *Jesus beyond Nationalism: Constructing the Historical Jesus in a Period of Cultural Complexity*, London: Equinox, 2009.

Vander Stichele, C., and T. Penner, eds, *Her Master's Tools? Feminist and Postcolonial Engagements of Historical-Critical Discourse*, Atlanta: SBL; Leiden: Brill, 2005.

Part Four

Extracts from New Testament Scholarship

Chapter 12

Scholars Reading the New Testament

Justin Meggitt on Living Standards in the Ancient World

Clothing

Clothing is an expensive item in pre-industrial economies and the first century was no exception to this rule. The stripping of the victim in the Good Samaritan provides an indication of its high cost, as does the logion recorded in Matt. 5:40//Luke 6:29 ... , and the division of Jesus' clothes amongst the soldiers at the crucifixion in all four accounts of the passion. The existence of numerous second-hand clothes markets throughout the Empire gives us another indication of its relative expense. The importance given to clothing as a means of articulating socio-economic distinctions in antiquity also suggests that it necessitated significant financial outlay.

It is not surprising, therefore, that the expense of clothing was a constant source of anguish for the poor, who tried to get as much as possible out of their vestments by patching and sharing what little they could afford. The experience of having inadequate clothing seems to have been common: Micyllus complains of being 'barefoot and half naked' in Lucian's *Cataplus*, and the poor in his *Saturnalia* voice a similar grievance. Lazarus, likewise had little in the way of clothes (Luke 16.19–31) ... To dream of short clothing presaged poverty in Artemidorus' *Oneirocritica*.

Juvenal's vivid description of the clothing of the protagonist of his third satire is particularly significant:

> ... the poor man gives food and occasion for jest if his cloak be torn and dirty, if his toga be a little soiled, if one of his shoes gapes where the leather is split, or if some fresh stitches of coarse thread reveal where not one, but many a rent has been patched.

Juvenal is not here describing the appearance of a beggar but that of a man with sufficient funds to keep a number of slaves: therefore, even allowing for the satirist's comical exaggeration, it is fair to say that the clothing possessed by most of the urban population was meagre. In the area of clothing, as with food, the non-élite city dwellers lived close to subsistence, if not below it.

Housing

Not only are we faced with the usual dearth of evidence from literary sources as we attempt to reconstruct something of the norms of non-élite housing in the first century, but, as MacMullen has observed, 'archaeology fails us, for no one has sought fame through the excavation of a slum'. The study of Graeco-Roman urban housing has tended to concentrate on prestigious *domus*. This is not entirely the fault of the ideological interests of the excavators as the flimsiness of most non-élite housing militates against its long-term survival, but, nevertheless, we must not allow our knowledge of the housing of the affluent few to influence our picture of the housing of the impoverished many.

The poorest had no housing as such and slept in the open air. Those slightly more fortunate lived in tombs, in spaces under the stairs of apartment houses ..., cellars and vaults, below bridges and theatre awnings, or in taverns. Some concentrated their own habitations, lean-tos ... built against the walls of permanent buildings, between the columns of porticoes, or beneath aqueducts, or dwelt in 'shanties' ... , outside the city proper ... and like their modern counterparts, those that erected such shelters lived in constant fear of having them torn down by the city authorities. The marginally more economically successful would inhabit a room in an *insula* or shared house. An *insula* was an apartment block and was common throughout the Empire (though not universal). Whilst the lower floors could be quite spacious and were sometimes rented by members of the élite the higher floors were progressively more sub-divided and more densely occupied. The highest floors consisted of tiny wooden *cellae*, which were rented on a daily basis. Such rooms offered little more shelter than the lean-tos, as we can see in Juvenal's description of the hapless Codrus, who lived in the roof of a block. The hellish nature of life in these cramped *insulae*, composed of 'chambers piled upon chambers', was proverbial. Tertullian, for example, belittled the Valentinians' conception of heaven by comparing it with such tower blocks. Conflagration and collapse were common. The desire for profit led to the construction of extra, precarious wooden floors, despite the efforts of Emperors to limit the height of such buildings. 'Cowboy builders' were rife ... Shared houses, which were far more common than has traditionally been supposed, had many characteristics in common with these *insulae*. Certainly conditions within them seemed to have been, on occasion, equally squalid and overcrowding was usual.

The *tabernae* (workshops) of some artisans were also a significant source of housing and within these small units the artisans, their families, and slaves, lived and worked. These buildings tended to be very modest and Hock is definitely inaccurate in assuming that each could hold 6–12 craftspeople ... Packer's estimate of an average of four people per unit seems much more likely.

Nearly all urban dwellers lived in these lean-tos, 'shanties', *insulae, tabernae,* and shared houses, or slept rough in the street. Given the awful conditions of overcrowding, shoddy construction, and lack of facilities we have just sketched, we can say, with some justification, that nearly the entire *plebs urbana* lived in 'appalling slums', as Brunt maintains ...

In their experience of housing, as well as their access to food and clothing, the Graeco-Roman non-élite suffered a subsistence or near subsistence life. Their labour, if they were lucky enough to actually have any, did not allow them to attain sufficient material resources for their lot to be otherwise.

[Justin J. Meggitt, *Paul, Poverty and Survival* (Edinburgh: T&T Clark, 1998), pp. 60–67, reprinted with the permission of Justin Meggitt and T&T Clark/Continuum]

Stephen Moore on Postcolonialism and the Book of Revelation

The Book of Mimicry

The phenomenon of mimicry is endemic to Revelation. The Book's representation of the Roman imperial order is essentially parodic, as we have noted, and parody is a species of mimicry: it mimics in order to mock. Do Bhabha's pronouncements on colonial mimicry apply, then, to Revelation's parodic strategy? Yes and no, it seems to me. In contrast to the scenario adduced by Bhabha in which systemic mimicry of the agents and institutions of imperialism perpetually threatens to teeter over into parody or mockery, Revelation presents us with a reverse scenario in which parody or mockery of the imperial order constantly threatens to topple over into mimicry, imitation, and replication. Revelation's implicit claim, as commentators never tire of telling us, is that Roman imperial court ceremonial, together with the imperial court itself, are but pale imitations – diabolical imitations, indeed – of the heavenly throne room and the heavenly liturgy. But commentators also routinely note that the heavenly court and liturgy in Revelation are themselves modeled in no small part on the Roman imperial court and cult (recall our earlier ruminations on Rev. 4–5) – which means in effect that the 'heavenly' order in Revelation is busily engaged in imitating or mimicking the 'earthly' order, notwithstanding the book's own implicit charge that the earthly is merely a counterfeit copy of the heavenly.

The latter observation borders on the obvious perhaps. Yet the obvious is not without interest in this instance. Revelation's attempted sleight of hand ensnares it in a debilitating contradiction. Christians are enjoined to mimic Jesus, who in turn mimics his Father ('To the one who conquers I will give a place with me on my throne, just as I myself conquered and sat down with my

Father on his throne,' 3.21), who, in effect, mimics the Roman Emperor, who himself (at least as represented in the imperial cult) is a mimetic composite of assorted royal and divine stereotypes. In Revelation, Christian authority inheres in imitation ('To everyone who conquers and continues to do my works to the end, I will give authority [*exousia*] over the nations, to rule them with an iron rod [cf. 12.5, in which the same Psalmic phrase is applied to Jesus himself] ... even as I also received authority from my Father', 2.26; cf. 20.4). But if the Roman imperial order is the ultimate object of imitation in Revelation, then, in accordance with the book's own implicit logic, it remains the ultimate authority, despite the book's explicit attempts to unseat it.

Mimicry and Monstrosity

On Revelation's own account, of course, it is Rome, the sea-beast, that is the consummate mimic – the mimic monster – with its seven heads and ten horns (13.1; 17.3), in imitation of the great red dragon (12.3, explicitly identified as Satan in 12.9 and 20.2), whose own appearance is in turn an imitation of various Near Eastern mythic prototypes. Furthermore, the unholy trinity of Satan, sea-beast, and 'false prophet' (for the latter epithet, see 16.13; 19.20; 20.10) mimics the holy trinity (strictly lower case, of course; we are not yet within spitting distance of Nicea) of God, Lamb, and prophetic spirit (for the latter, see 2.7, 11, 17, 29; 3.6, 13, 22; cf. 1.10; 4.2; 17.3; 21.10). In addition to the general structural parallel of two antithetical triads, certain characteristics ascribed to the sea-beast in particular mirror those ascribed to Jesus or God: note especially the Christlike 'resurrection' attributed to the sea-beast in 13.3, 14, also the thrice-repeated declaration that 'it was and is not and is to come' (which crops up twice in 17.18 and again in 17.11, in variant forms), parodying the thrice repeated acclamation of God as he 'who is and who was and who is to come' (1.4, 8; 4.8). Also notable is the depiction of the land-beast as also a lamb-beast: 'it had two horns like a lamb' (13.11). Revelation is engaging in subtle mockery of Satan and his elect agents here, it would seem, implying that they are best seen as distorted reflections of God and his elect agents.

Yet, as we have just observed, Revelation's deity cannot function as anchor for this mimetic chain, but is instead merely another link in it, because modeled on the Roman Emperor – and we have not even begun to consider the extent to which this deity is also a composite copy of Ezekiel's deity, Daniel's deity, and so on, themselves in turn ultimately constructed on the model of the ancient Near Eastern monarch. If the Roman imperial court is, in Revelation, merely a dim, distorted reflection of the heavenly court, the latter is itself merely a magnified reflection of the former and sundry other earthly courts, so that the seer's vision of heaven occurs in a mimetic hall of mirrors.

Again, this observation smacks of the obvious, and as such falls short of profundity. Yet the 'obvious' does not always command acknowledgement.

The difficulty of effectively exiting empire by attempting to turn imperial ideology against itself is regularly underestimated, it seems to me, by those who acclaim Revelation for decisively breaking the self-perpetuating cycle of empire. To my mind, Revelation is emblematic of the difficulty of using the emperor's tools to dismantle the emperor's palace. The seer storms out of the main gates of the imperial palace, wrecking tools in hand, only to be surreptitiously swept back in through the rear entrance, having been deftly relieved of his tools at the threshold.

[Stephen D. Moore, *Empire and Apocalypse: Postcolonialism and the New Testament* (Sheffield: Sheffield Phoenix Press, 2006), pp. 112–14, reprinted with the permission of Stephen Moore and Sheffield Phoenix Press]

Markus Bockmuehl on Reception/Effective History

My first suggestion is that New Testament scholars explicitly adopt the history of the influence of the New Testament as an integral and indeed inescapable part of the exercise in which they are engaged. Among the numerous benefits of this move would be a more historically embedded understanding of not just the background but also the foreground (so to speak) of the New Testament, including its reception and understanding in the patristic period and beyond. Instead of perpetually going behind the text, the whole battery of historical-critical and synchronic tools could be applied to approaching the New Testament from its meaning and function 'in front of the text', where it was in fact heard and heeded (or ignored).

New Testament studies on this view could find a focus in the study of the New Testament as not just a historical but also a historic document. Its place in history clearly comprises not just an original setting but a history of lived responses to the historical and eternal realities to which it testifies. The meaning of a text is in practice deeply intertwined with its own tradition of hearing and heeding, interpretation and performance. Only the totality of that tradition can begin to give a view of the New Testament's real historical footprint, the vast majority of which is to be found in reading communities that, for all their diversity, place themselves deliberately 'within the living tradition of the church, whose first concern is fidelity to the revelation attested by the Bible' [Fitzmyer]. And conversely, that footprint, for good and for ill, can in turn serve as a valuable guide to the scope of the text's meaning and truth …

It is encouraging to note that increasing numbers of scholars are recognising this concern as desideratum for the future prospering of New Testament studies, even if in both method and substance we surely have a long way to go. There is still much scope for fresh research here, of a kind that would build bridges both internally between synchronic and diachronic methods and also externally between biblical studies and historical theology as well as other disciplines. 'Effective history' (*Wirkungsgeschichte*) could offer a shared and focusing interest for subdisciplines ranging all the way from textual criticism to narrative criticism, from biblical theology to liberationist deconstruction. In the process it would enrich and cross-pollinate a great deal of insular academic discussion – providing a broader and less ephemeral base by reviving long-forgotten insights of exegesis and application, but without being forced to give hostages to either a one-dimensional 'history of the victors' or a revisionist veneration of all that was supposedly suppressed.

It is also worth considering whether a concerted move of biblical scholars into the area of effective history might not in turn persuade *systematic theologians* to think a little harder about the formal relationship of their dis-cipline to biblical studies. In this regard, one might want to initiate a sustained dialogue about Eberhard Jüngel's frequent dictum that systematic theology is nothing if not consistent exegesis. If that has any truth to it, what might be the effect on biblical studies of reconceiving both contemporary and historical theology primarily in terms of the interpretation and application of Scripture? Critically applied, *Wirkungsgeschichte* offers a hermeneutically sensitive and powerful instrument for interpreting both the reader and his or her text.

On a more pragmatic political note, effective history would at least enable New Testament scholars to give some substance to the rather hackneyed claim that their discipline matters because the New Testament is a canonical document of great influence.

It is of course true that to some degree the same hermeneutical diversity and incongruity observed in conventional New Testament studies would inevitably beset a study of *Wirkungsgeschichte* as well. We would not suddenly arrive at splendid agreement about the true meaning of the text in history. The effect, say, of Romans 13 in subsequent political thought, or of the Fourth Gospel in conciliar Christology, is by no means free from the sorts of hermeneutical, literary, and political ambiguities that affect the study of the New Testament itself. But the polyvalency of our findings would not as such invalidate the project. By agreeing to include in our remit the question of how the New Testament texts have in fact been read and lived, we would at least be engaged in a common exploration that would by definition embrace historical and reader-response concerns alike. Properly defined, such a study could in turn provide a commonly accessible subject matter and pool of insights for the different exegetical and hermeneutical approaches that are always likely to co-exist.

The need for such a pursuit of effective history is in fact coming to be recognised by scholars from a great variety of theological presuppositions ... The Evangelisch-Katholischer Kommentar series ... although it remains unclear if its conception ultimately makes the text's effective history the handmaiden of historical criticism or if the two stand in some other, more constructive relationship. In English-speaking scholarship it is good to see such issues at last coming to diverse expression in the recently inaugurated Blackwell Bible Commentaries, with their emphasis on reception history. At the same time, much systematic reflection about more and less appropriate *methods* of writing *Wirkungsgeschichte* will be necessary if work on these welcome initiatives is not to produce mere 'scrapbooks' of effects, a cacophonous post-modern catalogue of 'voices' without communication, in dialogue with only themselves.

[Markus Bockmuehl, *Seeing the Word: Refocusing New Testament Study* (Grand Rapids: Baker Academic, 2006), pp. 64–68, reprinted with the permission of Markus Bockmuehl and Baker Academic]

Shawn Kelley on Rudolf Bultmann and Reading Scholarship in Context

Behind Bultmann's theology one can detect the longing for a pure Western essence untainted by the corrupting spirits of the East or of Rome. Bultmann neither invented this longing nor is his attraction to it unique. I have argued that this longing permeates much modern thought, both in philosophy and in New Testament scholarship. To put the matter more precisely, I have argued that this longing is infused in the discourse that underlies some aspects of both philosophy and modern New Testament scholarship. There is, therefore, nothing unusual about finding this particular longing (for purity untainted by the alien) in the work of a biblical scholar who is deeply influenced by the history of his own discipline and by the philosophy of Martin Heidegger. The situation is made more complex, however, by the unfortunate fact that Bultmann's career exists in the shadow of Nazism. Much of Bultmann's writings, including his seminal essay on demythology, appear during the Nazi era. Furthermore, his own theological work is deeply and self-consciously influenced by a philosopher who was also a Nazi. Given the historical context out of which he was writing, it seems important to ask about the interaction between Bultmann's theology and National Socialism. Throughout this book I have tried to distinguish between racist intentions and racialised discourse. Once again I find this distinction helpful in posing the particular question of Bultmann's relationship to Nazism.

It is important to begin the discussion by recognising that Bultmann, unlike Heidegger, never flirted with Nazism and was, instead, a member of the Confessing Church. After the war it was commonly asserted that the Confessing Church actively resisted Nazi racism and oppression. I am persuaded by the revisionist view that the Confessing Church was far more ambiguous in its attitudes towards Jews and towards the regime ... Even if one accepts these scholarly revisions, as I do, this does not change the fact that, when faced with a choice, Bultmann did not choose Nazism. Unlike many intellectuals, Bultmann was not a supporter of the National Socialist 'renewal' of the German *Volk*. Furthermore, Bultmann, who rarely talked about politics, did make a series of statements critical of National Socialism. Bultmann's postwar statement, made after the regime's many atrocities had come to light, was far more critical than the statement of 1933. At the same time, his statement of 2 May 1933, made the day after Heidegger officially joined the Party … , stands in striking contrast to the numerous public statements made by intellectuals and religious leaders in support of the regime … He spoke out against the mistreatment of Jews … , against nationalism's excesses … , and against the dismissal of non-Aryan Christian ministers … He was never tempted to join the German Christian movement, which radically deJudaised the Bible, the hymns, and the Churches … Instead he was, from the beginning, deeply concerned that such a folkish religion … would replace or dilute Christianity … After the war he complained that the regime had oppressed both Jews and Christians … and had been hostile to scientific research … He also argued that blood and soil racism reduces humanity to the level of the beast … and that totalitarianism is radically opposed to the principles of human freedom … National Socialism took the most radical position possible on a variety of issues. There is no evidence that Bultmann himself was personally attracted to their fanatical radicalism, their rabid antisemitism or their unequivocal nationalism.

If the question is 'Was Bultman a Nazi?', then the answer is an emphatic 'No'. This does not mean, however, that he is diametrically opposed to everything they represent. There is a distinct ambiguity that comes through in his discussions of these issues, even in his criticisms of Nazism. So, for example, he argues that nationalism is a perfectly legitimate issue, but that the absolute nationalism of Nazism threatens to turn the people into an idol. Christians owe allegiance to the state and the *Volk*, but it should be ambiguous and critical … This framework leads him to ask the following question, 'Is our present struggle on behalf of the idea of nationality … a struggle for an abstraction or for something concrete?' … This question seems to confirm Baranowski's conclusion that while the Confessing Church wanted to defend itself against the encroachment of the Aryanised German Christian movement, it 'was equally concerned to avoid the appearance of a sectarian breakaway …'

Let us also look more closely at his defence of the Jews … while he is speaking out against unjust antisemitic actions he acknowledges the legitimacy of the Jewish problem and he accepts the need for national renewal and for the struggle for the German *Volk*. In other words, he seems to separate the violent antisemitism, which he blames on defamations, from the policies of the government, from Hitler himself, and from the Nazi revolution. The implication is that something important is going on but it is in danger of being transformed into something ugly. Although there is no evidence that he supported legalised antisemitism, he limits his criticisms to antisemitic actions without speaking out against the antisemitic laws that had already been promulgated. My point is not to criticise Bultmann's actions from the safety of my own study. His statement on behalf of Jews was both courageous and, given the spirit of the times, highly unusual. Instead I wish to emphasise that when Bultmann thinks about the issues and antisemitism, he necessarily employs the same intellectual resources that he employs in his theology and his exegesis. These intellectual resources, which emerge from a discourse which is racialised, limit his ability to repudiate, in a comprehensive manner, the central tenets of Nazi racism and antisemitism. His intentions are praiseworthy, but his intellectual resources severely limit the kind of critique he is able to launch.

[Shawn Kelley, *Racializing Jesus: Race, Ideology and the Formation of Modern Biblical Scholarship* (London and New York: Routledge, 2002), pp. 154–57, reprinted with the permission of Shawn Kelley and Routledge]

Notes

2 Reading Historical Documents Historically

1 D.C. Allison, *The New Moses: A Matthean Typology*, Minneapolis: Fortress, 1993; R.D. Aus, *The Death, Burial, and Resurrection of Jesus, and the Death, Burial, and Translation of Moses in Judaic Tradition*, Lanham: University Press of America, 2008.

2 J.M. Robinson, P. Hoffman and J.S. Kloppenborg, eds, *The Critical Edition of Q. Synopsis, including the Gospels of Matthew and Luke, Mark and Thomas, with English, German and French Translations of Q and Thomas*, Leuven: Peeters, 2000.

3 M. Casey, *Jesus of Nazareth: An Independent Historian's Account of his Life and Teachings*, London and New York, forthcoming 2010, chapter 2.

4 A very brief introductory selection might include B.H. Streeter, *The Four Gospels: A Study in Origins*, New York: Macmillan, 1930; R.H. Stein, *The Synoptic Problem: An Introduction*, Grand Rapids: Baker, 1987; E.P. Sanders and M. Davies, *Studying the Synoptic Gospels*, London: SCM, 1989; M. Goodacre, *The Synoptic Problem: A Way through a Maze*, London and New York: T&T Clark, 2001; D. Burkett, *Rethinking the Gospel Sources: from Proto-Mark to Mark*, London and New York: T&T Clark, 2004.

5 R.A. Culpepper, *The Anatomy of the Fourth Gospel: A Study in Literary Design*, Philadelphia: Fortress, 1983.

6 See, for example, S.D. Moore, *Poststructuralism and the New Testament: Derrida and Foucault at the Foot of the Cross*, Minneapolis: Fortress, 1994; A.K.M. Adam, ed., *A Handbook of Postmodern Biblical Interpretation*, St Louis: Chalice, 2000; Y. Sherwood, ed., *Derrida's Bible (Reading a Page of Scripture with a Little Help from Derrida)*, New York: Palgrave Macmillan, 2004; S.D. Moore, 'A Modest Manifesto for New Testament Literary Criticism: How to Interface with a Literary Studies that is Post-Literary, Post-Theoretical, and Post-Methodological', *Biblical Interpretation* 15, 2007, 1–25.

7 R.M. Fowler, *Let the Reader Understand: Reader-Response Criticism and the Gospel of Mark*, Minneapolis: Fortress, 1991, p. 132, n. 8; D. Margeurat and Y. Bourquin, *How to Read Bible Stories*, London: SCM, 1999, pp. 136–37.

8 J.G. Gager, *Kingdom and Community: The Social World of Early Christianity*, Englewood Cliffs: Prentice-Hall, 1975.

9 See, for example, B. Malina, *The New Testament World: Insights from Cultural Anthropology*, Louisville: WJK, 1983.

10 P.F. Esler, *Community and Gospel in Luke-Acts: The Social and Political Motivations of Lucan Theology*, Cambridge: CUP, 1987, p. 76. For criticisms see E.P. Sanders, 'Jewish Association with Gentiles and Galatians 2.11–14' in R.T. Fortna and B.R.

Gaventa, eds, *The Conversation Continues: Studies in Paul and John in Honor of J. Louis Martyn*, Nashville: Abingdon, 1990, pp. 170–88 (esp. p. 178); J.G. Crossley, 'Defining History', in J.G. Crossley and C. Karner, eds, *Writing History, Constructing Religion*, Aldershot: Ashgate, 2005, pp. 9–29 (20–21).

11 M. Bockmuehl, 'Review of Malina, *New Testament World*, third edition', *BMCR*, 2002.04.19, available at http://ccat.sas.upenn.edu/bmcr/2002/2002-04-19.html last accessed 10 Sept. 2009.

12 R. Stark, *The Rise of Christianity: A Sociologist Reconsiders History*, Princeton: Princeton UP, 1996.

13 J.T. Sanders, *Charisma, Converts, Competitors: Societal and Sociological Factors in the Success of Early Christianity*, London, SCM, 2000; J.G. Crossley, *Why Christianity Happened: A Sociohistorical Account of Christian Origins*, Louisville: WJK, 2006.

14 See further C. Osiek and M.Y. MacDonald with J.H. Tulloch, *A Woman's Place: House Churches in Earliest Christianity*, Minneapolis: Fortress, 2006, pp. 221–23.

3 Contemporary Historical Approaches to the New Testament

1 W. Arnal, *The Symbolic Jesus: Historical Scholarship, Judaism and the Construction of Contemporary Identity*, London & Oakville: Equinox, 2005.

2 N.T. Wright, *Jesus and the Victory of God*, London: SPCK, 1996, p. 79, n. 233.

3 J. Økland, *Women in Their Place: Paul and the Corinthian Discourse of Gender and Sanctuary Space*, London & New York: T&T Clark/Continuum, 2004, pp. 46–47.

4 C. Vander Stichele and T. Penner, *Contextualizing Gender in Early Christian Discourse: Thinking beyond Thecla*, London: T&T Clark/Continuum, 2009, pp. 4–5.

5 H. Moxnes, *Putting Jesus in His Place: A Radical Vision of Household and Kingdom*, Louisville: WJK, 2003.

6 '//' means parallel (text).

7 P.A. Harland, *Associations, Synagogues, and Congregations: Claiming a Place in Ancient Mediterranean Society*, Minneapolis: Fortress, 2003.

8 E. Said, *Culture and Imperialism*, London: Vintage, 1993, p. 8.

9 S.D. Moore, *Empire and Apocalypse: Postcolonialism and the New Testament*, Sheffield: Sheffield Phoenix Press, 2006, pp. 13–14.

10 For example, C. Myers, *Binding the Strong Man: A Political Reading of Mark's Story of Jesus*, Maryknoll: Orbis, 1988; H.C. Waetjen, *A Reordering of Power: A Sociopolitical Reading of Mark's Gospel*, Minneapolis: Fortress, 1989; T.B. Liew, *Politics of Parousia: Reading Mark Inter(con)textually*, Leiden: Brill, 1999; R.A. Horsley, *Hearing the Whole Story: The Politics of Plot in Mark's Gospel*, Louisville: WJK, 2001; S. Samuel, *A Postcolonial Reading of Mark's Story of Jesus*, New York and London: T&T Clark, 2007; C.I.D. Joy, *Mark and its Subalterns: A Hermeneutical Paradigm for a Postcolonial Context*, London: Equinox, 2008.

11 Myers, *Binding the Strong Man*, pp. 6, 11, 86.

12 T.B. Liew, 'Tyranny, Power and Might: Colonial Mimicry in Mark's Gospel', *JSNT* 73, 1999, pp. 7–31 (13, 23).

13 H. Bhabha, *The Location of Culture*, London & New York: Routledge, 1994, pp. 85–92.

14 P.A. Harland, 'Honouring the Emperor or Assailing the Beast: Participation in Civic Life among Associations (Jewish, Christian and Other) in Asia Minor and the Apocalypse of John', *JSNT* 77, 2000, pp. 99–121.

15 Moore, *Empire and Apocalypse*, p. 114.

4 Applying Methods Old and New

1 See G. Theissen, *The Gospels in Context: Social and Political History in the Synoptic Tradition*, T&T Clark: Edinburgh, 1992, p. 81.

2 R. Darnton, *The Great Cat Massacre and Other Episodes in French Cultural History*, London: Allen Lane, 1984, pp. 75–104.

3 See J.G. Crossley, 'History from the Margins: The Death of John the Baptist' in J.G. Crossley and C. Karner, eds, *Writing History, Constructing Religion*, Aldershot: Ashgate, 2005, pp. 147–61.

4 On the use of Esther stories in Mark 6.17–29 see R.D. Aus, *Water into Wine and the Beheading of John the Baptist: Early Jewish-Christian Interpretation of Esther 1 in John 2:1–11 and Mark 6:17–29*, Atlanta: Scholars Press, 1988.

5 For example, E. P. Sanders, 'Jesus' Galilee' in I. Dunderberg, C. Tuckett and K. Syreeni, eds, *Fair Play: Diversity and Conflicts an Early Christianity. Essays in Honour of Heikki Räisänen*, Leiden: Brill, 2002, pp. 3–41.

5 The Quest for the Historical Jesus

1 G. Theissen and D. Winter, *The Quest for the Plausible Jesus: The Question of Criteria*, Louisville: WJK, 2002.

2 D.C. Allison, *Resurrecting Jesus: The Earliest Christian Tradition and Its Interpreters*, London: T&T Clark, 2005, p. 150.

3 ' ... among his people' is the literal translation and used in several Bible translations. NRSV has 'among his relatives'.

4 The famous phrase 'For the kingdom and the power and the glory are yours forever. Amen' is missing from early manuscripts.

5 J.D.G. Dunn, *Jesus Remembered*, Grand Rapids: Eerdmans, 2003; R. Bauckham, *Jesus and the Eyewitnesses: The Gospels as Eyewitness Testimony*, Grand Rapids: Eerdmans, 2006; R. Rodriguez, *Structuring Early Christian Memory: Jesus in Tradition, Performance*, London & New York: T&T Clark, 2009.

6 R.W. Funk, R.W. Hoover and the Jesus Seminar, *The Five Gospels. The Search for the Authentic Words of Jesus*, New York: Macmillan, 1993, p. 36.

7 J.D. Crossan and J.L. Reed, *Excavating Jesus: Beneath the Stones, Behind the Texts*, New York: HarperCollins; London: SPCK, 2001, p. xv.

8 N.T. Wright, *The Resurrection of the Son of God*, London: SPCK, 2003, p. 636.

9 R.D. Aus, *The Death, Burial, and Resurrection of Jesus, and the Death, Burial, and Translation of Moses in Judaic Tradition*, Lanham: University Press of America, 2008.

6 The New Testament and the Origins of Major Christian Theological Ideas

1 A.E. McGrath, ed., *The Christian Theology Reader*, Oxford: Blackwell, 1995, pp. 7, 148.

2 M. Casey, *From Jewish Prophet to Gentile God: The Origins and Development of New Testament Christology*, Louisville: WJK; Cambridge: James Clarke, 1991.

3 L.W. Hurtado, *One Lord, One God: Early Christian Devotion and Ancient Jewish Monotheism*, Philadelphia: Fortress, 1988; L.W. Hurtado, *Lord Jesus Christ: Devotion to Jesus in Earliest Christianity*, Grand Rapids: Eerdmans, 2003; L.W. Hurtado, *How on Earth Did Jesus Become a God? Historical Questions about Earliest Devotion to Jesus*, Grand Rapids: Eerdmans, 2005.

4 A good place to start assessing the validity of both sides would be a debate between the two scholars in the *Journal for the Study of the New Testament*: M. Casey, 'Lord Jesus Christ: A Response to Professor Hurtado', *JSNT* 27 (2004),

pp. 83–96; L.W. Hurtado, 'Devotion to Jesus and Historical Investigation: A Grateful, Clarifying and Critical Response to Professor Casey', *JSNT* 27 (2004), pp. 97–104.

5 C. Rowland, 'Review of Crossley, *Why Christianity Happened*', *JTS* 59 (2008), pp. 765–67.

6 See further P. Athanassiadi and M. Frede, eds, *Pagan Monotheism in Late Antiquity*, Oxford: Oxford University Press, 1999.

7 Paul, the Law, Faith and Salvation

1 E.P. Sanders, *Paul and Palestinian Judaism: A Comparison of Patterns of Religion*, Philadelphia: Fortress; London: SCM, 1977.

2 J.D.G. Dunn, *The Theology of Paul the Apostle*, Grand Rapids: Eerdmans; Edinburgh: T&T Clark, 1998.

3 For entries into this hugely controversial and widely covered area of New Testament studies see, for example, M.F. Bird, *The Saving Righteousness of God: Studies on Paul, Justification and the New Perspective*, Milton Keynes: Paternoster, 2007; M. Zetterholm, *Approaches to Paul: A Student's Guide to Recent Scholarship*, Minneapolis: Fortress, 2009.

4 R. Stark, *The Rise of Christianity: A Sociologist Reconsiders History*, Princeton: Princeton UP, 1996.

5 J.T. Sanders, *Charisma, Converts, Competitors: Societal and Sociological Factors in the Success of Early Christianity*, London: SCM, 2000; W.A. Meeks, *The First Urban Christians: The Social World of the Apostle Paul*, second edition, New Haven and London: Yale UP, 2003.

6 J.G. Crossley, *Why Christianity Happened: A Sociohistorical Account of Christian Origins*, London: WJK, 2006.

8 Paul's Revolution for Our Times?

1 W. Blanton, 'Apocalyptic Materiality: Return(s) of Early Christian Motifs in Slavoj Žižek's Depiction of the Materialist Subject', *Journal for Cultural and Religious Theory* 6 (Winter 2004); J.D. Caputo and L.M. Alcoff, eds, *St Paul among the Philosophers*, Bloomington & Indianapolis: Indiana University Press, 2009.

2 A. Assmann, 'Preface' in J. Taubes, ed, *The Political Theology of Paul*, Stanford: Stanford University Press, 2004, pp. xii–xiv.

3 Taubes, *Political Theology of Paul*, p. 5.

4 Taubes, *Political Theology of Paul*, pp. 52–54, quotation p. 54.

5 Taubes, *Political Theology of Paul*, pp. 40–41.

6 A. Badiou, *Saint Paul: The Foundation of Universalism*, Stanford: Stanford University Press, 2003.

7 Badiou, *Saint Paul*, pp. 2, 44–45.

8 Badiou, *Saint Paul*, p. 17.

9 Badiou, *Saint Paul*, p. 23.

10 Badiou, *Saint Paul*, p. 7.

11 S. Žižek, *The Puppet and the Dwarf: The Perverse Core of Christianity*, Cambridge, Mass.: MIT Press, 2003, pp. 130, 135–37.

12 Žižek, *Puppet and the Dwarf*, pp. 49–50, 81.

13 S. Žižek, *On Belief*, London and New York: Routledge, 2001.

14 M. Lilla, 'A New, Political Saint Paul?' *New York Review of Books* 55/16 (October 23, 2008), pp. 1–9 (6).

15 D. Boyarin, *A Radical Jew: Paul and the Politics of Identity*, Berkeley: University of California Press, 1994, pp. 47–49.
16 Žižek, *Puppet and the Dwarf*, pp. 8–10 (cf. pp. 17–18).
17 Žižek, *Puppet and the Dwarf*, p. 81 (cf. p. 110).
18 T. Eagleton, *Reason, Faith, and Revolution: Reflections on the God Debate*, New Haven and London: Yale University Press, 2009, pp. 21–22.
19 Eagleton, *Reason, Faith, and Revolution*, p. 20.
20 Eagleton, *Reason, Faith, and Revolution*, p. 24.
21 Žižek, *The Puppet and the Dwarf*, pp. 8–10 (cf. pp. 17–18).
22 Žižek, *The Puppet and the Dwarf*, p. 9.
23 Badiou, *Saint Paul*, p. 2.
24 Lilla, 'A New, Political Saint Paul?', p. 8.
25 Žižek, *The Puppet and the Dwarf*, p. 113.
26 M. Bakunin, *Selected Works*, ed. S. Dolgoff, New York: Alfred A. Knopf, 1972, pp. 283–84.
27 Badiou, *Saint Paul*, p. 2.

9 What is 'Reception History'?

1 D.C. Allison, *Resurrecting Jesus: The Earliest Christian Tradition and Its Interpreters*, London and New York: T&T Clark, 2005, p. 9.
2 U. Luz, *Matthew 1–7: A Commentary*, Minneapolis: Fortress, 2007, p. 62.
3 A.C. Thiselton, *The First Epistle to the Corinthians: A Commentary on the Greek Text*, Grand Rapids: Eerdmans, 2000, p. 196.
4 Luz, *Matthew 1–7*, p. 62.
5 Thiselton, *First Epistle to the Corinthians*, pp. 285–86.
6 Thiselton, *First Epistle to the Corinthians*, pp. 283–84.
7 M. Bockmuehl, *Seeing the Word: Refocusing New Testament Study*, Baker Academic: Grand Rapids, Michigan, 2006, pp. 121–36; cf. p. 169.
8 C. Rowland and J. Roberts, *The Bible for Sinners: Interpretation in the Present Time*, London: SPCK, 2008.
9 Rowland and Roberts, *Bible for Sinners*, pp. 81–87.
10 Rowland and Roberts, *Bible for Sinners*, pp. 9–10.
11 Y. Sherwood, 'Bush's Bible as a Liberal Bible (Strange though that Might Seem)', *Postscripts* 2 (2006), pp. 47–58.
12 Sherwood, 'Bush's Bible as a Liberal Bible', p. 52.
13 J. Berlinerblau, *Thumpin' It: The Use and Abuse of the Bible in Today's Presidential Politics*, Louisville: WJK, 2008.
14 M. Krejci, 'The 2008 Primaries or How the Democrats Learned to Stop Worrying and Love the Bible in Politics', *SBL Forum*, available at http://sbl-site.org/Article.aspx?ArticleID=792 last accessed 10 Sept. 2009.
15 A. Bach, 'Bush's Bible: A Wild Beast Loosed upon the World', *Postscripts* 2 (2006), pp. 109–25 (119).
16 *Amnesty International Report 2009: Egypt*, available at http://thereport.amnesty.org/en/regions/middle-east-north-africa/egypt last accessed 10 Sept. 2009; R. Fisk, 'Police state is the wrong venue for Obama's speech', *Independent*, 3 June 2009.
17 Berlinerblau, *Thumpin' It*, pp. 60–74.
18 J.G. Crossley, *Jesus in an Age of Terror: Scholarly Projects for a New American Century*, London and Oakville: Equinox, 2008, pp. 58–100, 144–72, 189–93.
19 M. Krejci, 'An atheist's dilemma: should we bend the Bible for justice?', *SBL Forum*, available at http://sbl-site.org/Article.aspx?ArticleID=779 last accessed 20 Jan. 2009.

10 Methods and Questions in Reception History

1 U. Luz, *Matthew 1–7: A Commentary*, Minneapolis: Fortress, 2007, p. 62.
2 W.J. Lyons, 'Historical Criticism, Reception, and Study of the Bible in the Academy', paper delivered to the British New Testament Conference, Durham University, 2008. This will be published in a forthcoming issue of *JSNT* dedicated to reception history.
3 M. Huie-Jolly, 'Maori "Jews" and a Resistant Reading of John 5.10–47' in M.W. Dube and J.L. Staley, eds, *John and Postcolonialism: Travel, Space and Power*, London: T&T Clark, 2002, pp. 94–110.
4 Huie-Jolly, 'Maori "Jews"', pp. 95–96.
5 For the details see J.G. Crossley, 'For EveryManc a Religion: Biblical and Religious Rhetoric in the Manchester Alternative Music Scene, 1976–94', *Biblical Interpretation* (forthcoming).
6 See, for example, J. Berlinerblau, *Thumpin' It: The Use and Abuse of the Bible in Today's Presidential Politics*, Louisville: WJK, 2008, pp. 4–15.
7 For discussion with bibliography see J.G. Crossley, *Jesus in an Age of Terror: Scholarly Projects for a New American Century*, London and Oakville: Equinox, 2008, pp. 144–72, 189–93.
8 H. Lindsey, *The Late Great Planet Earth*, Grand Rapids: Zondervan, 1970, p. 77.
9 Available at www.leftbehind.com/channelseekgod.asp?pageid=785&channelID = 6 last accessed 10 Sept. 2009.
10 N. Chomsky and G. Achcar, *Perilous Power: The Middle East and U.S. Foreign Policy*, Boulder and London: Paradigm, 2007, p. 31. This is in the context of a broader discussion of the rise of Christian and Islamic fundamentalism in the same period with reference to broader social and economic causes.
11 J. Archer with F.J. Maloney, *The Gospel According to Judas by Benjamin Iscariot*, London: New York, 2007.
12 A.D. DeConick, *The Thirteenth Apostle: What the Gospel of Judas Really Says*, London and New York: Continuum, 2007.
13 BBC News, 'Judas "Helped Jesus Save Mankind"', 7 April 2006, available at http://news.bbc.co.uk/1/hi/world/americas/4882420.stm last accessed 10 Sept. 2009.
14 Archer with Maloney, *Gospel According to Judas*, p. 2.
15 Archer with Maloney, *Gospel According to Judas*, e.g. pp. 42, 66.
16 Archer with Maloney, *Gospel According to Judas*, pp. 29–31.
17 H. Räisänen, 'The "Effective History" of the Bible: A Challenge to Biblical Scholarship' in H. Räisänen, ed., *Challenges to Biblical Interpretation: Collected Essays 1991–2001*, Leiden: Brill, 2001, pp. 263–82.
18 K. Newport, '"Be Thou Faithful unto Death" (cf. Rev. 2.10): The Book of Revelation, the Branch Davidians and Apocalyptic (Self-)Destruction', in W.J. Lyons and J. Økland, eds, *The Way the World Ends? The Apocalypse of John in Culture and Ideology*, Sheffield: Sheffield Phoenix Press, 2009, pp. 211–26 (212).
19 Newport, 'Apocalyptic (Self-)Destruction', p. 225.
20 Luz, *Matthew 1–7*, pp. 61, 63.
21 B. Mack, *The Myth of Innocence: Mark and Christian Origins*, Philadelphia: Fortress, 1988, p. 365.
22 Mack, *Myth of Innocence*, pp. 367–68.
23 Mack, *Myth of Innocence*, p. 376.
24 Berlinerblau, *Thumpin' It*, pp. 1–2.
25 Huie-Jolly, 'Maori "Jews"', p. 97.
26 M. Lilla, 'A New, Political Saint Paul?' *New York Review of Books* 55/16 (October 23, 2008), pp. 1–9 (2).
27 Lilla, 'A New, Political Saint Paul?', p. 8.

28 G. Agamben, *The Time That Remains: A Commentary on the Letter to the Romans*, Stanford: Stanford University Press, 2005, p. 1.

29 A. Badiou, *The Meaning of Sarkozy*, London: Verso, 2009.

30 A. Badiou, *Saint Paul: The Foundation of Universalism*, Stanford: California, 2003, pp. 4–15.

11 How to Read New Testament Scholarship

1 W.J. Lyons, 'Historical Criticism, Reception, and Study of the Bible in the Academy', paper delivered to the British New Testament Conference, Durham University, 2008. This will be published in a forthcoming issue of *JSNT* dedicated to reception history.

2 H. Moxnes, 'Schleiermacher's *Life of Jesus*, 19th Century Nationalism, and the Present Challenge', in H. Moxnes, W. Blanton and J.G. Crossley, eds, *Jesus beyond Nationalism: Constructing the Historical Jesus in a Period of Cultural Complexity*, London: Equinox, 2009.

3 E. Renan, *The Life of Jesus*, Amherst, New York: Prometheus, 1991, pp. 110–11.

4 W. Blanton, *Displacing Christian Origins: Philosophy, Secularity, and the New Testament*, Chicago: Chicago University Press, 2007, pp. 129–65.

5 D. Georgi, 'The Interest in Life of Jesus Theology as a Paradigm to the Social History of Biblical Criticism', *Harvard Theological Review* 85 (1992), pp. 51–83 (76).

6 E.P. Sanders, *The Historical Figure of Jesus*, London: Penguin, 1993, pp. 2, 4–5.

7 C.V. Stichele and T. Penner, *Contextualizing Gender in Early Christian Discourse: Thinking beyond Thecla*, London: T&T Clark/Continuum, 2009, pp. 145–52.

8 S. Kelley, *Racializing Jesus: Race, Ideology and the Formation of Modern Biblical Scholarship*, London and New York: Routledge, 2002, p. 214.

9 E. Käsemann, *New Testament Questions of Today*, London: SCM, 1969, p. 186.

10 W. Arnal, *The Symbolic Jesus: Historical Scholarship, Judaism and the Construction of Contemporary Identity*, London & Oakville: Equinox, 2005.

11 N.T. Wright, *Jesus and the Victory of God*, London: SPCK, 1996, p. 93.

12 For full discussion see J.G. Crossley, *Jesus in an Age of Terror: Scholarly Projects for a New American Century*, London and Oakville: Equinox, 2008, pp. 179–81.

13 Kelley, *Racializing Jesus*, p. 221.

14 See, for example, J.G. Crossley, *Why Christianity Happened: A Sociohistorical Account of Christian Origins 26–50 CE*, Louisville: WJK, 2006, chapter 1.

15 B.J. Malina, *The Social World of Jesus and the Gospels*, London: Routledge, 1996, p. 41.

16 Malina, *Jesus and the Gospels*, p. 63.

17 R. Rohrbaugh, *The New Testament in Cross-Cultural Perspective*, Eugene: Cascade Books, 2007, pp. 89–90.

18 For two different but complementary approaches to this question of academia and power with bibliography see Crossley, *Jesus in an Age of Terror*; Stichele and Penner, *Contextualizing Gender*.

19 Available at www.andyrowell.net/andy_rowell/2007/11/audio-from-a-fe.html last accessed 10 Sept. 2009.

20 N.T. Wright, *The Resurrection of the Son of God*, London: SPCK, 2003, p. 737.

21 N. Chomsky, *Understanding Power*, P.R. Mitchell and J. Schoeffel, eds, New York: New Press, 2002, p. 242.

22 Chomsky, *Understanding Power*, p. 154.

Index